Claiming citizenship: rights, participation and accountability

SERIES EDITOR: JOHN GAVENTA

Around the world, a growing crisis of legitimacy characterizes the relationship between citizens and the institutions that affect their lives. In both North and South, citizens speak of mounting disillusionment with government, based on concerns about corruption, lack of responsiveness to the needs of the poor and the absence of a sense of connection with elected representatives and bureaucrats. Conventional forms of expertise and representation are being questioned. The rights and responsibilities of corporations and other global actors are being challenged, as global inequalities persist and deepen.

In response, this series argues, increased attention must be paid to re-examining contemporary understandings of rights and citizenship in different contexts, and their implications for related issues of participation and accountability. Challenging liberal understandings in which citizenship is understood as a set of rights and responsibilities bestowed by the state, the series looks at how citizenship is claimed and rights are realized through the agency and actions of people themselves.

Growing out of the work of an international network of researchers and practitioners from both South and North, the volumes in this series explore a variety of themes, including locally rooted struggles for more inclusive forms of citizenship, the links between citizenship, science and globalization, the politics and dynamics of participation in new democratic arenas, and the relationships between claiming rights and ensuring accountability. Drawing from concrete case studies which focus on how people understand their citizenship and claim their rights, the volumes contribute new, empirically grounded perspectives to current debates related to deepening democracy, realizing rights-based development, and making institutions more responsive to the needs and voices of poor people.

Series titles

D1498453

MELISSA LEACH, IAN SCOONES AND
BRIAN WYNNE | editors

Science and citizens

Globalization and the challenge of
engagement

Zed Books
LONDON | NEW YORK

Science and citizens: globalization and the challenge of engagement was first published by Zed Books Ltd, 7 Cynthia Street, London N1 9JF, UK and Room 400, 175 Fifth Avenue, New York, NY 10010, USA in 2005.

www.zedbooks.co.uk

Cover designed by Andrew Corbett
Set in FF Arnhem and Futura Bold by Ewan Smith, London
Index: ed.emery@britishlibrary.net
Printed and bound in the EU by Biddles Ltd <www.biddles.co.uk>

Distributed in the USA exclusively by Palgrave Macmillan, a division of St Martin's Press, LLC, 175 Fifth Avenue, New York, NY 10010.

A catalogue record for this book is available from the British Library.
US CIP data are available from the Library of Congress.

ISBN 1 84277 550 2 cased
ISBN 1 84277 551 0 limp

Contents

Foreword by John Gaventa

This volume explores a variety of themes related to how citizens engage in critical scientific debates and decisions that affect their futures, be they in specific policy issues about genetics, HIV/AIDS, occupational health, biotechnology or GM foods to broader processes of assessing the risks of new technologies.

Throughout, the volume contributes again and again to core themes of the *Claiming citizenship* series: how citizens both engage with and are constructed by policy processes; how rights are realized and how demands for new rights – such as, in this case, the right to safety or access to cognitive justice – emerge; whose realities and knowledges are used in the construction of standards of acceptable risk; the links between local and global processes and how they affect citizen mobilization; and how institutions respond to the multiple voices of the citizens they are meant to serve. In doing so, the volume poses critical challenges to how citizen participation is often conceptualized in policy discourse, which usually involves at best relatively passive contributions of lay knowledge and preferences to pre-defined and bounded technical processes. Instead, it offers a far more robust vision – one that involves understanding citizens as bearers of knowledge and agency, deeply linked to their own identities, cultures and even ontologies, and intertwined with global networks and solidarities.

The editors and authors of the volume address these issues through a richly textured combination of analysis and empirical case studies drawn from both North and South, including Brazil, China, India, New Zealand, Sierra Leone, South Africa, the United States, the United Kingdom and Zimbabwe. In so doing they link a wide spectrum of intellectual debates about science, citizenship, globalization, indigenous knowledge, policy, participation, risk and reflexivity. They do so in a way that itself is illustrative of one of the dimensions of citizen engagement they discuss, i.e. through mobilizing global networks that help to develop new forms of knowledge, vision and imagination.

Some of the researchers involved and two of the editors, Melissa Leach and Ian Scoones, are affiliated to the Development Research Centre (DRC) on Citizenship, Participation and Accountability, an international research network based at the Institute of Development Studies which brings together researchers and practitioners from Bangladesh, Brazil, India, Mexico, Nigeria and South Africa. The Citizenship DRC is funded by the UK

Department for International Development (DfID), with additional funding from the Rockefeller Foundation, which enabled the participation of some of the Northern contributors to this project.[1]

In October 2001 and again in December 2002, members of the DRC network joined with other academics (spanning the fields of anthropology, sociology, ecology, science studies and geography), science advisers, professionals and activists for two conferences involving almost one hundred participants to explore the themes now reflected in this volume. The DRC network also linked with other networks, including that formed around the Science in Society Programme of the UK Economic and Social Research Council (ESRC), in which the third editor, Brian Wynne, has been involved. The Science and Society Programme also co-funded the second conference at IDS.

This volume in turn is part of a larger series on *Claiming citizenship* emerging from the work of the Development Research Centre. Other volumes will explore related issues of struggles for more inclusive forms of citizenship, the politics and dynamics of institutionalized participation in new democratic arenas, and the relationships between claiming rights and ensuring accountability. Drawing from concrete case studies that focus on how people understand their citizenship and claim their rights, the volumes contribute new, empirically grounded perspectives on current debates related to deepening democracy, realizing rights-based development, and making institutions more responsive to the needs and voices of poor people.

As overall series editor and as director of the DRC, I would like to thank the editors and authors of this volume for contributing their work to the *Claiming citizenship* series. The energy, quality and professionalism reflected in this work are far greater than can be credited to the DRC itself. Rather, they reflect the commitment to the issues involved and the collaboration of many people from a number of organizations and networks around the world. In addition, special thanks should be given to those who have helped in the production of the manuscript, including Kathryn Perry, Oliver Burch, Lucila Lahitou and, of course, our colleagues and editors at Zed Books, whose support for this series is deeply appreciated.

John Gaventa, Series Editor
Institute of Development Studies

Note

1 Further information on the Development Research Centre on Citizenship, Participation and Accountability may be found at <www.drc-citizenship.org>.

ONE | Science and citizenship

1 | Introduction: science, citizenship and globalization

MELISSA LEACH, IAN SCOONES AND
BRIAN WYNNE

The need to clarify our understanding of the complex interfaces and inter-sections between science and citizenship is now more pertinent than ever. There have always been issues and controversies over how people relate to science, and how science reflects its human contexts; but these are now unfolding in a new, more pervasive and complex, and arguably more urgent, context. Globalization is changing the nature of science and technology, as it is being shaped by their developments: altering the intensity of innovation of new technologies, and the resulting constitutions and flows of knowledge and expertise, and the character and scope of risks and uncertainties. Globalization is also implicated in the changing nature and contexts of citizenship: internationalizing governance and the networks through which people might press claims, and forging new solidarities and forms of connection between once more disparate local groups. Moreover, as recent analyses of the molecularization of the life sciences have suggested (Rose 2001), politics and citizenship are themselves ever more intimately connected with the subtle shaping of human subjectivities that form the cultural undergrowth and underpinnings of the forms of politics of late-modern, globalized times.

With these changes, there is now an expanding array of overt engagements between science and citizens. Along with the recognition of the ways in which scientific discourses and notions of human agency and citizenship have for long been tacitly intertwined and mutual, these proliferating encounters force us to break down established analytical categories to recognize new synergies between expert and lay knowledges, new linkages between local and global processes, new relationships between state and non-governmental action, new networks of international activism, and a variety of hybrid forms of public and private control and ownership that frequently transcend national boundaries. Equally, many of the categories that might once have been used to think about these engagements in different parts of the world – North and South, developed and developing countries, indigenous and modern – no longer seem salient.

This changing context suggests a convergence between two loosely defined bodies of work which have, to date, remained rather separate. On the one hand, the field of science and technology studies has since the 1970s examined issues of scientific and technological practice and culture, as well as the specific technological products and risks of modern science, in 'Northern', largely industrial settings. On the other hand, development studies, especially their anthropological contributions, have engaged with similar issues in 'Southern' settings, but with perhaps a greater emphasis on agricultural and rural issues, on the connections between technology and livelihoods, and on the perspectives emerging from so-called 'indigenous' knowledges in relation to modern expert-knowledge interventions. Emerging separately, as they have, each of these fields of work has developed distinct theoretical and analytical traditions, and thus ways of conceiving of the relations between science and citizens. The necessary convergence between these bodies of work in an era of globalization invites a bringing together of these streams of analysis to explore ways in which they might mutually enrich, build on and critique each other. Science studies (the Sociology of Scientific Knowledge – SSK) have for over a decade addressed, and tried to encourage policy actors to recognize, the cultural dimensions of the interactions of 'lay' public knowledge with scientific knowledge over risk and environmental issues, health programmes and the like. The striking correspondences between this and anthropology's long-standing interest in the encounters between modern and indigenous knowledges have only recently been pursued. Moreover, the theoretical realization of these 'cognitive' interactions as much more than this, as encounters between different practical-cultural *ways of being* as well as ways of knowing – ontologies – has occurred in both disciplinary domains, but its implications have not been jointly addressed. 'Post-colonial science studies', for example (see, e.g., Anderson 2002; Verran 2002), have recently combined SSK and anthropological perspectives on encounters between indigenous cultures and modern environmental science and practice in ways that open up important new issues for modern scientific culture and its self-understandings. This bears upon wider processes of globalization.

This book has emerged from such ongoing conversations between scholars of science and technology studies, especially the more specialist field of SSK, and development studies, conducted through a series of meetings and exchanges over the last few years. By bringing together a group of authors who perhaps would not normally appear together in a single volume, we aim to explore the correspondences, convergences, potentials and – in some cases – divergences between their central intellectual issues and ways of approaching them. Perhaps because all the contributors to this book are engaged in some way in critiquing mainstream approaches

4

to the study and practice of development and science and technology, many commonalities emerged, although often refracted through different terminologies, different empirical concerns and different types of policy engagement. Considering these commonalities, differences and potential new avenues, the book casts new light on the ways we understand the institutions and governance of science in a globalizing world: the ways we understand questions seen as ones of risk and uncertainty; the ways we understand citizenship and public engagement with science; and the ways we understand issues of knowledge, practice, agency and expertise.

In turn, there arises a set of challenges for prevailing attempts to orchestrate deliberative and participatory processes around issues of science and technology. Thus, although it has been recognized sporadically over the years, the emerging correspondence between the concerns and perspectives of science and technology studies about the 'democratization of science' in developed societies on the one hand, and the focus of development studies on citizen participation in expert-led development programmes and policies on the other, remains to be developed and exploited. By far the most dominant way of describing the confrontations and issues between modern discourses and interventions and 'indigenous' actors has been as if these were purely cognitive processes. A liberal enlightened perspective has thus been to talk of overdue recognition of the saliency and validity of hitherto marginalized and disparaged forms of knowledge, often local in distribution and practical in focus. More recently, however, both anthropological and SSK insight have come to understand knowledge as cultural practice that sustains and is sustained by these cognitive idioms, but which crucially stretches beyond them alone. This has led scholars such as Latour and Stengers to advocate an understanding of the countless typical – and almost definitive of our times – conflicts between scientific and 'lay' knowledges as not just epistemic conflicts between ways of knowing, but as reflections of different ways of being, of practising and relating – of ontologies. Moreover, the 'reflexive turn' in social science and humanities cultivated the insight that what we see as representational knowledge is not simply that, but is also subtly performative, in that it inevitably reflects and tacitly projects models of the human subject into the public world. This is true of representations of nature as well as of social worlds.

Thus, whereas dominant understandings of the chronic latter-day crisis of public (lack of) legitimacy or mistrust of science see these as *cognitive* defaults, either on the part of the publics of science or modern rationality (the 'deficit model'), or on the part of science when it neglects valid non-scientific knowledge (Collins and Evans 2002), others see them as unrecognized ontological conflicts between incompatible ways of life. Thus, these

5

problems, whether in developed, developing-world or global settings, are a cultural challenge to dominant modernity and its hegemonist scientific culture. This implies a demand for self-reflexive humility, awareness and debate. This could be described as the main point of this book – to argue that this self-problematization and reflexivity of scientific institutions, and this recognizing of alterity in a respectful way in the face of proliferating local and global public alienation, is an essential move. It is of course an issue of scientific knowledge's mutual construction with global and local forms of power; but clarification here is key to generating the possible conditions of sustainable cultural, as well as technical, robustness through exploring different visions of globalization.

This book is divided into four sections. Following this brief introduction is an overview chapter that traces the varied contributions of science and technology studies and development studies to understanding science and public engagements with it. It examines the connections between strands of debate in these fields, and different theories of citizenship; connections that have rarely been made explicit before, but which help us move towards fruitful ways of understanding citizenship practice in today's globalizing world. Part Two offers a series of perspectives on science and citizenship from different standpoints. Part Three picks up the emergent themes in a series of case studies, covering issues ranging from medical genetics, agricultural biotechnology, occupational health and HIV/AIDS to transport technology and food security, in settings including rural Sierra Leone, urban Britain, China, South Africa, India and Brazil, as well as in international scientific, policy and activist networks. Part Four engages critically with the move to participation and democratization of science in both North and South, and illustrates some of the dilemmas involved through a series of short examples where citizens have been invited to deliberate on 'science and technology issues'. To convey the sense of conversation and ongoing debate between these fields of work, Parts Two to Four are preceded by a short editorial commentary, which both highlights some of the key issues raised by the chapters in each section and points to unresolved issues, further questions and new avenues of inquiry.

In the remainder of this introduction, we first highlight a series of emergent themes linking science, knowledge and governance which resonate in the book. In different ways, as we go on to show, these each suggest challenges for the ways in which we understand the relationships between citizenship and knowledge in a changing global context. A key issue raised in this intellectual context is also the relationship between the subtle dynamics of the formation of human subjectivities through 'representational' knowledges, and our ideas of citizenship in public contexts.

Science, knowledge and governance: emergent themes

Challenging modernist development A recurrent theme in the book is the recognition of the unacknowledged cultural contingencies of scientific knowledge as deployed in the framing, definition and attempted resolution of public policy issues. Depending on the setting and the institutions involved, these may be defined in terms of risk and regulation, or more broadly in terms of trajectories of modernist, technology-led development. By making explicit these cultural, institutional and power-laden processes underpinning science and technology agendas, and the forms of subjectivity and citizenship which they normatively embody, the book challenges any assumption that science is independent of society and politics, or that these ways of thinking about public policy issues are universal or inevitable. Indeed, the book brings to light a variety of ways in which modernist development and its policy trappings are challenged, both discursively and practically, along with the meanings of issues involving new technologies. In some settings, these challenges take the form of 'alternative development' or anti-globalization, or counter-hegemonist globalization movements of the kind highlighted by Escobar (1995), Sachs (1992) and others. Others emphasize a form of reflexive modernization and sub-politics as part of an emergent global 'risk society' (Beck 1992, 1995, 1998).

Increasingly, science and technology agendas and networks are being pursued on a global scale, whether through international public policy and agreements, or trade and commerce. Particular views of science, technology and policy are embedded in these new global networks. North-world authored globalization and commodification cultures are developing new kinds of global knowledge-culture and epistemic politics, as reflected, for example, in the proliferating attempts to enrol indigenous people in global scientific and commercial systems of research, with intellectual property rights to exploit these indigenous knowledges for profit. Yet as the book shows, science and technology issues are subject to a variety of alternative and sometimes incompatible meanings. Those that emerge from specific, localized cultural contexts have, in some circumstances, been linked and mobilized in new global networks – a case in point being the mobilization of 'indigenousness' and its knowledges themselves as part of the anti-globalization movement, and the objectification and standardization of such knowledges in global databases in order to 'protect' them as a global cultural resource.

Reframing dominant expertise Thus, science has been recognized as needing to accept its own cultural boundaries, frames and blinkers that obscure and patronize the intellectual and moral substance of other ways

7

of knowing. Whether in 'Southern' development contexts (e.g., Leach and Mearns 1996; Scoones and Thompson 1994) or 'Northern' settings (e.g., Irwin and Wynne 1996), work has challenged the dominant assumptions of scientific and other powerful institutions, and extensively documented the independent intellectual capacities and substantively grounded epistemic cultures of multifarious lay publics. Thus, the institutions of scientific knowledge have been invited – whether or not they have responded is a different matter – to recognize other kinds of knowledge framed within other practical cultural assumptions, meanings and life-worlds. Publics, whether rural farmers in Africa or users of health services in the UK, have been acknowledged as having not just other bodies of knowledge, but also *other ways of knowing* – different systems of meaning, saliency and value – that need to be taken into account. This cultural understanding of the globally multifarious eruptions of the public mistrust of modern science places a fundamentally different perspective on the issue from those that inform most public policy and private corporate culture across the world.

It has increasingly been recognized, however, in both the sociology of scientific knowledge (e.g., Verran 2002) and anthropology (e.g., Strathern 1999) that this is a matter of incommensurable practical human-cultural ways of being (ontologies), not only of different human epistemologies or preferred ways of knowing. Major, internationally reverberating social conflicts, in which public unwillingness to defer to presumptive scientific authority has been interpreted as public unwillingness or inability to 'understand' scientific knowledge or method, have been recognized instead to be cultural confrontations between different, incompatible ontologies. The projections of modern policy and scientific institutions of the 'public' as typically vacuous in epistemic terms can be understood instead as the projections of insecure institutions unable to adopt more self-reflexive orientations towards their own social relations and cultural parochialism. Such lack of open self-reflexivity can, of course, be seen as a means of power. From this view, those conflicts between powerful institutions acting in the name of scientific rationality and publics have thus been recognized as less a reflection of public ignorance and irrationality and more a reflection of different frameworks of meaning within which salient observations and propositional beliefs are defined and given standing.

Indeed, there is now recognition that publics have salient knowledges and critical perspectives that should be taken seriously as substantive inputs into the planning, design and implementation of scientific interventions and development initiatives previously assumed to be the sovereign domain of expert scientific bodies. These interactions take place in particular, and now often globalized, institutional contexts, however, where power relations shape the terms of engagement. For example, the global documentation, aggregation, archiving and databasing of 'indigenous knowledges' is seen by organizations such as the United Nations World Intellectual Property Organization (WIPO) and the United Nations Educational Scientific and Cultural Organization (UNESCO) as a means of protecting them from exploitation and perhaps extinction, and of recognizing rights to ownership of products that may lead to economic and other returns. But the translation into formal quasi-scientific terms itself poses dilemmas, representing knowledges in abstracted terms stripped from the contexts in which they have practical enactment, human identity and cultural reality. Indigenous knowledges are thus rendered formally commensurate with other abstracted and translated (scientific) knowledges that have been given a new, standardized 'global' (a)cultural collective potential being. Thus, by removing knowledge from context, the power of dominant framings and the potentials for commercial exploitation that they support are upheld. The implications for the 'subjects' or 'citizens' of such knowledge are problematic.

In both developing and developed society contexts, therefore, it has been accepted, at least in principle, that science can gain democratic public legitimacy only if it recognizes its own need to understand itself in relation to these other cultures, and to learn respectfully to negotiate with and accommodate to them, rather than dismiss them as vacuous, untrustworthy and emotive. Perhaps in reflection of their institutional power and privileged presumed influence in such issues, however, scientific institutions have proved to be very resistant to opening themselves up to such self-reflexive needs and opportunities. A number of chapters in the book explore and reflect on both the problems that such lack of open self-reflexive capacity engenders and the possibilities for increased institutional responsiveness and openness.

Meanings and practices of risk and uncertainty Directly connected with the preceding observations, another recurring theme in the book is how risk is understood and problematized. Much debate about the relationships between science and publics has been cast in terms of a narrow, technical definition of risk, one amenable to prediction, management and control by expert institutions and public policy. In this framing of the issues and debate, publics are assumed to be aware of (or to misunderstand) risks in these same technical terms, and thus a key challenge for policy is seen as that of educating publics and communicating risks in rational terms. As several chapters argue, however, issues whose meanings for publics may be more multi-dimensional and varied are presumptively framed as ones of

9

risk, as if this were an objective and universal public meaning. Furthermore, scientific and policy institutions often frame as 'risk' – implying calculable probabilities of known outcomes – what is actually uncertainty or even ignorance about the possible consequences of a given form of technological development, and ambiguity as to the proper meanings of the issue(s) at stake. These more challenging dimensions are thus concealed from formal public treatment and negotiation.

This institutional culture of denial of unpredictability and (thus) of lack of control combines with the expert denial of any epistemic capacity of lay public culture, and with the assumption imposed on the public that the meaning of the issue in hand is indeed one of propositional truth amenable to science – is this safe or not? In different substantive forms, this basic set of processes appears to encompass both developed and developing-world situations. Yet publics may have different meanings defining the issue, which may include their own problematization of the institutional culture of science and its presumptive imposition of scientistic meanings without recognizing public definitions of the issue. As several chapters show, this is so far from scientific institutional imagination that public dissent is taken only to confirm the starting assumption that the issue is indeed a scientific one like risk, and thus dissent is confirmation of public incapacity to understand that science. These self-defeating cultural reflexes of institutional science contribute to science's own public legitimacy problems, which are then blamed on someone else. As well as embodying tacit normative projections of the proper citizen, they contribute to the oblique forms of negotiation and shaping of public agency in such issues.

Debates framed in terms of risk also focus on the consequences of science and technology development. Thus, questions about the setting of science and technology agendas in the first place, about processes of innovation, and about whose priorities or visions of development or the good society these are to address, are left begging. The assumption is that public concerns are focused on risks and consequences rather than on the unstated and unaccountable human purposes, aspirations, priorities, expectations and aims that drive innovation-oriented scientific knowledge. This latter, hugely important domain of science – partly, of course, because innovation-oriented knowledge is usually controlled by the private sector rather than the public sector – has been simply excused de facto from any of the questions of public accountability, public involvement and participation that have swept those scientific fields associated with risks and consequences.

Risk discourse appears to have been less dominant in development contexts, at least to date. Some research efforts have concentrated more on diverse forms of technology innovation, farmer creativity and local knowledges that respond to particular social and livelihood priorities (e.g., Richards 1985). Both expanding on and drawing lessons from this work for other settings, several chapters in the book make the case for increased attention to public engagement in 'front-end' innovation questions. They also argue for a broader recasting of science and technology debates around notions of justice, rights, livelihoods and the aims and purposes of development, scientific innovation and societal change.

Participation, democracy and accountability Each of these emergent themes raises challenges for processes of deliberation and participation. There is a long tradition of participation in development planning and programmes, which has more recently been joined by a tide of new procedures such as consensus conferences, citizens' juries and deliberative panels, which are now being applied to science and technology issues in both North and South. It has become evident, however, that the tacit prior framing of the modes and scope of such participatory initiatives, through the imposition on these of particular framings of the science in question and of presumptive normative models of 'the citizen', can lead these proclaimed 'openings' to more democratic forms to have a disciplining and thus participation-closing role.

The features of this paradoxical 'new tyranny' of participation (Cooke and Kothari 2001), especially in relation to scientific knowledge and the sometimes uncritical enthusiasm for deliberative techniques, are analysed in this book in these terms, with a view to assisting a more realistic and reflexively aware integration of such mechanisms into more broadly based and robust approaches.

Experiments with participation and deliberation over science, as the cases in Part Four exemplify, have largely been locale-specific. Yet increasingly, science and technology issues, and public engagement with them, unfold over much larger, and globalized, political fields of technology politics and human ethics. This requires a move beyond a preoccupation with techniques and procedures to embrace a more fundamental political analysis of science and technology, encompassing issues of agency, power, accountability and democracy. As Sheila Jasanoff suggests (in her chapter), this would pose such questions as: Who is making the choices that govern people's lives? On whose behalf? In which forums and with which discourses? With what rights of representation? According to whose definitions of 'the good'?

A further issue raised in recent debates (Fairhead and Leach 2003; Hinchcliffe et al. forthcoming; Latour 2000, 2004; Stengers 1996; Whatmore

11

2002) has been the role of nature and technology as agents in democratic processes. This has been highlighted in response to the critique of relativist-humanist accounts of scientific knowledge as constituted only by dominant 'social interests'. In SSK, the coproduction or mutual construction thesis (Jasanoff 2004; Jasanoff and Wynne 1998; Latour 1987) has long recognized how objective materiality plays a shaping role in representative knowledge of nature, without mistakenly giving it sole agency. But exploration of the idea that material non-human realities play quasi-subject roles in public arenas has become an influential project, as in Latour's idea of the 'parliament of things'. This raises important questions about whether, and to what extent, notions of citizenship should be extended to encompass non-human objects. It also alerts us to attend to the implicit models or assumptions of natural objectivity and human subjectivity embedded in scientific knowledge–citizen encounters in today's globalizing world.

Performing citizenships

Therefore, these emergent themes concerning challenges to dominant notions of modernist development, representation (intellectual and political), objects and subjects, scientific expertise and risk, as well as the call for a broader, more politicized democratization of science, have important implications for how one understands citizenship. As we explore in the next chapter, mainstream approaches to 'citizen involvement' with science and technology have been based on implicit models of the citizen grounded in versions of liberal theory. In these, citizens are either expected to engage passively with expert scientific institutions, especially those linked to the state, or to participate in forums orchestrated by such institutions. This contrasts with a model of the citizen as a more autonomous creator and bearer of knowledges located in particular practices, subjectivities and identities, who engages in more active ways with the politicized institutions of science. Such citizens do not act solely as individuals, as in liberal theory, but through emergent, and sometimes global, social solidarities that may unite people around particular issues and visions, whether these be fluid and shifting with circumstances, or more lasting.

A range of normative terms that have entered the lexicon, many of which appear in the following chapters, such as 'practical reason' (Fischer *infra*), dialogue and a 'listening science', 'cognitive justice' (Visvanathan *infra*), and an 'epistemology of the South', reflect these more performative and embedded ideas of scientific citizenship. Although sometimes implicitly, these developments reflect a recognition that knowledge, including scientific knowledge and especially scientific knowledge as deployed in public arenas, is inalienably cultural in that it embodies, reflects and projects commitments of a human kind, which also shape human relations and identities, imagined communities and ontologies. These explicit representational forms also, in a performative manner, tacitly project into the public domain normative models of the human that become part of the cultural repertoire and thus have influence over real emergent human behaviour, human relations and human imagination. This performative cultural dimension of scientific knowledge is what Verran (2002) has called the tacit provisional performance of human ontologies in the making. In short, scientific engagement makes citizens, but in more complex ways than often acknowledged.

Such tacit, oblique and emergent performance, as well as the more overt performance of citizenship in relation to science – and difficulties for scientific institutions in accommodating this – are now being played out in many different settings and around many different issues across the world. Thus, for example, the UK public controversy over genetically modified (GM) crops and foods has been insistently defined by scientific and policy institutions as an issue of risk, with a more recent elaboration to include what are accepted as legitimate public ethical concerns about 'tampering with nature' or 'playing God'. These ethical concerns have been dealt with, however, by framing them as individual emotive concerns, which are deemed a private matter on which people should decide for themselves, and act by individual choice in the marketplace. There is absolutely no acknowledged *public* dimension to this ethical concern arising from scientific-institutional culture itself. Thus, public responsibilities are seen to lie in identifying and managing the risks, and public opposition is identified with anti-science or misunderstanding of science. This default role for science – risk science – sequesters human political and cultural responsibilities, issues and agency as if these were discoverable, resolvable and replaceable by science. It is precisely the political, ethical and cultural dimensions of GM technology, however, and what it implies for broader societal futures, which have become the focus for citizen action and mobilization around the world. Public concerns and autonomous, active citizenship are also responding to the perceived inadequacy and untrustworthiness of scientific institutional culture. This could be of much wider relevance to the issues engaged in this collection.

Chapters in this book examine a range of cases where citizens are engaging with science, with a range of responses from expert institutions and a range of effects on the governance of science and technology. Overall, the book argues that such multivalent performative dimensions of citizenship should be recognized for what they are, while the hidden framings and implicit practices and meanings of scientific institutions should be rendered explicit and accountable to democratic debate and negotiation with those whose subjectivity they represent and shape. In the context of globalization, this book, drawing on the confluence of development studies and science and technology studies, sets out an agenda for analysis and action in terms of confronting and rendering more sustainable and legitimate scientific and technical cultures, creating new forms of knowledge network, and through the corresponding forms of human solidarity, enhancing democratic global citizenship.

2 | Science and citizenship in a global context

MELISSA LEACH AND IAN SCOONES

Introduction

Shifting science–society relationships are highly relevant both to contemporary practices of citizenship and their expression, and to questions concerning the dynamics of 'participation'. Just as political and economic changes are altering the contexts, arenas and ways in which people perceive and act on citizenship rights, so too are scientific and technological changes and the new risks and opportunities they present. Scientific and technological issues present particular challenges and opportunities for participation: on the one hand they are associated with claims to highly specialized, professionalized knowledge and expertise that may serve to exclude, yet on the other hand recent scientific controversies have also created new demands and opportunities for concerted citizen engagement in decision-making. At least in some contexts there is seen to be a new mood of public cynicism and critique of 'expert' institutions and their knowledges, and demands for new sorts of dialogue and public empowerment in the scientific realm.

Today these issues are reflected perhaps most clearly in the extensive academic, policy and media debates that explore contemporary relations between risk, science and society. In this chapter, we outline approaches that are helpful in exploring these issues in a globally comparative frame. The justification for this approach is twofold. First, these issues have to date been explored through distinct traditions of work associated with science and technology studies (STS), focusing predominantly on 'Northern' contexts, and development studies (DS), focusing predominantly on the global 'South'.[1] This suggests a need both to explore the cross-context 'translatability' of theories and debates and the possibilities of cross-learning between them. Second, a comparative approach allows an exploration of how citizenship and knowledge claims are emerging around different issues – from biotechnologies and road development to biodiversity and health technologies, for instance – in different settings, according to particular histories and contemporary dynamics in the relationships between science, state, international political economy and society.

In this chapter, we provide a review of some of the dominant lines of work in STS and DS that reflect on the relationships between science and citizenship. First, we consider major emphases in how each has conceived of the relationships between experts and lay knowledges, revealing some important contrasts in their approaches. We then go on to examine how different notions of citizenship have been incorporated into these debates, whether explicitly or implicitly. Through this discussion, we also address how diverse strands in the theoretical literature on citizenship (and the theories of democracy that link to these)[2] provide different lenses for thinking about science, knowledge and the engagement between different perspectives. As we show, approaches to participation and deliberation, now central to thinking and action in a scientific context in both North and South, are underlain by particular concepts of the citizen, which variously enable and constrain their transformative potential. Today, these processes take place in a globalized context, and in a third section we reflect on how this context forces us to redefine further the relationships between science and citizenship. We show in this context why it is necessary to go beyond static, universalized and essentialized notions of citizenship and a singular notion of the state, to embrace a more fluid, decentred and experience-based notion of both citizenship and expertise, but without losing sight of the historical, political and institutional structures that shape often highly contrasting forms of engagement.

Perspectives on knowledge and expertise

In order to explore these issues, we begin by considering the different analytical traditions for approaching knowledge and expertise relationships in STS and DS. While STS has relatively recently come to an interest in lay knowledge and experience-based expertise, DS by contrast draws on a much longer tradition of work examining local knowledge and practices and their conceptual and social underpinnings.

A recent review by Collins and Evans (2002) identifies two main waves in science studies to date. The first aimed at understanding, explaining and reinforcing the success of science, without questioning its basis. Science was held to be authoritative, objective and universal, and an unquestionable basis for expert-led decisions. Despite critiques from the early 1970s by academics, this perspective continued to dominate in many policy contexts. Thus perceived crises of legitimacy in science among publics were deemed to be the result of public misunderstanding of science, a 'deficit' in public knowledge that should be filled through science education.

A second wave of science studies, however, focused on challenging the assumptions and practices of science. In a variety of works sharing a social constructivist approach (e.g., Barnes et al. 1996; Haraway 1991; Knorr-Cetina 1981), science – its framing of questions, experimental methods, styles of investigation, modes of reaching closure, treatments of risk and uncertainty – was reconceptualized as a social and political activity. A prominent line of work focused on the details of 'laboratory life' (e.g., Latour 1987; Latour and Woolgar 1979) and examined the sets of practices that came to constitute science, and the ways these acquired authority in particular settings (Knorr-Cetina 1999; Pickering 1992). By emphasizing the way in which scientific knowledge was like other forms of knowledge, this work challenged the distinctions made between scientific experts and non-experts. Yet in this work the emphasis was on demystifying the practices of science, and parallel research attention was not applied to other knowledges in the public realm.

Nevertheless, an important strand of social science work did argue that public understandings of science were more sophisticated and nuanced than they had been given credit for, and that these understandings focused not just on the content and methods of science, but also on forms of its institutional embedding, patronage and control (Irwin and Wynne 1996; Wynne 1992). It also explored cases where laypeople had explicitly engaged with and contested science and its advice by conducting their own research and experiments (for instance, in 'popular epidemiology' concerning issues of toxic waste pollution; Brown and Mikkelsen 1990). Drawing attention to what has come to be labelled 'citizen science', this work demonstrated how publics now engage critically with the scientific perspectives of expert institutions, either through funding or orchestrating their own scientific investigations, or through lobbying to transform research questions (e.g., Fischer 2000; Irwin 1995).

Debates about citizenship and science in European settings have also been strongly influenced by Ulrich Beck's 'risk society' thesis and its subsequent elaborations (e.g., Beck 1992, 1995). Beck and others have been arguing that contemporary public critiques of scientific expertise are symptomatic of a broader, more fundamental set of social transformations, requiring new forms of sociological theorizing. The risk society thesis suggests that publics are increasingly concerned with risks that are no longer 'external', but continually thrown up by systems of industrial technology and its governance themselves. The scientific and bureaucratic apparatus charged with knowing and managing risk continues to operate according to ideas of predictability, so there is a mismatch between the character of hazards and what Beck terms 'relations of definition': the legal, epistemological and cultural power matrix in which discussions of science and technology are conducted (Beck 2000: 224). In the process, society has become 'reflexive', compelled by this mismatch to question its foundational principles (including ideas of scientific rationality) in an automatic, boomerang-like reflex. Reflexivity can in turn lead to (but is distinct from) conscious public reflection, scrutiny and dissent, which draws attention to ways in which public institutions with inadequate procedures more often legitimize than counter hazard.

For Beck, science not only creates the problems but also the analytics required to recognize and overcome them: reflection is enwrapped in the terms of modern, expert science. Yet, as a number of critics have pointed out, this obscures attention to alternative knowledges, sciences and forms of social order that may exist in the public realm (Caplan 2000; Wynne 1996). In a similar way, most work on citizen science has seen it as alternative science, conforming with its broad categories, paying less attention to the ways in which publics' knowledges develop in embedded relationship with local social processes and differences, concepts and moralities (see Leach and Fairhead 2002).

Collins and Evans (2002) acknowledge in their review that by breaking down any theoretical distinctions between expert and public knowledges, seeing all as partial perspectives, the social constructivist view makes it difficult to define who should legitimately take part in decision-making in science and technology issues. They therefore propose a 'third wave' of STS that focuses on expertise and allocates it a privileged role in decision-making. Such expertise, however, is reconstructed to include not just certified specialists but a range of uncertified specialists with a variety of forms of 'experience-based expertise'. These could include members of the public who, they argue, can frequently bring valuable 'contributory expertise' to a given decision-making process. They also argue, however, that to be legitimate this expertise has to be continuous with Western scientific rationality: they thus exclude, for example, astrology, theology and other 'fringe' sciences, and discount attention to 'folk knowledges', whose concepts and practices are discontinuous with those of Western science. Perhaps more importantly, the focus on knowledge and epistemology obscures from view more fundamental questions of ontology, or of the 'mutual embedding of natural knowledge and social order, their co-production' (Jasanoff 2003a: 392). Different forms of expertise may not easily combine, as they may represent fundamentally different lifeworlds and ways of framing an issue. Furthermore, by focusing on particular decisions and the propositions supposed to inform them – such as 'Is it safe?' – Collins and Evans arguably neglect the broader negotiation of public meanings and identities that are frequently disputed (Jasanoff 2003a; Wynne 2003).

In contrast, interest in these broader questions of human meaning, as well as in 'folk rationalities' and the sociocultural embeddedness of public knowledges, has been central in debates about rural people's knowledge in the developing world.[3] This analytical tradition is rooted in social anthropological work from early in the twentieth century, which detailed knowledge systems concerning issues such as health, agriculture and ecology in the context of broader ethnographies of society and culture (e.g., Evans-Pritchard 1937; Richards 1939). It thus emphasized how knowledge and beliefs about technical issues were largely inseparable from cosmology and local religion on the one hand, and questions of social order and prevailing relations of authority on the other. Central to this work has been exploration of local concepts, metaphors and idioms, examining how these make sense in relation to their particular social and cultural settings.

What came to be called 'indigenous knowledge' (IK) from the early 1970s has been seen in ambiguous relationship with Western science in its modernist guise. It has sometimes been depicted as a valuable and complementary resource to be repackaged in the terms of modernizing, expert scientific institutions (Brokensha et al. 1980; Chambers et al. 1989), much in the same way as 'third wave' STS seems to envisage. This perspective has stimulated numerous efforts to collect and collate stocks of valuable local technical knowledge concerning soils, plants, ecology and so on, sometimes assembling this in international 'banks' and networks. It has also underlain an interest in local classification systems, and various approaches to valorizing and incorporating the 'complementary' or 'contributory' expertise of rural people into technology development in terms of agriculture and environment, such as through participatory technology development or farmer field schools (e.g., Farrington and Martin 1988). In these, local knowledge and Western science are envisaged as complementary partners, filling gaps in each other's arenas of expertise.

At other times, indigenous knowledge and Western science have been portrayed as rooted in incommensurable concepts and framings, necessitating a more comparative framework of analysis (Fairhead 1992; Scoones and Thompson 1994). This work has shown how rural people's knowledge frames technical problems and agendas, and defines what relevant data to include or exclude from consideration, in particular ways that reflect social and political circumstances. It has shown how dispute and debate over technical issues in local settings are interlocked with social difference (for example, in terms of gender, age, ethnicity) and with struggles over control of resources, and over socio-political authority, and how local knowledges develop through practice, experience and 'performance' (Nyerges 1997; Richards 1989). In this respect, work on rural people's knowledge mirrors the tradition in STS of treating science as practice and performance (Pickering 1992). These practice-based analytical approaches, however, have been pursued in parallel in DS and STS, applied to different actors in different settings by different academics, with very little engagement between them.[4]

Work in developing-country settings also underlines the fact that public dissent and lack of trust in expert institutions is not so new, and not uniquely a feature of late industrial modernity in the West (Latour 1993). For instance, long-term anthropological/ecological/historical research in low-income countries of Africa, Asia and the Caribbean, whether concerning pastoralism, forest management, soils or water, has frequently exposed major disjunctures between the knowledge and perspectives of land users and those underlying and reproduced through national and internationalized science and policy (e.g., Brockington 2002; Fairhead and Leach 1996, 2003; Homewood forthcoming; Leach and Mearns 1996; Scoones 1995; Stott and Sullivan 2000). Local people have reflected on, responded to and resisted 'inappropriate' technologies and development plans in a variety of ways (Peet and Watts 1996). Public experiences and critique of science and of risk-framing as being part of the legitimization of powerful institutions date back to early colonial times, and now thrive, for instance in terms of concerns about forests in West Africa (Fairhead and Leach 2000), or water and dam development in India (Mehta 1998).

Perspectives from DS also suggest that works in the contemporary risk society tradition over-state the novelty of the risks faced by late industrial society, and the incapacity of 'relations of definition' to recognize them. Risks, hazards and uncertainties have long been experienced in developing-country settings in the constant interplay of ecological and bodily processes, capricious markets, government politics and international engagements (Mehta et al. 1999). Here too they have long been inadequately appreciated by the sciences informing management of public health, rangelands, watersheds, soils and vegetation, which have frequently been premised on ideas of predictability and managerial control. The narratives constructed through such sciences of control themselves presuppose and project particular social categories, or notions of the citizen or non-citizen: for instance, the poacher, the slash-and-burn farmer, and so on. Furthermore, many of the risks and uncertainties faced by people in developing countries emerge as a consequence of their position in global political-economic processes – whether those linked to colonialism or contemporary neo-liberal regimes (e.g., Nugent 2000), or to global environmental problems such as climate change, whose origins lie in richer industrialized countries (e.g., Adger et al. 2001).

These strands of work in DS have grown out of a concern with rural people's basic needs in agriculture, natural resources and health. These have not been the sort of high-tech issues that have dominated debates in STS, which have been decidedly circumspect about the possibilities of lay publics contributing valid knowledge to technology development. Apart from those forms of lay expertise seen as continuous with formal science, and as having a contributory role, other forms of public knowledge still tend to be seen as ignorance, misunderstanding or unfounded fears, which need to be managed by science communication, education or political processes. Yet the DS literature suggests that publics may bring important perspectives to debates about science and technology, which may be more about the broader socio-political agendas they represent and the alternatives thus excluded than about the technology per se. While the notion of valid 'contributory expertise' differentiates between certain citizens who have the right to participate and others who do not, taking lessons from DS work to embrace the broader notion of 'contributory perspectives' suggests broadening – or indeed abandoning – this distinction. This in turn raises questions about the relationships between science, citizens and political participation, which our next section works through from a different starting point, that of debates about citizenship.

Perspectives on citizenship and science

Contemporary debates about the changing relationships between science, public knowledge and different forms of expertise raise prospects for new forms of public engagement, whether in setting agendas for, conducting or applying the results of science and technology development. In recent years, there has been an explosion of participatory, deliberative and inclusionary approaches to decision-making about scientific and technological issues in the context of risk, and many claims have been made about the need for, and ways to, 'democratize science' and promote citizen involvement with it. But who are the 'citizens' in these approaches, and what sort of participatory engagement is envisaged? Citizenship has been theorized in many ways and according to diverse traditions of political philosophy.[5] Here we summarize how several dominant lines of thinking construct the notion of citizenship, indicate connections to particular theories of democracy, and consider how these are reflected – whether explicitly or, more often, implicitly – in debates about science and knowledge in STS and DS. We identify how these in turn suggest different approaches to, and justify different traditions of, participation.

Liberal perspectives We begin with liberal perspectives. Put briefly, in liberal thought citizens are entitled to universal rights granted by the state. Citizens are seen as individuals who act rationally to advance their own interests, while the state's role is to protect and enforce their rights. Rights are deemed universal in the sense that every citizen has equal rights vis-à-vis the state, including rights to participation through electoral democracy. Exercising rights is seen as the choice of citizens, on the assumption that they have adequate resources for rights-claiming. Public participation is therefore seen as something to which all citizens have an equal right, and as conducted by individuals through engagement in democratic politics, overseen by a state whose benevolent motives are unquestioned.

This mode of theorizing has been coproduced with the emergence of Western liberal democracies. As other works have shown, however, different historical trajectories may strongly challenge the universality of rights in other contexts, given the particular experiences of colonialism and the way in which legal and political institutions define some as 'citizens' and others as 'subjects' or non-citizens (Mamdani 1996; see also Kabeer 2001).

From the liberal perspective the state is seen as a benevolent protector of individuals, including, as Marshall's classic work (1950) emphasized, protecting them against major risks. The state is given a role in reducing uncertainties emerging out of the processes of capitalism, requiring various forms of welfarism. In the contemporary era and from a liberal perspective, a similar role might be imagined for the state to intervene in risk amelioration, and for state-sponsored science to guarantee the safety of citizens, through food safety regulations, pollution risk management and so on. Liberal understandings of citizenship thus hold faith in the modern state's expertise, and science has become its core currency in the technology arena. Liberal theories of democracy connected with these defer decisions to elected elites, who historically have been highly reliant on accredited scientific and technocratic expertise.

It is this kind of perspective on citizenship which underlies the 'deficit' model in science studies and policy, established so authoritatively with the 1985 report of the Royal Society, which treats public scepticism about science as due to a deficit in people's knowledge and understanding of it. The assumption is that individual members of the public would come to respect and appreciate official scientific expertise if they could only be brought to understand this through education and the effective communication of science. In a European context, 'science shops' (Irwin 1995), whereby members of the public can consult accredited experts on issues that concern them, reflect such a view, as well as a liberal emphasis on people's rights to access formal scientific knowledge. In DS, a liberal perspective underlies much recent development thought, whereby citizens are conceived as beneficiaries, customers and users of services provided by a developmental state or, following the Washington consensus, liberalized markets. As Cornwall and Gaventa (2001) have shown, much 'participatory' development has been attempted within this framing, with participation seen in terms of individuals choosing among an array of options and services, but not playing a major role in setting agendas of policy or technology development.

Communitarian perspectives In strong contrast to liberal notions of citizenship, communitarian thought centres on the notion of the socially embedded citizen and membership of a community (Sandal 1998; Smith 1998). Individual identity is therefore subsumed to that of a group, and the common good is prioritized over the pursuit of individual interests. The emphasis is on the pursuit of local agendas, with the state appearing more distantly, if at all.

A communitarian perspective in DS is evident – though usually implicitly – in many approaches to community development and locale-specific projects. In these, an external donor agency, non-governmental organization (NGO) or branch of the state may focus on a particular geographical area or group of people for the planning and delivery of development interventions. In such approaches, the 'community' is often constructed as if it were bounded and relatively homogeneous, with people acting together for a common goal. This is particularly evident in approaches to community-based natural resource management, for example. It frequently follows that knowledge is assumed to be held by the 'community', and that knowledge is seen as an important definer of group identity and cohesiveness. Drawing on a long tradition of highly localized, village-based anthropological studies, much work on indigenous technical knowledge and 'ethnoscience' aims to document such knowledge as an input into community development processes. A communitarian perspective also allows for lay knowledges, however, to be seen as culturally embedded and geographically specific, and to be associated with different precepts and problem framings from Western science and its associated notions of modernization and development.

A parallel, though distinct, set of ideas underlies communitarian movements in Europe and North America, such as those focused on anarchist or broadly 'alternative' eco-lifestyles. Here again, the focus is on community self-sufficiency in terms of governance, with knowledge seen as a community and local resource. In terms of science and technology it is this line of thinking that underlies advocacy of 'radical' or 'alternative' technology and a philosophy of 'small is beautiful', supporting local economic development (Schumacher 1973). While these traditions of communitarian thought have focused on the local, a communitarian perspective also helps

23

comprehend manifestations of what might be seen as 'global' citizenship. Local expressions of communitarianism frequently incorporate global imaginations, captured in the expression 'think global, act local'.

In developing-country contexts, participation has generally been constructed around and conducted within a community-level project frame, resting on the assumption that citizen participation emerges through being a community member. A large repertoire of techniques and methods has evolved since the 1980s in such contexts to facilitate the expression of community concerns and the elicitation of local knowledge. Participatory Rural Appraisal, for example, has become the sine qua non of development practice the world over (Chambers 1993, 1997; PLA Notes 1988 onwards). Only much more recently, and especially since the early 1990s in the wake of Agenda 21 initiatives (Selman 1998; Selman and Parker 1997), have such approaches and their associated constructions of the participating citizen become popular in the North.

Civic republican perspectives Civic republican thought bridges aspects of the liberal and communitarian traditions, situating individuals as part of collectivities that press claims in the political realm. It recognizes a diversity of interests within society and assumes that citizens will form factional groups around these. Citizenship is thus related to a common civic identity based on common public culture, and individual obligations to participate in communal affairs (e.g., Habermas 1984, 1996; Miller 1988). This participation is not confined to representative political systems as in liberal thought; rather civic republican thought promotes deliberative forms of democracy as a complement or alternative to representative democracy (e.g., Bohmann and Rehg 1997; Dryzek 1990, 2000). A notion of the common good is seen to emerge out of a rational debate among free citizens in which different claims have their say and give way to collective agreement.

Much work on citizen science is underlain implicitly by a civic republican perspective. Such work draws attention to how claims and interests related to knowledge and experience emerge and are refracted through political dialogue. Factional groups, united by common experiences of science, technology and its risks, may press claims based on their experiential knowledge, as in the actions of HIV/AIDS activists, toxic waste campaigners, 'NIMBY' protest groups or parents concerned about vaccine risks and side effects.

The recent move towards deliberative and inclusionary processes explicitly invites such claims-making in new forums, whether citizens' juries, consensus conferences, scenario panels, and so on (e.g., Bloomfield et al.

2001; Holmes and Scoones 2000; IPPR 1999; NEF 1998; and see Part Four of this book). Given that public issues involving science and technology are always pervaded by uncertainty and involve social and ethical judgements, plural perspectives and deliberative processes may be needed in order to reach socially legitimate and acceptable decisions (Munton 2003).

Many questions arise, however, about how such dialogues are convened and framed. Civic republican thought generally assumes that nation-states provide the organizing frameworks for political dialogue, and by implication the epistemological basis for such interactions. Some commentators have pointed critically to the tendency for Deliberative and Inclusionary Processes (DIPs) to remain very much within the orbit of mainstream scientific discourse, with their questions, problem-framings and modes of argumentation defined accordingly (e.g., Scoones and Thompson 2003; Stirling, this book). This tendency can perhaps be better understood by reflecting on its civic republican underpinnings, where the state is seen as coherent, rational and ordering, suggesting a reliance on scientific expertise as the basic framework within which judgements will be reached. Sometimes, of course, such encounters between citizens and accredited experts will result in the reframing of the debate, as when HIV/AIDS activists in the USA succeeded in expanding the range of perspectives deemed credible within scientific research about the issue (Epstein 1996). Very often, however, deliberative forums remain couched within a particular framework, silencing other perspectives and agendas. The assumption of free debate and 'ideal speech' contained within much civic republican thought (Habermas 1984, 1996) betrays naivety about the politics and power relations of such encounters.

In the North, the move to participation in decision-making in science and technology, as more broadly, has thus been bound up with an extensive debate about political interests and their expression in the public sphere through deliberative democracy. In contrast, and surprisingly, the much longer-standing concern with participation in developing-country settings has only late in its history come to reflect in any depth on the politics of participation, and on participation beyond the community and project level. Only recently are a range of arguments that citizens should be more active 'makers and shapers' of development agendas emerging from critiques of liberal 'users and choosers' perspectives (Cornwall and Gaventa 2001). Equally, emerging from a dissatisfaction with the communitarian emphasis on independent local settings is concerted reflection on how processes of local and national governance involving state and other institutions may be made more participatory (Cornwall 2002; Gaventa and Goetz 2001).

These emergent perspectives on participation in developing-country settings resonate strongly with civic republicanism in their construction of citizenship, showing many similarities with perspectives on deliberative democracy in the North. Not surprisingly, they confront many of the same dilemmas. In relation to science and technology, recent attempts to invite citizen participation in policy processes – for example, in national desertification or biodiversity conservation strategies – face similar problems of domination by powerful, mainstream problem-framings, as do such processes in Northern settings (e.g., Fairhead and Leach 2003; Keeley and Scoones 2003). In all settings, moreover, there is a pervasive tension between public engagement with a particular decision and a broader challenge to the whole policy process, opening it up to public scrutiny and making it more legitimate and inclusive (Wynne 2003). As the experience of the 'GM Nation?' debate in the UK in 2003 showed, public concerns were very much centred on these broader issues, critiquing the wider discourses and practices of public institutions and the ways they impose particular meanings.

Citizenship and identity Although they do so in different ways, liberal and civic republican thought both promote citizenship as universal, distinguishing this from particularistic group identities. Such perspectives are critiqued by theories of difference and identity. Many feminists and others associate citizenship with group identities based on specific forms and experiences of difference – such as those linked to gender, race, disability, locality, and so on (Young 1989, 1990) – creating a perspective that Dryzek (2000) terms 'difference democracy'. From such perspectives, claims about universality and the rationality of dialogue are critiqued as promoting the biases of powerful groups. Standard approaches of deliberative democracy are extended and modified to attend to counter-processes of exclusion and to recognize highly differentiated needs, such as through a 'politics of presence' (Phillips 1993, 1995). These perspectives also stretch the definition of the public realm into the private sphere, in that personal, embodied experiences become central to the construction of identities and political positions. Knowledge in such accounts is very much bound up with the constitution and expression of identity. For instance, certain strands of eco-feminist thought in both North and South link 'women' with distinct experience-based forms of ecological knowledge derived from their everyday interactions with their local environments (e.g. Mies and Shiva 1993). Many discussions of indigenous peoples and their forms of self-representation similarly ground identity in particular forms of ecological knowledge. While drawing attention to knowledge differentiation, however, these perspectives tend also to depict knowledge as rather static and essentialized. Much work in a DS context has documented the struggles of such marginalized groups in relation to broader state and development processes and the science they are based on, which are seen as biased towards the interests of dominant groups (such as men, urban industrial elites, corporate capital, and so on) over key resources such as water, genetic resources or forests (e.g., Blaikie and Brookfield 1987; Bryant 1992; Rocheleau et al. 1996).

This DS work bears strong parallels with work on environmental justice in European and North American settings. This similarly draws attention to the unequal effects of science and technology-driven processes, and their contribution to the marginalization of certain groups and places. The knowledge deployed in such struggles is seen to emerge from particular experiences of specific places, and to be derived from everyday, lived experiences; for example, of pollution, disease dynamics and so on (GECP 2001; Schlosberg 1999).

Certain forms of identity and difference – most notably gender, reflecting the important contributions of feminist thought – have received prominent treatment in both STS (e.g., Harding 1991, 1998) and DS (e.g., Kabeer 1994). In contrast, other dimensions – notably race – have been surprisingly downplayed in both, although perhaps for different reasons reflecting the respective histories of each (for STS, see Skinner 2002). A recent collection, however, fruitfully brings together scholars of science studies and anthropologists with international interests to reflect on how 'race' and 'nature' are invoked together to justify particular forms of social categorization and control, as well as challenges to these (Moore et al. 2003).

While these perspectives on citizenship and identity bear parallels with civic republican thought in the emphasis on interests (linked to knowledge) and the mobilization of these in claims on the state, the greater emphasis on difference, and the power structures within which these are embedded, leads to less optimism about reaching consensus through rational political dialogue. These perspectives draw attention to a political economy of knowledge that legitimizes and privileges certain kinds of expertise over others, and in which people have differential access to material resources and political power through which to press their concerns. Thus, identity politics and engagement in scientific and policy processes are frequently pursued through social movements – such as the many evident in the environmental arena (Offe 1985; Wapner 1996; Yearley 1994). While movements may present their driving interests, knowledge and identity in essentialist terms, however (as indeed some analysts do), it is problematic to assume that actors cannot make demands on the basis of more than one identity, or indeed take part in more hybrid forms of political engagement.

Such criticisms have in particular been put forward by those taking post-structuralist approaches to the question of citizenship and identity.

Citizenship practice and subjectivities A number of post-structuralist theorists have challenged essentialist ideas about collective identity. Instead, they argue that people have a multiplicity of overlapping subject positions, as 'female', 'farmer', 'Hindu', and so on, each more or less contingent, in which each dimension shapes the others. Subject positions both arise from and shape everyday practice, but may also be acquired through identification with broader discourses. Group political identity is produced through identification with others who hold particular subject positions in common. Citizen action thus draws upon particular political identities at particular moments (Laclau and Mouffe 1985; Mouffe 1992, 1995). This gives rise to a fragmented and contingent notion of citizenship as realized in the enactment of political action. While citizenship also continues as an idea or principle to 'give a sense of inclusion ... what it means to be included is now a highly contingent matter' (Ellison 1997: 709). Furthermore, rather than being directed at a singular notion of the state, such action may be directed towards more diverse and dispersed sites and spaces. This perspective thus becomes even more pertinent in the context of globalization, where terrains of governance are increasingly fractured, as we consider in the next section.

The emphasis on practice in these notions of citizenship has many strong resonances with the so-called move to practice in constructivist STS from the 1980s onwards. This work emphasizes how knowledge and its authority come into being only through particular practices, and the specific networks of actors and objects that they involve (see Haraway 1991; Latour 1987, 1993; Pickering 1992, 1995). More broadly, the emphasis in STS on the social construction of scientific knowledge and the existence of plural, partial perspectives on any given problem is highly compatible with this way of conceiving of citizenship, even though, as we have seen, there has been rather little work on understanding citizen knowledge and perspectives in the STS field. In DS, by contrast, such analysis of knowledge-as-practice as there has been focuses on the domain of lay knowledges rather than on accredited expertise. In actor-oriented approaches, particularly well developed in issues of agricultural technology (e.g., Long and Long 1992) and ecology (e.g., Nyerges 1997), a similar picture emerges of multiple and shifting subject positions that come into being through and enact particular forms of knowledge. Interactions between these – as, for instance, when farmers and agricultural extension workers interact, or in so-called participatory development encounters – may create new forms of knowledge and practice in an unpredictable and contingent way that thoroughly undermines aspirations to controlled, blueprint, planned development interventions (Long and van der Ploeg 1989). For this reason, orchestrated attempts at public involvement often unravel, unleashing unanticipated outcomes and further processes of change.

For some commentators, this conception of the decentred, free-floating subject tends – at its extreme – to dissolve into extreme relativism, nihilism and the politics of despair, failing to allow for the possibility of forms of solidarity, shared practices and meanings beyond those of a dissociated individual subject (Ellison 1997; Lash et al. 1996). The extreme post-structuralist position thus threatens to eclipse the broader idea of citizenship as about inclusivity and political involvement. It is in attempting to rescue a notion of citizenship from this morass that Ellison comments:

> Citizenship no longer conveys a universalist sense of inclusion or participation in a stable political community; neither does it suggest the possibility of developing claims organised around a relatively stable set of differences; nor, for that matter, can the term be made to conform easily to the living out of a series of socially constructed identity positions on the decentred social subjects. Instead, we are left with a restless desire for social engagement, citizenship becoming a form of social and political practice born of the need to establish new solidarities across a range of putative 'communities' as a defence against social changes which continually threaten to frustrate such ambitions. (1997: 712)

Citizenship is thus redefined in more performative terms; in effect, as *practised engagement through emergent social solidarities*. Such solidarities frequently emerge in response to threats of various kinds. These forms of engagement, involving new processes of social and political interaction, are, as Ellison emphasizes, likely to be 'increasingly messy and unstable' (ibid.).

A politics of this kind is not dissimilar to the politics that Beck, Giddens and others (Beck 1992; Beck et al. 1994; Giddens 1990) have associated with the conditions of late modernity, and the emergence of the 'risk society'. As society responds reflexively to the emergence of new risks, it is argued, so new forms of sub-politics emerge. While Beck draws attention to the breakdown of traditional social forms in this context, however, and to the linking of reflexivity to an ongoing process of individualization, the risk society thesis gives less attention to the building or regeneration of social solidarities (Ellison 1997). This may reflect the particular origins of the thesis in late-twentieth-century Europe, but it is not necessarily applicable elsewhere (Adam et al. 2000; Caplan 2000). Indeed, a variety of experiences, many of them in developing-country settings, reveal the creation and re-creation of solidarities that are by no means stable, but which contribute substantially to social and political processes over particular periods in particular places: solidarities among people threatened or displaced by large dams or infrastructure development, for example. Emergent social solidarities may in turn connect people and groups in different sites, albeit temporarily. For example, what is described as the 'anti-globalization move-ment' consists of a range of diverse solidarities around particular issues, expressed in practices of engagement with particular institutions in both local and global settings (Held and McGrew 2002; Klein 2000).

It is notable that such a perspective on citizenship potentially fractures the established social and democratic link between citizenship and social equality. Instead, as Ellison, paraphrasing Beck, suggests: 'there may be "reflexivity winners and losers". Some groups may be more adept than others in adjusting to more fluid social and political forms, constructing and reconstructing solidarities which further a variety of claims across space and time according to the dictates of social change' (1997: 212). Citizenship is then associated with those who are able to participate, and who do 'practise engagement', which suggests in turn a category of contex-tual non-citizens who do not. This may be for a variety of reasons, whether through deliberate non-engagement, through political marginalization, through lack of resources, or through a sense of distance and alienation from the debates being pursued in the public realm. Citizenship practice – and non-citizenship – thus needs to be seen as historically constituted, its conditions of emergence shaped by particular social, material and political relations. For example, hunters in Trinidad have brought their experience-based expertise of wildlife dynamics into critical engagements with state- and donor-led biodiversity science through citizenship prac-tice, whereas in Guinea, despite the prevalence of similar forms of local knowledge and state-sponsored science, such citizenship practice has not emerged. The reasons for this can be traced to the ways in which social relations of science have developed, linked to the nature of colonial and post-colonial state-building and then to degrees of donor dependence, as embedded in each country's political, educational and media traditions (Leach and Fairhead 2002).

Such a perspective on citizenship as practised engagement links to a view of participatory democracy that emphasizes the capacity of citizens to participate and engage in decisions that affect their lives (Pateman 1970). Some commentators distinguish such genuinely participatory democracy, in which citizens bring their own perspectives and experiential expertise to bear, from deliberative democracy, which often constructs rational debate within dominant expert framings (Gaventa, pers. comm.). Participatory democratic theory also, as Sirianni and Friedland note:

> stresses the educative function of participating in community and political affairs for creating the kinds of citizens capable of sustaining democracy. Through active participation, citizens become more knowledgeable about the political system, develop a greater sense of their own efficacy, and widen their horizons beyond their own narrow self interest to consider a broader public good. (2000: 23)

In other words, practising citizenship is also a learning process that creates and enhances citizenship capabilities (Merrifield 2002).

Such a conception of citizenship as practised engagement through emergent social solidarities is helpful in conceptualizing current public responses to science and technology and the risks these present. It is in these terms, for instance, that the forms of public response to genetically modified (GM) crops in India can be best understood. Moreover, engagement with scientific controversies may now be a key context where citizenship practices are played out in new, important ways in an era when other issues have been depoliticized or given over to the play of liberal market forces.

There has, however, been rather limited attention in most STS and DS commentaries to the implications of such reconfigured forms of citizenship for public action in issues of science and technology. As we have seen, much of the debate about participation and deliberation has drawn instead, we would argue, on overly static and essentialized notions of the 'public', 'community', 'state', 'interests' and 'knowledge'. These problems, and the need for a more historicized account of citizenship as practised engagement, become even more pertinent in the context of globalization, a subject to which we now turn.

Globalized contexts for science and citizenship

While debates on participation in science frequently take place in particular locales, the world is now too connected, and science and policy too globalized, for citizenship practice to be confined to a local level. Equally, in the context of contemporary globalization it is not appropriate to characterize 'late industrial society' as specific to certain geographical locales, as the risk society thesis has tended to do. Rather, relations of definition of and responses to risk are quintessentially locked into globalized scientific and policy fields. This pervasive international context creates an important common arena for study that transcends North–South divides. Yet many comparative questions arise concerning the strikingly different capacities

31

of different countries and groups to negotiate their interests in such internationalized contexts.

Despite the fact that science and technology are commonly seen as central to processes of globalization – for instance, through the development of information and communication technologies – most debates on globalization have been surprisingly silent on how science and knowledge relations are transforming in a contemporary globalized arena. Perhaps this relates to prevailing assumptions about the universality of science, dislocating it from context and place. Nevertheless, a number of strands of contemporary theorizing about globalization in general offer important insights into how the globalized scientific field, and citizens' engagement with it, might be understood.

There are various dimensions to the globalization of science. Rosenau (1990) describes the growing importance (alongside states) of a world of transnational sub-politics, with its dimensions including a prominence of transnational organizations, transnational problems dominating the political agenda, transnational events, the development of transnational communities, and transnational structures such as various forms of network. Many transnational actors relevant to science have emerged, whether corporations involved in scientific research and commerce (creating risks, defining what is risky and what is not), or international organizations with a scientific mandate, such as those regulating scientific and technology issues. International conventions, agreements and deliberations, such as those dealing with biodiversity conservation, biosafety and so on, co-evolving with scientific committees and with the politics of their operation, are conducted at least partly through the practices of science (Fairhead and Leach 2003).

Especially given the transformations wrought by information and communications technology, Castells (1996) argues further that dominant functions are increasingly organized through networks and flows that link them up around the world. Today, scientists across the world are linked through e-mail-based networks, as well as through the more traditional forms of professionally based workshops, meetings and conferences. Such networks together can have a powerful influence on the framing of debates and the direction of scientific and technological research, through the creation of 'epistemic communities' (Haas 1992) or advocacy (Sabatier and Jenkins-Smith 1993) or discourse coalitions (Hajer 1995).

As a result of these increasingly prominent global actors and networks, there is evidence of a growing alignment of science and policy that does not rely on orchestration by any particular international organization, state or localized institution. The sense is more akin to Hardt and Negri's (2000) characterization of an 'empire' dominating contemporary world politics, premised on an increasingly decentred, deterritorialized form of global governance. This is prescribing particular forms of harmonization in the science-based regulation of science and technology. For example, in debates about genetically modified organisms (GMOs), globally organized science is being used to justify harmonizing standards to risk assessment and the removal of barriers to trade. Such moves also act to create a global field of epistemic relevance into which researchers find themselves drawn in order that their work might have credibility and standing.

Even where the international political-economic interests appear more diffuse and harder to pin down, internationalized concepts can powerfully influence local debates, albeit mediated through complicated scientific and policy relationships and networks linking national research traditions, donors, NGOs, development projects, national and local media, and so on. Sometimes the effect can be to silence local discourses, or rather for their evidence, concepts and categories to be co-opted into terms that more or less fit internationalized ones. This is the case, for example, in Guinea, where the internationally salient concept of 'biodiversity' has been operationalized in a variety of national and local scientific and policy discourses. All of these share the notion of 'managing biodiversity' as something separate from and threatened by people, thus writing out or reinterpreting farmers' perspectives on the ways they live with and manipulate plant variety in everyday life and landscapes. These farmers' perspectives continue to animate local discourses and social relations, but in a way rather dislocated from public policy processes (Fairhead and Leach 2003). In a similar vein, Hayden (2003) describes how the neo-liberal framing of the International Convention on Biodiversity, which assumes that 'nature protection' requires payment for ecosystem goods and services, and people to profit from using nature, is totally at odds with how Amazonian 'indigenous peoples' frame nature protection.While international concepts sometimes serve to oversimplify or obscure local debates, however, they can also sustain them in powerful ways. As anthropological work on globalization has pointed out, rather than opposing local knowledges to a homogenizing movement of cultural globalization, there is a need to look at how precepts that appear as universal are in fact represented and interpreted in quite different ways in different locales (Robertson 1992). Thus, while appearing to have a common meaning, international concepts can mean different things to actors in different local contexts. They can be appropriated creatively as vehicles for localized movements, as has been the case, for example, with the use of 'sustainability' ideas by activist groups in India (Visvanathan, pers. comm.).

These conceptual appropriations suggest one set of ways in which globalization is now shaping apparently localized movements around science and technology. Others include the linking of local knowledge claims and movements through international networks and organizations, with 'indigenous peoples' perhaps representing the case par excellence.

These linkages, however, take place in a context of increasing deterritorialization due to mass migrations and transnational flows of products, images and ideas, creating what Appadurai (1991) has termed a 'global cultural ecumene' or what Hannerz (1990) terms a 'world in creolisation'. In this despatialized world, claims around the territorial or local basis of knowledge or practice are no longer taken for granted. And where such claims are made they need to be questioned as to their social and political meanings (Gupta and Ferguson 1992). This casts a new, more critical light on what is meant by 'local' or 'indigenous' knowledge.

Globalization, then, renders theories of citizenship situated solely within the context of the nation-state (whether of liberal or civic republican persuasion) as highly limited. One response to this has been the construction of the notion of a 'global citizen', responding to global problems and linked with others across national borders through citizen action (Edwards and Gaventa 2001). The sense of inclusivity that underlies the idea of citizenship emerges here through inclusion in the idea of an integrated world community. There is also a sense, as in Beck's (2000) construction of 'world risk society', of citizen reflexivity emerging in response to global, transnational risks and threats, such as those linked to global warming, for example.

A perspective on citizenship as practised engagement of social solidarities – as developed earlier – allows for the possibility of global citizen action but in ways that are often contingent, fragmented and diffuse, emerging through the expression of aspects of people's global and local identities. Rather than recourse to the establishment of global institutions to guarantee global citizenship rights, these are claimed and might be institutionally supported through more diverse actions linked across different sites (Appadurai 2002b; see also Robins, this book).

Moreover, as Robertson (1992) argues, globalization may be generating new forms of reflexivity, as through the mass media and other forms of interaction people come to pay more conscious attention to the world as a single place. For example, in a project to translate global environmental problems into a set of meaningful indicators for Lancashire County Council (McNaghten et al. 1995), it became clear against all preconceptions that people felt a sense of solidarity with Bangladeshi farmers who would be affected by rising sea levels as a result of global warming. This thoroughly contradicted the idea that people will be persuaded to do anything about global climate change only when negative impacts on them, personally, can be demonstrated. In this case, more transnational expressions of citizenship challenged prevailing constructions of the citizen as an individual, self-interested consumer within the context of a nation-state. Citizens' movements have also emerged that are motivated by global visions, but ones that run counter to, and critique, dominant forms of globalization, such as the 'counter-hegemonic' globalization movement of Porto Allegre.

Bauman (1998) argues that globalization and localization are not only two aspects of the same thing, but also driving forces and active expressions of a new polarization and stratification of the world's population, a new sociocultural hierarchy dividing those who are free to move from those who are 'chained to the spot' – or forced into (globally shaped) localities against their will. In effect, this is an argument about those who can assume global citizenship – through taking advantage of new networks, movement and communication forms, and compressions of space and time (Giddens 1990; Harvey 1989) – and those who cannot. Nevertheless, it is important not to write off these so-called 'localized poor' as non-citizens in a global context. Even those apparently excluded from global citizenship are still subject to the effects of global processes, possibly leading them to form different sorts of social solidarities on different scales and in different ways. There is evidence of these emerging, for example, in cases where disenfranchised valley farmers face flooding by large dam construction, or where marginalized smallholders are subject to policies promoting industrialized, biotech-based farming.

Contemporary discussions of participation in a global setting often emphasize mechanisms such as the representation of local or special interest groups (for example, indigenous people, women, pastoralists, small farmers, and so on) in international convention meetings. They also emphasize global consultations with people as 'consumers' of development, as in the 'Voices of the Poor' exercise of the World Bank (Narayan 2000). In such approaches, people are supposed to participate and express their knowledge and perspectives in internationally convened forums. They rest either on a liberal conception of citizenship, replacing the usual emphasis on the nation-state with the globe, represented in turn by supposedly impartial international governance institutions such as the World Bank, International Monetary Fund (IMF), Convention on Biological Diversity (CBD) or World Trade Organization (WTO), or accept a form of identity- or interest-based citizenship in the global arena.

The limited literature that has reflected critically on these approaches highlights how the power dynamics at play replicate and exacerbate those evident in participatory approaches in local settings (e.g., Brock et al. 2001).

Taking a different perspective on science and citizenship suggests that sites of engagement may be far more diffuse and transient, but nevertheless contain potential for the development of multiple and interacting solidarities in a global context. For example, in the opposition to GM foods, groups working on themes from property rights to sustainable agriculture to health and food safety in settings as diverse as rural India and Europe are finding areas of common – or at least overlapping – ground, facilitated by a huge array of e-mail networks, meetings and other forums, to raise and reframe the debate about food and agriculture futures. In this way, 'everyday sites of social resistance' (Lefebvre 1991) may become linked in new, often unpredictable ways, recasting the rather mechanistic, instrumental view of participation as one that is more decentred, less orchestrated and, with this, more political. In turn, such engagements may create, through repeated practice, experiential learning and the building of solidarities, new forms of citizenship engagement that provide – at least for those who become involved – the possibilities for envisaging alternative science and technology agendas.

Such processes of globalization further underline that the North–South distinctions that have pervaded so many debates on science, risk and participation do not hold up in practice. As the issues and examples considered in this chapter have shown, experiences of extreme vulnerability and marginalization from science/policy processes are common to groups of people in Europe and the USA as much as in Asia and Africa, while the latter, too, have their groups of 'scientific citizens' contesting official perspectives in Euro-American, reflective, 'risk society' style. Other distinctions – between issues, prevailing scientific cultures and histories, and positions in international political economy, for example – may be of greater significance in shaping the evidently highly diverse patterns of public engagement (and disengagement) with science appearing across the world.

Cognitive justice, science and citizenship

The demands of many citizens' movements, whether or not orchestrated through international connections, are for what might be termed 'cognitive justice' (Visvanathan, this book) in the scientific field. Such demands do not represent an anti-science or anti-technology agenda; nor are they necessarily against the particular high-tech scientific developments, such as biotechnology, that have caused such public controversy over possible risks. Rather, the demand is for the right for different forms of knowledge and their associated practices and ways of being to coexist, and to carry weight in the decisions that affect people's lives. The idea of cognitive justice provides a useful way of thinking about the broader social and political field in which struggles over issues involving science and technology take place. As a relational concept, it provides a frame for advancing democratic practice and for recognizing the claims of communities, groups and networks that may be articulated in terms outside the remit of science. In this sense, it goes beyond a narrower, but potentially useful in some circumstances, notion of 'knowledge rights', which has more absolute, non-negotiable and individualized connotations.[6] At certain times, and around certain issues, knowledge rights might be a candidate for inclusion together with the political, social and economic rights that currently dominate discussions of citizenship, and which comprise the rights-based agenda in development. While such rights would be formally granted through institutional and legal processes, they would be made real only through the practices of citizens claiming and using them (Nyamu 2002). This may, in turn, rely on the realization of other rights, such as those in the economic or political realm; although in other circumstances knowledge rights may be a means to extend other forms of rights-claiming.

The broader idea of cognitive justice, however, helps overcome some of the potential pitfalls of a narrower emphasis on knowledge rights. Cognitive justice would not be confined to possessing or accessing knowledge as if it were a commodity linked to individuals, as a liberal conception of citizenship – and many 'rights to information' campaigns – would suggest. Nor would it simply imply bringing 'contributory expertise', continuous with dominant scientific perspectives, to a given decision. Nor would it be only about citizens pressing claims based on their experiential knowledge, as a civic republican perspective would suggest. Nor would it be confined to expressing essentialized knowledges associated with particular local, community, or identity-based groups. Rather, it would encompass the legitimacy of struggles to pursue particular ways of life, knowledge, perspectives and practice; to use these as ways of building solidarities with others, and for cognitive representation in processes of scientific experimentation and decision-making in science and technology issues. Such a perspective, grounded in a conception of citizenship as practised engagement, could serve to enrich innovation-oriented science and the setting of science and technology agendas, as well to render protection-oriented, precautionary science and risk assessment more socially inclusive and legitimate.

Furthermore, cognitive justice in terms of public issues involving science can be seen as mutually constitutive of participatory forms of democratic practice more generally. As Jasanoff (2003a: 397) argues, there are a number of compelling reasons why citizen engagement is necessary, and must necessarily extend beyond the addition of 'contributory expertise' to particular decisions. Citizen engagement is, she suggests, necessary: to uphold the standards of democratic society where such engagement should be the rule rather than the exception; continually to test and contest the framing and direction of expert-led decision processes; to subject institutional interests and biases to public scrutiny; to establish culturally appropriate bases on which knowledge and decisions are assessed; and to enhance civic capacity to reflect on and respond to the broader challenges of modernity. In short, cognitive justice suggests new forms of practised, engaged citizenship, both in terms of issues involving science and technology, and more broadly.

Notes

1 Although recently scholars from an STS tradition have engaged with themes concerned with post-colonial techno-science (Anderson 2002), as well as the relations between science and other knowledge systems (e.g., Verran 2001, 2002).

2 This chapter cannot attempt to provide a full account of theories of democracy and their relationship to citizenship-knowledge debates. For recent reviews see, for example, Held (1987, 1995); Dryzek (1990, 2000); Mansbridge (1999); Phillips (1993).

3 This discussion of the differing roots of work on indigenous knowledge as compared with citizen science draws on Leach and Fairhead (2002) and Fairhead and Leach (2003). See also Keeley and Scoones (2003).

4 A few notable exceptions: studies that have treated rural people's and scientists' knowledges together within the same ethnographic, practice-oriented framework include Fairhead and Leach 2003; Keeley and Scoones 2003; Murdoch and Clark 1994; Wynne 1996.

5 In this chapter we are not attempting a full review of concepts and theories of citizenship, nor their philosophical underpinnings. For fuller reviews of contemporary literature on citizenship, see, for example, Ellison (1997); Jones and Gaventa (2002).

6 Our thinking on this issue has been considerably enriched both by conference discussions and the subsequent e-mail exchange between Barbara Adam and Sheila Jasanoff, from which points in this section are drawn.

TWO | **Beyond risk: defining the terrain**

Commentary

MELISSA LEACH, IAN SCOONES AND
BRIAN WYNNE

Recent controversies and forms of engagement between science and publics cannot be understood in the narrow technical terms of 'risk' and disputes about it. Even when it is acknowledged that uncertainty, rather than risk in terms of calculable probabilities, pervades scientific issues, they frequently remain cast in these same narrow technical terms. The chapters in this section argue for, and show, a variety of ways of moving beyond these narrow definitions of scientific issues, and the notions of citizenship they embody, to encompass more of the dimensions of human meaning and concern which are found to pervade encounters between science and publics in all parts of the world.

Thus Jerry Ravetz argues for a shift from 'risk' to 'safety'. This extends his earlier notion of post-normal science, characterized by complex problems, uncertainties and strong value commitments, and requiring an extended peer community and mutual learning through dialogue. He argues that concerns with safety increasingly animate encounters between science and society, safety being a more vernacular, qualitative concept which embodies political, moral and relational concerns as well as technical ones. In Ravetz's view, safety is a constitutional issue in terms of the responsibilities of the state, of the same order as freedom of speech or human rights. This embodies a notion of citizenship as linked to claims to safety, in relation to a state.

Whether safety is the appropriate term for seeking this move beyond risk was widely debated in the meetings that have informed this book; however, the chapter does underline the basic point that politics and science must be seen together. Equally, other chapters in this book would question the degree to which the state can act as the primary guarantor of safety in relation to science, in the context of rapid processes of privatization and globalization.

If Ravetz has introduced an argument for the politicization of science and science–society encounters, Fischer explores further the epistemological relations between scientific and public rationalities. He contrasts the technical rationalities that tend to frame public policy debates about science and technology, often defining these in terms of risk, with the

41

sociocultural rationalities of publics. These emerge from lived experience as embedded in people's social worlds, and are guided by a logic of practical reason which integrates the social and the technical, and relates judgement on any issue to its relations with 'the good way of life'. These dimensions are systematically ignored by technical risk discourses which Fischer thus argues are 'irrational'.

Fischer's reference to 'the good way of life' as a basis for epistemology is taken further by Wynne in his critique of risk as the assumed framework of meaning imposed on public issues involving science. The essence of Wynne's argument is that people's sociocultural rationalities are about more than epistemology – knowledge or ways of thinking; they are about ontologies, or ways of being. At the same time, representations of risk, while imposing presumptive meanings that obscure and disable people's ontologies, also impose their own: they actually project implicit models of the human, and in that sense are tacitly performative of human ontologies. This has important implications for citizenship: while citizenship practices may emerge from people's own ways of being, particular constructions of the citizen are also imposed through risk discourses whose influence reflects real relations of power in national and, increasingly, international contexts.

A further aspect of breaking free of the risk discourse straitjacket which Wynne underlines is the need to problematize as part of the citizenship agenda the front-end purposes of innovation, and the human purposes driving this. Wynne draws examples from the large anthropological litera-ture which has documented more 'autonomous' processes of creativity in local cultural settings to illustrate how innovation can be driven by diverse human meanings and purposes. As he notes, however, with globalization the sources of innovation and forms of agency constructing and driving innovation are increasingly distanced and obscured from those expected to make use of it.

These themes are picked up by Shiv Visvanathan, who argues that we need to go beyond the normal rhetoric of participation to an understanding of the democratic implications of cognitive representation and empower-ment. This can be seen in terms of popular struggles for cognitive justice. This is not to fall into the trap of an anti-science and technology discourse, but to recognize the plurality of knowledge systems, and the underlying relationships between knowledge, livelihoods and ways of being. He argues for the recognition of the rights of alternative epistemologies and sciences in a more democratic imagination of science and citizenship.

3 | The post-normal science of safety

JERRY RAVETZ

Safety: a new element of politics and science

For a very long time we have been led to believe that the discoveries of science would be automatically applied for the benefit of humanity. By means of some 'hidden hand', the scientific discoveries made by independent researchers are converted into developments in technology and medicine that advance human welfare. We now know that scientific advance is not spontaneous, but is directed by externally set priorities. Questions of the purposes and assumptions driving science, and the power behind them, have to be addressed more openly and urgently.

The motto 'knowledge is power' goes back a long way, especially in connection with science. But now we must ask, who has the power that derives from science, and for whose benefit is it used? The converse is that 'ignorance is impotence'. To that we ask, who is kept in ignorance, how and, again, to whose benefit?

Neither of these questions is simple, nor are the answers straightforward. There is no need to suppose a conspiracy to control power or create ignorance. And we can assume that individual scientists are at least as moral and idealistic as the ordinary run of humanity. But the contract between science and society is managed by large, established institutions, whose imperatives involve power and profit in the increasingly important arenas that they themselves are creating. Unless we look at science-in-society in those terms, we are inhabiting a fantasy world of universal good intentions. We must acknowledge that science has become a means of production rather than an adventure, and that the great mass of researchers are just workers rather than explorers. Such developments bring politics directly into the governance of science. But there is another new feature that makes science, in one crucial aspect at least, essentially political.

The traditional goals of science, knowledge and power are now being enriched by a third: safety (Ravetz 2003). As science has enabled ever greater control over the age-old dangers of disease, famine and calamities, it has produced new threats, some potentially catastrophic and others insidious. The state of personal and societal safety, which in recent generations we have come to take for granted as a right, is now threatened by the unexpected consequences of advances in our science-based technology. Not

43

just the application of science but our scientific knowledge itself is now the subject of debate and concern in relation to safety and survival.

The preservation of safety is not merely a new function for science; it is one that injects politics directly into the contract between science and society. For those institutions that use science to protect the public are in a position of trust. When they fail in that task, they, and also the science and scientists that they have deployed, are seen to have betrayed that trust. In this way, science in its functions of assuring safety (we may call it regulatory or precautionary science, or just safety science) is exposed to moral protest and outrage as it never was before. This explains the sudden emergence of public mistrust of science at the turn of the millennium. There is a sense among the public that science has failed to provide protection from new dangers, many of them generated by science itself. And worse, science (as an institution related to government and commerce) has failed to acknowledge its responsibility either for their creation or for its failure to protect.

One way in which official science has secured and maintained a protected position in relation to safety has been through nomenclature and concepts. A particular discourse, ostensibly based on science, has been established to the exclusion of others based on personal experience. Thus there has been an effective creation of ignorance, as other perspectives on the issue have been inhibited from development and expression. Over the last half-century, in the industrial sphere the traditional concept of 'safety', dependent on straightforward science, craft skills and professional judgements, was supplanted by 'risk'. To some extent this was inevitable, as novel and complex industrial installations required ever more sophisticated methods for the analysis of their hazards. Civil nuclear power was the leading example of this tendency; the routes to disaster are so numerous that refined mathematical analysis provides the only hope of an assessment of their risks. But then the official discourse became dominated by 'risk', with its connotations of being a precise, quantitative measure. Older ideas of 'danger' and 'safety' were generally displaced, and relegated to untutored popular discourse. Thus the choice between the two sets of terms, with their associated concepts, involves the politics of technology and its regulation. This is at the core of the struggle for the survival of modern civilization against all its destructive tendencies. Key words have power; their absence produces impotence.

Not 'risk' but 'safety'

I therefore suggest that we carry the campaign into the terrain of nomenclature and concepts. 'Risk' is a technical term, which as commonly used presents a reduced, artificially bounded and simplified picture of the problem: probability and cost. There is a precise definition of risk: the product of the probability of an occurrence of harm, multiplied by the cost of that harm should it occur. The precision is only in the concept; in any real example, the difficulties of measurement and quantification, on top of those of defining the situation for analysis, make risk analysis a highly imprecise affair. For any real hazard involves a complex syndrome of possibilities, together with potential steps for prevention, containment, mitigation, remediation and compensation; and each of these has its own socio-technical system incorporating a variety of traditions and values.

The true complexity that is ordinarily described as 'risk' would be better characterized by the traditional terms 'safety' and 'danger'. We can approach 'safety' through the apparent paradox that there is no such thing as a zero risk. This maxim is thrown at those objecting to some proposal that they consider dangerous, as if they were demanding an unattainable perfection. Of course that is not so. To understand 'safety', we can ask, why it is safe to cross a busy road at one point and dangerous at another? The traffic is there, and the risk of an accident is non-zero at both places. But in one place the risk-reduction system is functioning with competence and integrity, and in another it is not. So being 'safe' amounts to saying that it's OK to be there. Thus, in contrast to the clinical concept of 'risk', 'safety' is a complex attribute. It is analogous to 'quality', since it is after all an aspect of quality. Both concepts are pragmatic, recursive and moral.

'Safety' cannot be reduced to a certified expertise in techniques of quantitative puzzle-solving. It is essentially post-normal (Ravetz 1993, 1999), as it involves complex and hence non-quantifiable uncertainties, along with strong value commitments. Therefore, problems of safety require an extended peer community and mutual learning through dialogue. This has implications for citizenship as well as for science. Social scientists have noted that in discussion of genetically modified (GM) food and crop risks, for example, ordinary people rarely use the term 'risk' unless prompted to do so, instead using the less colonized terms 'harm', 'danger' or, more typically, and significantly, 'unknown consequences' (Marris et al. 2001). Also, safety is the concept that is appropriate for real regulation; thus in the UK we still do not have the 'Health and Acceptable-Risk Executive', but rather the Health and Safety Executive (HSE).

The methodology of safety science

Changing our conceptual focus from 'risk' to 'safety' enables us to gain clarity on the post-normal character of the problems. A full appreciation of a 'safety' problem necessarily involves its complex character. To take a familiar example, a dangerous road crossing involves a variety of road users (and abusers!), together with their associated groups and institutions, plus all those official bodies with (frequently conflicting) tasks and perspectives for the place. Each interest will have its own conceptual framework for characterizing the problem, deriving from its own remit, culture and traditions. To some extent they will be speaking in different languages. It is, of course, possible to impose a single 'scientific' analysis and conclusion; but in practice that will be just another stakeholder's voice. There will be an effective solution when all the different sides learn to listen to each other, to reach a creative solution that minimizes the perceived cost to each, and then collectively to 'own' the solution so that it can be genuinely put into practice. Of course, it is quite possible that in some cases such a happy state of affairs is not achieved. Then at least one side goes through the post-normal educational experience, and with non-violent means (in this case, demonstrations and walk-ons) might coerce the other into resuming negotiations in good faith. Of course, the experts have a part to play in all this. But they will be more useful to the extent that they see themselves in a context where the scientific-technical issue is defined by purposes that are ambiguous and conflicted. Then they will also more easily see themselves as others see them, a precious gift to anyone.

The trajectory of safety science

One key difference between safety science as a post-normal inquiry and traditional science is the source of its problems. In 'basic' science they are created by the investigators. In industrial science and research and development (R&D), they are presented by managers to researchers; the criteria of quality reflect the intention of profitable development. But safety science exists in the policy domain, and so has a very different trajectory. A problem is born when someone discovers that something seems to be dangerous, despite everyone assuming that it is safe. It could be an unusual medical complaint, or a device that goes wrong even when properly used, or signs that some natural or socio-technical system is not in good shape. What should they do? The perceptions may well be ambiguous, and the causes are likely to be indistinct or unknown. The discoverers may make a report to some organization, perhaps the responsible firm or perhaps some regulatory agency or inspectorate. They get fobbed off. What next?

It is important to realize that from the nature of the situation, without anyone being consciously indifferent or malevolent, the authorities are in a catch-22 trap. To check out every single report of this vague nature would stretch the resources of any regulatory agency. Many such reports are beyond verification. There are also the possibilities of powerful vested interests becoming offended, and then bringing political pressures to bear.

So it is easiest for the staff to dismiss those reports that don't fit into known categories, and which don't seem to present any serious threat. The effective policy becomes based on the assumption that 'absence of conclusive evidence of harm' is the same as 'conclusive evidence of absence of harm'.

I should make it clear that with the previous sentence I am not asserting that all regulatory agencies are suborned and corrupt. Not long ago, people in the UK would have been shocked even at the suggestion that a regulatory agency could be influenced by an external interest. But we are all wiser now, thanks to the blunders and scandals of the mid-1990s. It is now common knowledge that risks arise, or safety is compromised, when one interest produces a situation whereby others are placed in danger. It is a commonplace that accidents do not merely 'happen', but occur through failures of the systems of anticipation and prevention. No regulatory effort can prevent all conceivable risks from ever being realized; judgements of what is feasible necessarily enter decisions, and the pressures exerted by powerful interests are a fact of life. In this sense, it is correct to say that risks are imposed, or, equivalently, that danger is an essential aspect of the exploitation and expropriation that are an inherent feature of unequal societies.

Returning to our narrative, a standard response by the regulators is to tell the aggrieved person that their evidence is 'merely anecdotal'. The implication is that they should come back when they have prepared a properly documented case. But to do that is beyond the resources of almost all individuals, and so they are left with their anecdotes and their worries. Until, that is, someone else hears about it; perhaps a neighbour or workmate, or perhaps a journalist. Then there is a collection of anecdotes, followed by the creation and mobilization of a collective identity and a corresponding sense of agency, and the beginnings of a safety campaign. What we might call 'housewives' epidemiology', carried out with (carefully planned) questionnaires to neighbours, is a natural start. But caution is in order. For a long time in the UK, a citizen who publicly reported the identity of dangerous pollutants in a river was considered far more culpable than the private firm that had put them there in the first place.

Once a safety campaign has started, the regulators are on the back foot. Unless they move very swiftly to accommodate the campaigners, they are forced into the position of defending a situation that an increasing number of people believe may be dangerous, and is therefore definitely not safe. The whole problem is set for confrontation, where reputations are at stake and (for a time) power politics dominates over science. In the ensuing debate, the scientific information is mixed in with issues of competence, legitimacy and probity. The evidence itself becomes enmeshed in legal and administrative processes. Investigative journalism and even the 'liberating' of confidential data can play their part. Can we still call this 'science'? Yes, that is all one phase of the post-normal science of safety.

If someone can rescue the situation so that a reasoned debate can take place (and that can and does happen), then the subsequent inquiry is quite different from that of traditional research. For 'normal' research scientists have the luxury of declining to study problems for which there is not a good prospect of a definite answer. As has been said, science is the art of the soluble. In the case of safety science, the inquiry must go ahead and find the best answer, even if it is far from conclusive. Further, until there is a good idea of what is actually causing the problem, the inquiry will be largely exploratory. The sorts of questions that are asked are of the form 'what if?' (Ravetz 1997), and the answers are necessarily speculative to some degree. And in the end, the best that can be achieved is better evidence on which a judgement must be made. The uncertainties cannot be banished, nor the value loadings eliminated.

This imperfect evidence is fed into a discussion, which again is very different from the evaluation of results in research science. For what is at stake here is not the character and quality of an item of knowledge, but the best practicable decision on the management of a problem in the real world. Results from laboratory experiments may be quite rigorous and exact, but their relevance to the messy world of variable natural systems and corruptible human institutions cannot be taken for granted. Because of these differences from the laboratory, the discussions in safety science must be of the post-normal sort. In the absence of an 'extended peer community' with their 'extended facts', it is all too likely that the decision will reflect the limited experience of those who inhabit a tidy world of well-behaved natural processes and well-behaved laboratory assistants.

Understanding 'safety science' in this way, we can see the severe limitations of the concept of 'risk management'. For this is an activity that is left to experts, whose mindset is that of, and whose natural loyalties are to, the expertise and the bureaucracy. In the case of known, standard and routine risks, the experts are usually adequate, or at least very nearly so, for doing a good job. But when safety is at stake, involving communities of people who need protection and not merely reassurance, then a different, post-normal type of inquiry is appropriate and necessary.

Safety and the corruptions of science

'Safety' could become a powerful organizing principle, a sort of heuristic, complementary to 'sustainability' or 'precaution'. It could provide a coherent basis for action in many issues in the politics of science, around which many issues in the politics of science could be organized. For safety is both eminently pragmatic and profoundly moral. The issues of technological dangers as they are now experienced bear a striking resemblance to the issues of child abuse and its cover-ups in the Roman Catholic Church. In both cases, the overwhelming majority of the workers have integrity, but the institution regularly puts its own short-term interests ahead of the welfare of its supposed clients. Then the responsible officials are corrupted by the requirements of their role, regardless of their personal inclinations. In the religious case, paedophile priests have been protected and their victims further victimized; and in the scientific case, scandalous dangers are all too frequently covered up by the agencies, while those they are charged to protect are kept in a state of ignorance and impotence, along with humiliation and isolation. This is most easily seen in the case of scientific medicine, where professional loyalties seem all too often to override elementary considerations of humanity and decency. In the UK, we have seen the scandals of retained body parts (Alder Hey and elsewhere), of sanctioned incompetence in special surgical units (Bristol), and of the persecution of bereaved mothers not explicitly as witches but as cases of the pseudo-scientific 'Munchhausen's syndrome by proxy'.

Even when their cover is blown, the guilty parties find it impossible to comprehend that they have betrayed their calling, and that they are viewed as profoundly immoral by those whose trust they had previously demanded and obtained as of right. The outrage of their victims is bewildering to them; they are sure that there must be some mistake. For, vested with the authority either of revealed religion or of objective science, they believe that they must of necessity continue to enjoy the legitimacy that had previously been unchallenged. But they are wrong. It was out of such a sense of betrayal of trust that the Reformation began nearly a half-millennium ago, and the winds of change now roaring through the Roman Catholic Church are a strong echo of that previous tumult.

Up to now, science has not been in a situation of being vulnerable to such deep corruption. Even when the Bomb caused moral disquiet, and the discovery of manifold threats to the global environment caused alarm, there was never any reason to suspect the systematic, institutional corruption of the leadership of science. And, just as in the case of the priesthood, there is every reason to believe that the ordinary workers are no worse, and quite possibly much better, in their morals than the ordinary run of humanity.

There is an interesting anti-parallelism between the cases of the Church and of science. The former seems to be an example of Lord Acton's dictum that power corrupts and absolute power corrupts absolutely. This would seem to be the pattern when powerful individuals encounter no restraints in indulging in any of the seven deadly sins for their own personal gratification.

49

In the case of science, the phenomenon is at the institutional level, and the effect is more subtle. Here, responsibility tends to corrupt, and responsibility without power corrupts absolutely. Those with responsibility for maintaining the institution, without any power to change it for the better, are the worst corrupted. This may be the sort of situation that Hannah Arendt (1963) described as 'the banality of evil' in connection with Eichmann and the Holocaust. It well describes the reflections of the legendary concentration camp commandant, who wondered how they could sleep at night, those people who gave him the terrible orders he had to obey. In science, so far at least, the problems are far less severe. The corruption occurs when institutions that are nominally applying objective knowledge for human benefit are actually caught up in playing the very different game of purveying information and misinformation on behalf of their political masters.

A textbook case of such corruption was recently revealed to the British reading public some months after it erupted in the USA. This involved the US army and the Food and Drug Administration (FDA). It started when the army felt the need to show that 'we' are prepared against anthrax, and started a programme of compulsory vaccination of service personnel. All that needs to be told here is that the firm manufacturing the vaccine had already stopped production, after five years of unanswered recommendations and warnings from the FDA about manifold failings in the quality of its production. There was the usual cycle, of a few people falling ill, at first believing that they were isolated and wrong, then discovering their common cause, finding allies in the media and Congress, and eventually battling it out with the army and the FDA, whose scientists duly mouthed their lines about the proven safety of the vaccine. Now we are in the phase of class-action suits (Reid 2002). It is all so familiar! We have had it with Gulf War Syndrome, and now the servicemen exposed to radioactive fallout in the earlier tests of nuclear weapons.

Safety politicizes science

What is new in the present period is that the public has become wise to the game of denial and reassurance, and in the UK at least has adopted the principle 'Don't believe it until it's been officially denied'. In the UK, we went through a historical turning point in the mid-1990s. Time after time we saw the chief officers of the relevant services, veterinary or health, appearing on TV to give solemn assurances to the public that there was no danger of Bovine Spongiform Encephalopathy (BSE) spreading to humans. These assurances were based on the combination of objective science and their professional integrity. When pressure groups and the media observed that this disease had already spread to cats, far more similar to people than to cows, they were brushed aside. Those who claimed a public health danger from BSE were traduced and victimized. Then it all fell apart, and on a fateful morning in March 1996 the Minister of Health admitted that the spread of BSE from cattle to humans was a very real but 'non-quantifiable' risk. Safety and trust had been lost, and policy-critical ignorance had emerged as the dominant consideration in a profound crisis.

In the UK we have had two sorts of luck. The first is that the disease seems likely now to be limited in its extent. What might have been a devastating, unimaginable plague may afflict only some hundreds or a few thousand at worst. For this deliverance we have no one to thank, either in science or in government, only our luck. Further, the British science leadership happened to have enough members with the independence of outlook necessary to appreciate that the crisis of trust and legitimacy was grave. Among these, Robert May took the lead in initiating reforms in the practice of policy-relevant science. He, at least, would not be offended if some nongovernmental organization (NGO) representative asked, 'Why should we begin to trust you now?' As a result, the UK is a case of a society that has actually learned at least some things from its disasters, and where (given all the extreme difficulties of reforming entrenched social institutions) there has been some partial but none the less genuine progress.

Indeed, the flexibility of the British governing establishment has been brilliantly displayed in the recent report from the Cabinet Office, 'Risk: Improving government's ability to handle risk and uncertainty' (2002). This calls for reforms designed to improve competence and to restore trust, and also specifies administrative machinery for ensuring that the reforms actually happen. One might call this post-normal science in everything but spirit and intent. It is not merely that the approach is top-down; one could hardly expect a government report to recommend launching into uncharted political waters, advocating a new set of institutions to deal with a problem that does not actually threaten governance as we know it. Nor should one cavil at the absence of the term 'safety', since as yet this is absent from all official discourse.

The clue to the limitations of the official approach is the absence of any discussion of how the present crisis of trust has arisen. Implicitly, it is all a question of deficiencies in management, which can be remedied by these well-intentioned administrative means. Within this sanitized bureaucratic reality, there is no room for the idea that risks are imposed by some interests on others, because power, privilege and profit derive benefit thereby. The traditional 'good shepherd' self-image of the governors is maintained, though with the modification that we now need to talk to the sheep and not merely push them around.

51

What could all this awareness and sophistication mean for the emergence of a new politics of science based on a notion of safety? First, we see that 'safety' is now one of the accepted entitlements of members of modern societies. It ranks with the 'Four Freedoms' enunciated by Franklin D. Roosevelt during the Second World War: freedom of speech and of religion, and from hunger and fear. Safety is a product of our modern industrial age. Until the last century, life for the masses was all too frequently 'nasty, brutish and short' (although not solitary), and even the elites had death as a constant companion. But a steady process combining many factors, including nutrition, public health and less brutalized schools and workplaces, has given the world's rich a measure of safety, along with comfort and convenience, that was previously unimaginable, but which is now taken for granted.

As it manifests itself only imperfectly, and within political cultures still characterized by inequalities and antagonism, it is only natural that the requirement of safety can sometimes lead to bizarre or counter-productive outcomes, as in the rise of a 'blame culture'. As an example of inherited inequalities of power in relation to safety, we have recently been reminded that our hundreds of child fatalities on the roads are largely the product of poor children being hit by the cars of rich male drivers. The huge damages occasionally awarded by American juries are just a form of payback, when almost all other approaches, especially those within accepted political channels, are seen as futile.

As part of the globalization of industry and culture, safety also becomes globalized. The struggle for safety is widely pursued by aboriginal and oppressed peoples, using the slogans and the camcorders provided by their NGO allies. They point the accusing finger at their impotent and corrupt governments, along with the multinational firms. But these are now increasingly forced to adopt a convincing rhetoric of respect for peoples and for nature in the cause of 'sustainability' or planetary safety. Here too the scientific, the pragmatic, the political and the moral are integrated.

Safety science: a new focus for politics?

Science is a very large and variegated social institution, performing a great variety of functions. It has always been recognized as providing both knowledge and power. Each of these was performed within particular social contexts, always and inevitably characterized by inequalities of wealth, status, power and privilege. The occasional protests against a class-bound natural science, which tended to surface in times of social instability (such as the English Civil War and the French Revolution), never got very far at all, because the challenge could succeed only by destroying science and much of society with it.

The emergence of safety as a crucial political issue provides a new element in the relations of science with society at large. What we might call 'safety science' is actually a small sector of the whole enterprise, but in the perspective of the public it is becoming crucial. We might think of it as the visible conscience of science. When there is a scandal of the corruption of safety science, the enlightened vision of the whole scientific enterprise is betrayed. Moreover, it is in connection with safety that ordinary people have their main experience of science. The mass consumers' revolts against conventional food and conventional medicine, both sectors relying on science in many ways, show that the politics of safety can be very powerful indeed.

Critics of our modern industrial system have focused on its roots in the brutal exploitation of peoples, and its continued disruption of the higher cultural and moral values of humanity in many ways. These negative features could be argued to be relics of a primitive past, which would soon be corrected by the material prosperity and social freedoms that accompany science-based modernity. But it now appears that to ensure safety for humanity and the planet there will need to be some very drastic changes in the way that the industrial system is managed and conceived. We not only have the threats of global climate change and instability, and of the manifold forms of pollution from 'waste', together with the runaway technologies of information, both electronic and biological. We are already living on our luck, and we will certainly need more as time goes by and crises accumulate. To imagine all these dangers as 'externalities', in the manner of mainstream economics, is worse than a sick joke. Further, we see that attempts to ensure safety, at any level from the local to the global, encounter fierce resistance from existing vested interests in the protection of their short-term profits and privileges.

In these new struggles, where the industrial system can no longer pretend to be the solution but lies at the heart of the problem, safety science can become a crucial form of scientific practice. There are enormous methodological problems in these post-normal situations; there are few certainties about the best way to cope with the bewildering variety of dangers. To resist the corruptions of responsibility without power, scientists will need an understanding that is far removed from the simplicities of textbook education and normal-science research. And, helped by the institutions and technologies of advanced, relatively democratic and open societies, the public will be able to judge the competence and integrity of safety science as clearly as that of other institutions entrusted with the protection of its safety. What sorts of democratic politics and science will emerge from this new awareness is, as yet, impossible to predict.

4 | Are scientists irrational? Risk assessment in practical reason

FRANK FISCHER

Introduction

The division between those with and without knowledge has become a primary social tension (Beck 1992). The issue is of particular importance in environmental and technology policy-making, generally heavily laden with technical questions. Elsewhere, I have argued that this is the critical question upon which the possibility of participatory democracy hinges in a world of technical and social complexities (Fischer 2000).

Can citizens actually participate? We know less about this than the discussions of citizen participation would suggest, as they are typically framed by outmoded understandings of both science and politics. From the conventional view, the issue looks doubtful. But from a post-empiricist understanding of science and politics, the question becomes more complex and, depending on how one understands participation, much less unthinkable (Fischer 2003b).

Modern-day debates about environmental and technology policy focus on risk. The empirical techniques of risk assessment and risk–benefit analysis have been introduced to bring intellectual rationality to bear on such deliberations. In particular, they are designed to counter what is seen as citizens' inability to decide rationally on such matters, as reflected in their worries about such issues as the siting of nuclear power plants or hazardous waste incinerators. With the blessing of economic and political leaders, the scientific community has fashioned sophisticated statistical decision techniques to compare risks in ways that provide a basis for informed policy decision-making (Covello 1993). Towards this end, the concept of 'acceptable risk' has been advanced to help people see the irrationality of their anxieties about flying in a plane after driving the car to the airport, statistically seen to be much more dangerous than flying. Or worrying about the effects of chemical fertilizers on the lawn while smoking a cigarette.

Risk assessment, however, has failed to do the job. Indeed, confronted with such assessments people seem only to have got more worried. While this has reconfirmed the conviction of many that ordinary citizens are irrational in matters pertaining to science and technology, it has also led others to examine more carefully why citizens respond the way they do.

Such research, generally called 'risk communication research', was initially supposed to find ways to convince citizens of the risk analysts' decisions. Unexpectedly, though, it has uncovered a substantial body of information to show that people merely respond to the risky situations in a different way (Kasperson and Stallen 1991). Instead of focusing on the technical information at hand, citizens process it from a sociocultural perspective. Whereas risk experts see citizens as incapable of digesting technical findings, and thus susceptible to irrational fears, others have argued that their reactions are simply based on another form of rationality. In this view, the problem rests on a limited understanding of the nature of risk, rationality and community decision-making processes (Fischer 2000; Wynne 1996).

Technical knowledge in a sociocultural context

What, then, is this other form of rationality? In their work on environmental risk assessment, Plough and Krimksy (1987) contrast the expert's technical rationality with the concept of 'cultural rationality'. 'Technical rationality', they explain, is a mindset that puts its faith in empirical evidence and the scientific method; it relies on expert judgements in making policy decisions. Emphasizing logical consistency and universality of findings, it focuses attention in public decision-making on quantifiable impacts. 'Cultural rationality', in contrast, is geared to, or at least gives equal weight to, personal and familiar experiences rather than depersonalized technical calculations. Focusing on the opinions of traditional social and peer groups, cultural rationality takes unanticipated consequences to be fully relevant to near-term decision-making, and trusts process over outcomes. Beyond statistical probabilities and risk–benefit ratios, public risk perception is understood through a distinctive form of rationality, one that is shaped by the circumstances under which the risk is identified and publicized, the standing or place of the individual in his or her community, and the social values of the community as a whole. Cultural rationality, in this respect, can be understood as the rationality of the social-life world. It is concerned with the impacts, intrusions or implications of a particular event or phenomenon on the social relations that constitute that world. Such concerns are the stuff upon which the environmental movement is built.

What does this tell us about the ordinary citizen's approach to risk? For the layperson, the concept of risk is understood as much in terms of qualitative, affective characteristics as it is in terms of quantitative relationships. Psychological research into the perception of risk shows citizens' understandings of risk to be made up of a rich, multi-faceted perspective that includes some twenty affective characteristics (Slovic 1992). According to this research, the more involuntary, unfamiliar, unfair or invisible the risk, the more likely it is that citizens will oppose it (Kasperson and Stallen 1991).

Focusing on how ordinary laypersons cognitively process uncertain information, social psychological research demonstrates the ways in which citizens draw on past experiences in making assessments. Given the complexity of most policy issues, especially technological ones, citizens tend to fill knowledge gaps with information about social process, or what has been called the 'social process theory' of cognition (Hill 1992). Of particular importance, in this respect, are their own experiences and those of the social groups to which they belong.

Not all people, of course, have the same experiences. It is possible to think of a continuum across which people with different levels of experience can be distributed. Individuals such as public administrators or political activists will have considerable experience with particular issues or problems. They develop relatively abstract and well-integrated knowledge structures that actively guide their perceptions and expectations in future decisions. These 'schemas' inform such individuals or groups about how events are expected to unfold, as well as how particular people ought to act in given sets of circumstances (Conover 1984; Fiske and Taylor 1984). They also explain how substantive issues in a particular area of politics interrelate or how decision-making procedures are expected to operate. Members of the lay public spend much less time dealing with and thinking about policy issues and thus hold different schemas. Their ability to perceive and analyse the various dimensions of comparable issues, as a result, is necessarily far more limited, often giving the impression that they are uninformed. What the research shows, however, is that in such situations citizens mainly rely more heavily on procedural than on substantive schemas. Citizens turn to often well-developed, generalized procedural schemas that can be applied to a range of different situations, from political decision-making to committee work in the office.

The move to sociocultural rationality and its emphasis on process is most apparent in the case of uncertain data. Uncertainty opens the door for competing interests to emphasize different interpretations of the findings. 'Wicked' problems such as 'NIMBY' (Not In My Back Yard), moreover, generate normative as well as empirical uncertainty. The question of how to define a situation is as problematic as the question of what to do about it. Competing definitions emerge from multiple, often conflicting, perspectives. Normatively, politicians and activists advance in such cases counter-arguments about the nature or definition of the problem itself. Empirically, each side engages in the politics of expertise, employing the same or similar data to suit their own purposes.

And where does this leave the public? Consider the empirical dimension of the problem. If two experts stand before an audience of citizens and argue over the empirical reliability of a given set of statistics, what basis does the citizen have for judging the competing empirical claims? In such situations, citizens are forced to rely more on a sociocultural assessment of the factors surrounding a decision. And not without good reason. Although scientific experts continue to maintain that their research is 'value-neutral', the limits of this view become especially apparent once they introduce their technical findings into the socio-political world of competing interests. In the absence of empirical agreement, there is every reason to believe that interested parties will strongly assert themselves, advocating the findings that best suit their interests. In such cases, at least in the immediate situation, there is nothing science can do to mediate among such claims. One can call for more research but, as experience shows, there is little guarantee that further research will bring either certainty or timely results in a particular conflict.

The presence of cultural rationality is especially strong when there is reason to believe in the possibility of deception or manipulation, which has often proven to be the case in environmental politics. In a world of large industrial giants with vastly disproportionate power and influence compared to that of local communities, it comes as no surprise to learn that citizens are wary of the kinds of distorted communications to which such asymmetrical relations can give rise. Where citizens have compelling reasons to suspect that a risk assessment is superficial or false, they can only turn to their own cultural logic and examine the results in terms of previous social experiences. Turning away from the empirical studies themselves, they ask questions such as: 'What are our previous experiences with these people?' 'Is there reason to believe we can trust them?' 'Why are they telling us this?' (Perhaps even, 'Why don't they look us in the eye when they tell us this?') Such questions are especially pertinent when crucial decisions are made by distant, anonymous and hierarchical organizations. Citizens want to know how conclusions were reached, whose interests are at stake, if the process reflects a hidden agenda, who is responsible, what protection they have if something goes wrong, and so on. If they believe the project engineers and managers either don't know what they are talking about or are willing to lie to serve the purposes of their company, workers or citizens will obviously reject the risk assessment statistics put forward by the company. For example, if they have experiences that suggest they should be highly distrustful of particular plant company representatives or plant managers, such information will tend to override the data themselves. From the perspective of cultural rationality, to act otherwise would itself be irrational.

Most fundamentally, cultural rationality, as an informal logic deduced from past social experiences, tells citizens whom they can trust and whom they can't. Citizens' and workers' understandings of large-scale technologies are rooted in the socio-historical context in which they are embedded and experienced (Fischer 2003a). Technology itself is encountered as more than an assemblage of physical properties; it is experienced as an interplay between physical properties and institutional characteristics (Wynne 1987). As such, the ordinary social perceptions and assessments of technological risks by workers and citizens are rooted in their empirical social experiences with the technology's managerial decision structures as well as historically conditioned relationships, interpreted and passed along by members of their own groups and communities. When the social relations of the workers and managers are pervaded by mistrust and hostility, the uncertainties of physical risks are amplified.

As the basic social glue that holds people together, trust is an essential component of modern sociocultural knowledge (Giddens 1990: 79–111). Expressed as confidence in some attribute or quality of a person, thing or statement, trust helps us orient to one another; it serves as a basic social cement of groups and societal integration. In modern societies, where institutions and practices are based on 'abstracted' expert knowledges, trust takes on special importance. Because such knowledges are 'disembedded' from the local contexts to which they are applied, people are left to trust in the validity of the knowledge and the competence of the expert who administers it (ibid.). Surrounded by expert systems whose validities are said to be independent of time and space, we usually have little choice but to rely on the decisions of faceless authorities. For instance, such trust permits us to take the elevator to the top of a skyscraper, even though we know little about the principles of architectural design or building codes. Indeed, our entire existence is circumscribed by similar situations, whether it concerns flying in a plane, driving a car, eating food in a restaurant or visiting a doctor.

Where the level of trust is low, however, cultural rationality will most likely caution citizens to be sceptical or resistant. Our sociocultural experiences are, in this way, factored into our interpretations of the experts' technical data on risk. Such data, after all, are not only a statement about the degree of danger we face, but also a statement about the degree of danger that another group has placed us in. On this aspect of risk, the technical findings are themselves silent.

While laypersons tend to rely heavily on sociocultural rationality, it is crucially important to note that few people act or think exclusively in one mode of rationality or the other. Such modes typically change with circumstances. For example, Sandman (cited in Hadden 1991) has demonstrated this with a simple test. He asked experts to imagine themselves in situations in which they were not in control of the surrounding circumstances and to think of themselves as fathers rather than as engineers and businessmen. In such cases, the experts were themselves found to abandon the technical rational model of decision-making for the sociocultural rational mode. That is, they themselves responded in their own roles as citizens. For the experts as well, the evidence they were given was insufficient. When it came to protecting their own families, the matter of trust required knowing more about the social processes behind the reported evidence. Such an exercise makes it clear that cultural rationality is a different kind of knowledge that has to be taken into account in any decision-making process.

At this point, we can recognize that the critics who argue that the environmental movement is grounded more in social critique or political ideology than in good science are not entirely wrong (Douglas and Wildavsky 1982; Rubin 1994). Without entering terminological disputes, the concept of sociocultural rationality bears a family resemblance to the concept of ideology. As used here, it might even be understood as the deductive rationality of a belief system. In so far as citizens interpret risks from the perspective of sociocultural experiences, they do so within a belief system. As deductive distillations of their experiences, these beliefs supply them with guidelines for action based on past experiences. Thus, in situations that are unclear, uncertain or anxiety-provoking, citizens are especially open or amenable to such appeals, and the environmental movement stands ready with ideological assistance.

What the critics fail to recognize or acknowledge, however, is that such a sociocultural perspective is inherent in the nature of the decision process. That is, in such situations there is no alternative but to seek out such normative guidance. Interpretations of how the social system works are precisely the kind of information that citizens need to help them link together their own knowledge and experiences into meaningful understandings of a particular situation. As the move to basic cultural orientations is in significant part a response to the fact that science cannot supply the needed answers, it is thus anything but irrational. Although critics portray the environmental movement as merely appealing to the lesser instincts of the citizenry, their own call for more emphasis on science rather than ideology fails to grasp this point. Wittingly or unwittingly, it serves itself as an ideology.

Criticizing the role of ideology in environmental decision-making, Rubin (1994) and others make the mistake of only ascribing to it a utopian interest in social change. In doing so, they fail to see that the belief systems of environmentalism fill a much more basic and practical need. While environmentalism is about change, the critics neglect to appreciate that these ideologies work on another level as well. Rather than just political rhetoric designed to challenge societies that 'greens' don't like, environmentalism also provides citizens with interpretive knowledge about how the basic institutions of society work and offers tactics for change. More than just wild-eyed utopian contentions, the ideology of environmentalism helps to orient many citizens to problematic situations around them – in particular to the question of whom should they believe and trust.

Missing is the recognition that in some situations people are in need of just such orientation. When confronted with risky circumstances, they look for help in understanding how they came about, how the system that created them really works – not just how officials say it works – and thus whom or what they should worry about. Reliance on established ideological perspectives offers quick, shorthand guidance. Much more than half-truths distributed to defend a particular set of interests, such belief systems represent the interpretive synopsis of a long history of experiences with social phenomena. In a complex world, they serve to simplify basic messages down to a few manageable premises that can serve as guidelines for thought and action. Which is not to say that people shouldn't or don't reflect on the content of these beliefs, at least over time. But in uncertain situations that require action without the luxury of time, they help to give people a basic orientation. And the ideologist, of course, makes a point of being there to help them. This holds as much for the ideologist of the free market as it does for the environmentalist.

Beyond uncertainty: rationality in practical reason

The case for cultural reason is generally made in terms of uncertainty: in the face of uncertainty, people have to turn to their social experiences to fill in the gaps. Without the information needed to make a rigorous empirical assessment, they make predictions based on extrapolations from their ordinary knowledge. Which in some cases can be quite prescient. Some people are even good at it.

But the case for cultural reason can be even stronger. Indeed, it can be grounded in epistemology. Here we have replaced the formal conceptions of scientific logic with the informal logic of practical reason. Indeed, this is what the citizen is already doing, and in the social world there is nothing irrational about it. Practical discourse is, in fact, the mode of reason geared to the everyday world of social action.

By practical reason I refer here to the work of the ordinary-language philosophers who have set out to understand how we think and reason in the everyday world, especially in the absence of ultimate values and with incomplete knowledge. Much of the work has, moreover, been advanced to deal with the very problem facing risk assessment. Confronting the question of how the activities of society proceed without the assistance of the kind of rationality called for by science, they have sought to reconstruct the informal logic of everyday discourse. That is, how do ordinary people deliberate and argue about questions of action? It may be the case that the kinds of decisions dealt with in the everyday world cannot be proven with the kind of rationality of science, but to judge them as irrational is to throw the baby out with the bath water. As Toulmin (1958), Scriven (1987) and others have made clear, such a judgement rests on a logical error. The positivists have simply falsely imported into the everyday world the epistemology of another domain. In Scriven's (1987) words, 'the classical models of reasoning provide inadequate and in fact seriously misleading accounts of most practical ... reasoning – the reasoning of the kitchen, surgery and the workshop, the law courts ... office and battle field'. To be sure, common or ordinary reasoning frequently has components that can usefully be represented by the formal logics of induction and deduction. The problem is, as he explains, 'they are only components, and a completely distorted picture of the nature of reasoning results from supposing that these neat pieces are what reasoning ... is all about'.

But can we be more precise? What exactly is an informal logic of practical reason? Many people have a good intuitive sense that such a logic exists without being able to say more precisely what it looks like. Towards this end, we can turn to Toulmin's (1958) approach to practical reason, or the 'logic of good reasons', especially as elaborated by Taylor (1961) and adapted to policy analysis by Fischer (1995a). From this view, we can understand a complete judgement in the practical world to involve four interrelated levels of evaluation, extending from the very concrete to the abstract (or the other way around). If we pursue the scheme from the concrete to the abstract, it begins with a very familiar question: Does a particular programme, project or policy fulfil a particular norm or standard? Which in ordinary language might simply be approached as the question: Does it work? Here we can easily interpret the goal of a risk assessment as an effort to answer this question: Does a particular action meet certain acceptable standards of risk? It is a question to which all the techniques and methods of empirical analysis can be brought. Called here technical verification, it is a question that the mainstream risk analyst takes to be the essence of rationality.

The problem with risk assessment is that it stops here. For a practical judgement, however, the evaluation must move on to the justification of the norms and standards against which the programme is judged. That is, the

61

legitimacy or validity of the standards has to be tested, a task that is carried out through three additional discourses. The first of these discourses can be called situational validation. Concerned with the context to which the norm and standard is applied, evaluation at this level asks whether there is anything about the decision which requires that an exception be made to the rule or judgement rendered at the level of technical verification. Here we find a classic example in the case of risk assessment, namely 'NIMBY'. Beyond the question of an empirical assessment, which might or might not show a nuclear power plant to be safe, some oppositional groups argue that, while it might be good in some places, it should not be sited in their area. This could be for purely self-serving reasons (for example, to protect their community from any question of doubt), or it could be because of some physical characteristic of the area; for example, a geographic fault line running through it (Hill 1992).

Beyond an assessment of the situational context, the evaluation logically moves to societal vindication, concerned with the contribution of the particular project or policy to the existing social system. This involves stepping outside a particular value or belief system and asking whether it has instrumental or contributive value for the social order as a whole. Whereas in first-order discourse the issue concerns a particular programme and the affected group(s), the frame of reference changes in second-order discourse to the impact on the society as a whole. Here, we find prominent arguments – those of corporate leaders and governmental officials – about the contributions of technology to economic growth and thus to the general social well-being. Nuclear power, it is argued, is needed to fuel an expanding economy in the face of coming oil shortages or perhaps even to deal with the challenge of global warming. Environmentalists, on the other hand, point to both the risks of a major disaster and question the need for the envisioned levels of growth that would have to be supplied with greater supplies of energy. Which leads to the fourth level of discourse: ideological choice.

Whereas the industrialists anchor their argument to functional considerations of the existing system, environmentalists typically point to a different way of life. Here we confront the role of ideology in the positive sense of the term. The essence of the green critique is to assess the existing system from the point of view of ideal principles and values, the stuff of fourth-level discourse – and to offer an alternative vision of how we might live together sustainably. This could include lower levels of consumption resulting from less emphasis on materialism or a more spiritual relationship with nature.

The essential point here is that all four discourses are part of a complete

Logic of practical reason	Discourses of nuclear power
Ideological choice (Because of)	Environmental critique of industrial society and mass consumption; soft energy paths
↑	
Systems vindication (Because of)	Energy needs of industrial society versus issues of security and risk
↑	
Situational validation (Because of)	Siting problems; NIMBY
↑	
Warrant (Since)	Risk assessment; safety standards
↑	
Data ⟶ Technical ⟶ Conclusion verification	

Figure 4.1 Beyond risk assessment to practical reason

or comprehensive judgement; all have a valid role to play in questions about risk. Where technical risk analysts offer data that fit into the first level of the evaluation, they fail to see that that such data are only components of a full evaluation. In judging citizens 'irrational' because they ignore formal risk assessment and discuss instead the kind of society in which we live, the technical analysts miss the fact that they also address an essential component of the complete assessment. In so far as risk analysts reject such information as irrelevant, arguing that the citizen cannot follow the argument, they can in fact themselves be judged as 'irrational' from the perspective of practical reason. Indeed, from the perspective of practical reason we can understand the statement that the acceptability of a statement or judgement is, in the last instance, dependent on its relationship to the good way of life. Involving the justification of the standard or norm against which the measurements were made, the line moves directly from technical verification to ideological choice (see Figure 4.1).

Scientists have to learn that judgements based on qualitative risk assessment, as an applied research methodology, are always situated in the world of action and are thus part of a practical/normative discourse. Practical reason, as a different kind of deliberative logic, is always integrating the social and technical. For particular analytical purposes, they can be separated, but only artificially; in the assessment process they must be brought back together. That is, scientific findings have to be judged within both the local and societal contexts to which they apply. Instead of understanding practical discourse as an inferior form of reason relied on in the face of

63

empirical uncertainty or a general inability to deal with the intellectual rigours of technical analysis, the risk analysis community has to come to grips with the fact that the acceptability of their findings must ultimately be judged by normative standards. Scientists fail to see this because of their irrational attachment to one component of a larger assessment. They have a contribution to make, but so do citizens.

From this perspective it becomes necessary to rethink and restructure the relationship between risk experts and citizens. In place of the traditional hierarchical, top-down relationship supported by technical rationality, the expert has to enter into an interactive, coproductive relationship with the relevant citizens (Callon 1996). More than an issue of democracy, it is seen here to be a requirement of problem-solving. Citizens, in short, have a type of information not available to experts – or at least they have no privileged position in this matter. The expert can at best function here as a citizen expert (Fischer 2000).

The task is to set up an extended dialectical conversation between the theoretical knowledge of the experts and the sociocultural information of the citizens. Towards this end, we need more knowledge about the epistemics that interconnect citizens and experts and how experts can function to facilitate such a conversation. The place to begin such investigations is with the innovative experiments in participatory research, such as those that have emerged in the developing world. It is here that we find an especially important reason for bringing development studies to bear on science studies, and the task of rethinking the role of expertise (see Part Four).

Conclusion

This chapter has explored the tensions between experts and citizens in the assessment of technological and environmental risks from an epistemological perspective. A good deal of the discussion about this issue, as we have seen, has focused on the purported inability of citizens to participate 'rationally' in the decision process, in particular the citizen's inability to grasp or accept scientific findings and their implications for rational policy-making. Rather than concentrating on the 'facts', environmental movements are said to concentrate on espousing ideology. Rejecting or ignoring the technical issues at hand, they are seen to refocus the analytical process through an ideological lens. The analysis here has turned the question around and applied the informal logic of practical reason to the scientific mode of decision-making. This has permitted us to question the rationality of the scientist rather than the citizen. Contrary to the standard take on the issue, we have in the process seen that ordinary citizens rationally focus on important questions that scientific experts ignore or neglect. Practical discourse assists in revealing the systematic connections between the scientists' technical data and the particular social situation, the societal system and the way of life. Indeed, practical reason makes clear that the connection is more than just logical, it is essential and necessary. This helps us better to understand the scientific risk analysts' need to integrate the citizen's perspective into their own analysis. Towards this end, the discussion concluded with an appeal to the developing methods of participatory inquiry as a way to facilitate such an integration. Participatory research, already a part of the inventory of citizen strategies emerging in both developing countries and global civil society, is seen to offer important insights into the process of rethinking the relationship of the expert to the citizen, as well as developing new and innovative methodological strategies for confronting the challenge ahead.

Are scientists irrational?

5 | Risk as globalizing 'democratic' discourse? Framing subjects and citizens

BRIAN WYNNE

Introduction

Ever since public controversies over new sciences and technologies became a defining part of the public domain from the late 1960s in industrial society, the issues have been defined as 'risk issues', or 'scientific issues', as if the only salient question is the propositional scientific one: is the practice in question effective and safe enough? After dogged institutional reinvention of the repeatedly discredited 'deficit models' of the public, which attributed the public failure of scientific reassurances over such new techno-scientific commitments to various forms of public misunderstanding (Wynne 1991), a watershed appeared to have been reached in March 2000, with the *Science and Society* report of the internationally influential UK House of Lords Select Committee on Science and Technology (House of Lords 2000). This crystallized an already widespread but diffusely emerging set of understandings, that public scepticism, mistrust or resistance to scientific assertions about such socially shaping technological programmes was not due to public ignorance, and required two-way understanding and dialogue rather than the prevalent norm of one-way 'correctional' idioms of communication. A new and bracing need also for scientific understanding of publics was defined as crucial for 'restoring' an anxiously craved state of public trust.

Reflecting these tidal shifts, a huge flowering of practical and analytical work aimed at such public engagement, dialogue and mutual understanding between science and publics has erupted since the late 1990s. Although not recognized as such, this has partly been playing catch-up with similar moves begun a decade or more earlier in development work, albeit usually in more immediately vernacular domains such as agriculture and land-use issues than with respect to new technologies and sciences.

This shift embodies the potential for new, more constructive models and practices of citizenship, human subjects and, correspondingly, of knowledge and 'epistemic agency' as a key, novel dimension of citizenship. In this chapter, however, I caution that this radical apparent potential is compromised by deeper, less manifest cultural assumptions and commitments framing most such initiatives, and that these problematic foundations have yet to be identified, confronted and changed. I argue that this failure – masked so far by the extravagant investments of enthusiasm, energy and expectation pouring relentlessly into new participatory initiatives by which citizens may influence science, and in expectation thereby render it more legitimate and robust – is founded on two factors.

First, 'participation' has an exclusive focus on downstream risk or impacts issues as distinct from upstream research and innovation,[1] reflecting the false assumption that public concerns are only about instrumental consequences, and not also crucially about what human purposes are driving science and innovation in the first place. Second, it reflects an assumption that the public meanings, or issue definitions, are naturally and properly the sovereign domain of authoritative expert institutions, and that citizens have no capability or proper role in autonomously creating and negotiating such collective, and potentially more diverse, public meanings. Thus, standardized and supposedly objective universal public meanings are imposed – 'risk issues' – which also imposes a normative, standardized model of citizens.

I develop this line of analysis and explore its validity and implications in the context of globalization processes where knowledge and technology feature. As a key intellectual resource in doing this, I draw upon the sociology of scientific knowledge (SSK), and especially the reflexive turn in social sciences and humanities generally. This includes especially the performative dimension, recognizing that even scientific representations of 'objects' (such as 'risk') as a reference to an external real world are more than mere representation. They also embody tacit projections of human subject worlds, relationships, agency and capacities of the human subject through such unspoken cultural projection, and these tacit projections are forms of material intervention into intersubjective human ontologies as well as nature (Verran 2001, 2002). This reflexive-constructivist perspective on scientific knowledge, however, is not at all anti-realist; it is avowedly realist. It refers to a reality that is contingent, open, complex, hybrid and ambiguously human-natural together, and always non-completed – endemically in-the-making, in both its human and its natural categories, as well as its substantive material features.

I first outline how risk discourse, as scientific idiom, dominates the public definition and treatment of the social issues of new techno-scientific trajectories such as energy, genomics and biotechnology, nanotechnology and the like. This risk discourse in modern societies (and by presumption of its authors, also in emergent 'global' contexts) is automatically imposed as the natural and universal objective representation of public issues (and hence of public concerns) as their natural public meaning, which, it is implied, all proper citizens would recognize. This unquestioned starting point, colonizing as it is more and more areas of public life (Power 2004), then leads to the further presumptive imposition of models of the 'citizen' on those publics by interpreting their responses to these (presumptively deemed) 'risk issues' as *'risk perceptions'*. This further affirms that the exclusive meaning of the issue is indeed 'risk', since those public responses must have been to (their own understanding of) those risks as 'we scientists know them really to be'. That such resistance might be caused by the public experience of finding its own, different meanings to be flatly ignored and denied is never even imagined as a different, more challenging basis of public dissent. Citizens are just not imagined to have such autonomous capacities by institutional actors, who are immersed in and agents of the discourse culture that reflects the assumption that the objective, natural meaning is 'risk'. This rigid failure of institutional-cultural imagination has not hitherto been challenged by the processes of participation and dialogue that have been developed.

I thus argue, consistent with the critical appraisal of the fashionable development discourse of participation – 'the new tyranny?', as Cooke and Kothari (2001) have asked – that virtually all of the mushrooming commitment to public citizen engagement in 'science policy' or 'scientific-technical issues', or to 'democratizing science', is something of a mirage, at least thus far. It imposes severe and unspoken framing limits around these new processes, such that the continuing failure to *democratically sensitize* science, and its persistent non-accountability to publics even in the new (if still limited) 'participatory' ethos, is omitted from critical attention.

I then try to address what further issues arise when we try to globalize our perspective in a way that avoids the hegemonistic assumption that modern scientistically framed public meanings (such as 'risk') are naturally universal and objective. Again, I try to retain focus on implicit models of the agency, capacities, needs and 'civic qualifications' of the 'public' or the 'citizen', as these can be seen to be embodied and performed silently in those dominant discourses and their framings in those more expansive and even less well-defined global processes.

In order even to begin this, we need to address the combination of three recent historical trends or transformations. These developments of the last twenty or so years are:

- neo-liberal intensification of globalization, in several dimensions, which renders straightforward comparative assessment of North and South cases and situations problematic, since it is the forms of increasing global *integration between* North and South which may be significant;

68

- pervasive intensification of the commercial culture of scientific research and knowledge;
- the growth, North and South, of ideas of 'legitimation crisis' around scientific expertise, and the policy response to enhance democratic participation in what were exclusive scientific-technical domains of decision relating to public issues.

The new 'publics of science' in a globalizing knowledge economy world include, for example, indigenous peoples as prospective partners in global bio-prospecting for lucrative 'global' innovations such as Western-world medical therapies, or HIV sufferers and at-risk groups in India or Africa (Hayden 2003; Karnik 2001; Oldham 2004). If existing understandings of risk and science as presumed frameworks of meaning – and 'citizen science', 'citizen' and 'public–science dialogue' – are inadequate for legitimate handling of the human and technical dimensions of these issues even in the modern developed world, then how much more so is this true globally? When we try to encompass the increasing intensity, extent and sheer diversity of these new global networks being enacted through scientific-technical discourses in agriculture and food, health, environmental management, bio-prospecting and biodiversity or human genetic databases, and even areas such as information or materials technologies, it becomes even more urgent to ask how existing concepts could possibly be viable, and how to improve on them.

Science, risk and public worlds: constructing representation

The discourse of risk, as scientific discourse, has become a defining feature of late modern society public policy culture. The November 2002 UK Prime Minister's Strategy Unit report on 'Risk: improving government's capability to handle risk and uncertainty' confirms the definitive spread of risk discourse right across public life, and recognizes the need to enlarge processes of public and stakeholder input into what are now called 'risk management' processes, to correct previous failures of the conventional 'technocratic' model. These extensive, deliberate and well-intentioned participatory moves tend to obscure the questions that need to be asked about the more subtly anti-democratic implications of translating more multifarious, messy, vernacular and contested issue definitions into monolithic 'risk' terms.

This emphasis on the need to enhance radically positive citizen engagement with science was also stimulated in the European Union (EU) by the 2001 European Commission President's *White Paper on Governance*, mainly by the experience of EU failures in policy handling of what were called 'risk issues', or even 'scientific issues' (see, e.g., European Commission 2002: 9, 23/Action 35).

This increasingly pervasive technical-scientific risk discourse was until recently confined to esoteric technical fields such as engineering, insurance and regulation of chemicals and pharmaceuticals. This recent spread has also, of course, spawned the avowedly less technicist 'risk society' discourse in social science (Beck 1992, 1995, 1999; Adam et al. 2000), as well as the sprawling international social science research industry on public 'risk perceptions' (Krimsky and Golding 1992; Slovic 2001). Even the more qualitative forms of this social science may also paradoxically reinforce the assumption I wish to challenge, that these issues are indeed naturally matters of 'risk'.

Thus, regardless of precise definitions, risk has become a defining discourse identifying the *meaning* of public issues concerning scientific research and development (R&D) and innovation trajectories in fields carrying increasingly intense and powerful potential social, environmental and cultural implications. While even the technical, let alone the social, meaning of what we call 'risk' as an object of risk assessment and management is always open to social definition and construction (Brunk et al. 1991; Wynne 1989), this basic epistemic and social contingency is obscured by the dominant scientistic cultural reification of risk as if it were an independently existing object with is own autonomous meaning, to be revealed, analysed and controlled as such by scientific discipline.

Thus institutionalized risk discourse reifies its constructed object twice over: once in defining the objective and universal meaning of public issues as risk issues; then in presuming that selected definitions of what is to count scientifically as risk are objective, natural and universal representations. This presumptive projection of 'objective' public meaning also involves a corresponding projection of the 'public' as a supposedly free subject of that meaning. Moreover, as we shall see, the ways in which risk and uncertainty are defined in institutional culture and its discourse impose a further tacit and unaccountable projection of 'citizens' and their capacities, and the ways in which they relate to contingency, lack of control and responsibility.

Elsewhere, I have tried to account for the power of this contingent reification as a historical matter (Wynne 2002). It may appear strange that complex global issues such as those concerning genetically modified (GM) crops or nuclear power could be reduced to issues of risk as defined by institutional authorities, who claim to have all the risks scientifically identified and controlled. It is evident, however, where this reductionist assumption originates and how it has gained credibility when one recognizes that this form of discourse was institutionalized for human activities such as early mercantile shipping accidents and losses, and later for single, precisely defined engineering plant design and control. In both these cases, the object in need of control, and the losses to be suffered, were indeed relatively unambiguous, very well bounded and well defined. What was at risk, and from what, were unambiguous questions for these original contexts. It is easy to understand how they might have become routinely reified as if objectively existing, rather than being recognized as the contingent product of human framing of their meanings and boundaries. Yet as a discourse of the supposed universal and objective meaning of the issues relating to such ramifying and multi-faceted questions as GM crops, climate change or biodiversity, this cultural assumption embodied in the very discourse itself runs into deeper trouble than could have been imagined by simply extrapolating from its origins. The object of meaning when we consider global biotechnology or biodiversity is not remotely as simple or as unambiguous as the object at issue in shipping losses, or any other insurance issue; and the same is true even for the risks of loss of control of a nuclear power plant or aerospace technology.

Thus, there is an apparently unseen but extensive openness of meaning underlying the self-consciously scientific public discourses of 'risk issues', and there are immense pressures to routinize and reify a supposed unambiguous 'object' in the face of deep ambiguities as to what the object(s) of attention and meaning should be. This largely unrecognized tension may require fundamentally different approaches from simply presuming a scientific meaning. Yet this predicament appears not even to have been understood, and not just by modern policy and scientific actors involved in the governance of such issues, but also by too many social science experts on risk. If people try to bring other meanings to the issue, they are likely to be excluded and patronized by expert institutions and some social science as *misperceiving* the 'true' object (Marris et al. 2001).

Although this point has been rehearsed often enough elsewhere (Marris et al. 2001; Wynne 2001), however, perhaps a corollary point has not been clearly stated. This is that part and parcel of the discursive imposition of an assumed universal objective meaning to such public issues is the corresponding imposition of a model of a standard citizen, who supposedly sees and lives such objective, standard meanings. This is not only a *standardizing* model of the citizen. It is also a model that defines citizens as being essentially incapable of exercising such meanings for themselves in autonomous social interaction in autonomous social worlds.[2] In other words, it is a model of the citizen that pre-empts and curtails crucial dimensions of democratic citizenship, and instead hands this over to institutionalized science and the power structures that may lie behind it. This is one of the dimensions I envisage when referring to science as having been allowed to assume the role of being the *culture* of modern policy, not only of *informing* it (Wynne 2002). It corresponds also with the problematic reduction of questions of public meaning to ones only of propositional uncertainty or conflict (Collins and Evans 2002, 2003; Wynne 2003).

In collecting together the disparate elements of the ways in which dominant scientific discourses of risk implicitly project and impose corresponding normative models of the 'public' and thus the 'citizen', we can say that these normative human projections include:

- a standardized model of the citizen as one who naturally sees the core meaning of the issues being dealt with as 'risk' issues, and 'risk' as defined by institutional science;
- through all the proliferating initiatives under the banner of democratization of expertise, the outer horizon of imagined citizen concerns is about the consequences of our innovations. This is a purely instrumental model of human existence – about means of control and security – which omits any more substantial questions of appropriate and worthwhile human ends. Thus innovation, and the human purposes, ends and visions that shape and inspire it, is seamlessly excluded from the proper realm of democratic agency of the citizen in the scientific, globalized knowledge-economy world. This omission actually flies in the face of expressed public concerns about the unaccountability and invisibility of just such driving human purposes in new sciences and technologies;
- thus also an instrumentalized model of citizens as centred on safety as their central end and meaning in public life;
- as illustrated below, a model of citizens as incapable of dealing with uncertainty, and expecting scientifically informed institutions to protect them from it;
- a model of the citizen as intrinsically unable to construct independent social meanings through autonomous relationships and negotiated worlds outside the ambit of powerful, expert-led institutions and discourse-makers, and their versions of public meaning and framing of issues;
- in more specific terms, the assumed global validity of Western-developed scientific risk frameworks often leads to the inadvertent transfer within the relevant scientific discourse of parochial North-world social models of 'citizens' such as 'high-risk' groups, and the implicitly imposed saliency or irrelevance of local contextual social conditions such as poverty and malnutrition.

Locating 'risk': some cases

It is interesting to look at the ways in which one recent and in many respects path-breaking global anthropological collection on risk (Caplan 2000) makes headway against this hegemonic monovalency of risk discourse on modern social and policy issues. Caplan does recognize that the dominant risk, and risk-society, discourse of modern public policy presumes a very Northern, scientifically centred societal set of meanings to such public issues. Instead of assuming that scientific and technological risks define the field, her collection of case studies turns to such fields as ethnic minorities, sexual practices in Africa, prostitutes in London, soldiers in Northern Ireland, and Amazonian peoples' experience of 'risk', contrasted to risk-society conceptualizations. Such globally diverse cases help to show the importance of 'context' as *substantive* to the meanings of such issues for their actors; the very process typical of (social and natural) scientific approaches, of distinguishing 'real' content (the defined risk object) from secondary 'context', is already rightly shown to be problematic.

These are all welcome departures from the dominant approach's uncritical reproduction of assumptions about objective and universal, acultural risk meanings, which latter approach reinforces a natural sense of legitimacy to the particular forms of globalization associated with it.

When we examine some of the theoretical underpinnings of these cases, however, we find some more limiting commitments. Thus, for example, in one case concerning diabetes self-management and new biomedical paradigms, which are more complex and multi-dimensional than earlier ones concerning the factors involved in diabetic stability and health generally, Cohn (2000) appears to take for granted that these more multi-factorial theories have made diabetic patients less able to identify with expert perspectives and practices. Expert and patients' frameworks are still assumed to be naturally centred on 'risk', when, especially for patients, but also for clinicians, there are many other dimensions of quality of life and social relations involved. Thus, not only are 'citizens', or patients, assumed to be dealing with a simpler world than that which experts confront – when the opposite can also be said to prevail – but also the basic, objective meaning of the issues for each participant is still implied to be solely 'risk' and 'control'.

In an utterly different case, Nugent (2000) makes the valid point that Beck's 'risk society' thesis imposes a questionable universalization of modern North-world society's parochial insecurities and obsessions about risks such as nuclear power or genetic biotechnologies. Nugent points out that this hugely influential, self-consciously reflexive social science perspective neglects its own modern society's long-standing proactive ways of inflicting new kinds of risk on marginalized peoples such as those of the Amazonian basin, and other peoples of the world under various forms of colonial and neo-colonial economic rule. Nugent cogently describes how the kinds of risk now given prominence under modern society's 'risk society' are themselves not the first kinds of 'global, manufactured risk' and are not universal, certainly not in terms of their priority in other global contexts. Nugent says that: 'what is designated by Beck as the authentic marker of reflexive modernization – uncertainty, risk – has a non-standard form, one which is intimately related (through colonial domination) to the European form explored by Beck, but which also challenges the idea that the locus of the exploration of reflexive modernization is Europe' (ibid.: 233). He goes on to criticize the sociological reification of 'risk' as if a universal object, suggesting that this undermines the possibility of a critical social science.

Having laid the grounds for a more humanly rich discursive repertoire than that of risk, however, Nugent appears to betray himself by simply differentiating but not really challenging the very same basic 'risk' discourse. This consolidates the same institutional assumption that I criticized earlier, that the true objective meaning of such public issues to their human subjects is, or should be, risk; the differentiation of the substantive risks said to be involved when encompassing the Amazon as well as Europe does nothing to alter this more fundamental presumed singularity of meaning. Thus, all the divergent issues and meanings of colonial domination, brutality and expropriation, land tenure, trading terms and cultural annihilation are condensed by Nugent into the point that there is a differentiation of risk experience between the centre and the margins of modern neo-liberally globalizing society. Nugent still domesticates all this under the term 'risk', however, which is thus by default still given 'natural' sovereignty as the defining discourse and presumed meaning. His failure to follow through on a promising opening only underlines the need to force such objectivist discourses into idioms that are sufficiently broad, rich and inclusive – and, as openly as possible, seen to be contingent and human – that they can be adequate public vehicles for negotiation about alternative human meanings, visions and ends – that is, also about alternative models of human subjectivity and citizenship – which are trying to make themselves heard as legitimate public voices. The more global and comprehensive such discourses claim (even if by default) to be, the more strongly this enforcement of open contingency and ambiguity is probably needed. Nugent seems to have taken one positive step in this direction, enriching and decentring the available risk discourses, but then appears to conclude that the only options are binary: either discourses of risk almost as a defining feature of modernization; or, alternatively, primitive supernatural discourses of the 'traditional demons' (ibid.: 247).

So to reduce the situation to these polar opposites seems to invite retreat into the scientistic fallacy that the only human meanings that are imaginable are those of risk (however science defines this) as objective universal. Likewise, the model of the imaginable citizen, her agency, autonomy and intellectual and moral capacities, is thus pre-emptively diminished to one where meanings are naturally given by science, and corresponding instrumental aims of control and automatic constructs of natural civic political and intellectual dependency follow from that.

A valuable antidote to this unspoken and probably unintended capitulation is that of Karnik (2001) about HIV/AIDS and India. She is interested in meanings, and explores how cultural meanings of HIV/AIDS have been constructed and transmitted globally. Two aspects of her analysis are especially interesting here. The first is that, in her account, the (social) categories of risk such as 'high-risk groups' which shape HIV medical and social research and policy practice in India were taken uncritically from Western practice, and then, as it were, tautologically confirmed themselves as meaningful categories for India too. (This seems to be a case of 'imagined subject' akin to Anderson's [1991] politics of *Imagined Communities*.) For example, prostitutes and their working-class (not middle-class professional) clients such as truck drivers were monitored as a presumed high-risk group, and the results were interpreted as confirmation of this high-risk status for India, without any comparative testing among other Indian client groups. Other possible social categories of 'high risk', deriving from different possible contributory causes of HIV under specifically Indian conditions – say, groups with endemic diseases and immune-system weakness due to extreme poverty, lack of hygiene or malnutrition; or other groups with no Western equivalent suffering similar levels of sexual exploitation to prostitutes – were simply not imagined, so not tested for, so not seen. By default, the original, North-world-derived tacit human premises were inadvertently confirmed and reproduced as unaccountable cultural processes of globalization, transferring notions of subjectivity and of society concealed in the scientific discourse of the issue.

This spotlights how dominant hegemonic discourses of risk embody tacit power and cultural relations, and transmit these through their global 'scientific' status and and – as Karnik also shows – through consequent international networks of training, recruitment and accreditation. This throws into sharp relief the ways in which discourses of risk embody and project assumptions about social and cultural context, which in turn embody particular models of the salient 'public' or 'citizen'. Internationalization, with its connotations of free collaboration, sharing and assistance, thus becomes under these conditions a vehicle of inevitably unaccountable and hegemonistic globalization.

A second relevant aspect of Karnik's article is how 'public participation' may inadvertently obstruct richer discourses of the meanings of such public issues. She argues that activist groups have positively obstructed the articulation and uptake of richer discourses of the HIV/AIDS issue which might link it as a biomedical reality in its context to such broader human issues as poverty, gender politics, history (for example, colonial dependencies) and culture. Karnik argues that global HIV/AIDS activists in India adopt explicitly critical discourses that uncritically reproduce the basic categories of HIV/AIDS risk as developed in Western society, and add references to poverty, gender and exploitation, if at all, only as afterthoughts. Thus, they basically reinforce the same Western cultural categories in Indian society, and exclude any *analysis* of the connections between the local widespread poverty and destitution, diseases and weak immune system performance, and HIV. They end up restricting their arguments to the call for the availability in India of Western drugs (as happened recently also in South Africa). The point Karnik makes is not that this political campaign is unjustified, but that its protagonists have instead restricted the public discourse to Western-oriented biomedical risk and control matters, and the corresponding tacit cultural categories and relations as defined above. Thus, they effectively preclude the political-economic conditions of poverty, destitution and dependency, and how to alleviate these, from being a key part of the issue in the developing world. Robins (see Chapter 8) deals with similar issues in South Africa. In other words, within the misplaced assumption of universality of scientific knowledge, the developing world is socially defined in the image of Western science's original assumed social context, which leads to the automatic deletion of important local realities such as chronic damage to immune systems from malnutrition and poverty – and of important global realities that cause these local conditions. Global exploitative economic relations and injustice, and North-world moral indifference, are effectively naturalized.

Crucially, Karnik argues further that this has thereby impoverished (rendered more reductionist, more globally standardized and more monovalent) the prevailing *science* as well as the politics of HIV/AIDS in all its diverse contexts. Thus, with tragic irony, science's supposedly special virtue of *unbiased sensitivity to reality* has been inverted, leaving it and its policy users unable to see and respond to the varieties of (social and natural) reality in which it exists. There may well be a more general lesson about science, culture and democracy here.

The processes that Karnik describes for globalized networks of risk and protection discourse about HIV/AIDS may well be a productive starting point for researching the global processes currently under way to try to incorporate new global knowledge actors in the form of indigenous peoples in areas such as the Amazon, where commercial bio-prospecting using indigenous knowledge of nature to identify attractive development objects as priorities for lucrative Western health markets is giving rise to complex new forms of global knowledge network.

What Karnik characterizes as a more enriched kind of science, which reflects and embodies less hegemonistic, more contingent diversities of human-cultural narrative, she describes for a 'risk'-oriented scientific-medical programme – HIV/AIDS. As she puts it:

> It is possible to continue to recognise the importance of AIDS as a single pathogenic disease and also recognise that the term itself, along with its related conceptual baggage (high-risk groups, therapies, vectors, etc) is historically and culturally contingent ... Such a view makes the world at once smaller, bringing people together while also enabling us to see the very important differences of class, gender, race/ethnicity, and sexuality, that separate us. It is an understanding that allows medical practice and science to open themselves to new ideas, instil a notion of self-reflexive rigour, and try to grapple with a complex world in a more complex way. (2001: 344)

This more flexible, open and intellectually rich kind of scientific culture would also implicitly entail more enriched understandings and normative projections – and material performances – of society and of citizens. The same kind of vision could inform sociological and practical understanding of, and intervention in, *innovation*-oriented fields such as GM sciences and technologies, as well as in a field such as HIV, which is more *protection (risk)*-oriented. Then, we might also imagine the substantive conditions and human ends and purposes – hence the scientific and technological shape – of such innovations to be more influenced by situated contextual sensitivities in scientific research cultures (more than simply 'risks' and consequences) than has been the case.

Scientific knowledge as policy culture: imposing public incapacity

Institutional treatments of uncertainty as a scientific and a public issue offer particularly graphic examples of just how deeply entrenched and resistant to counter-evidence and challenge are the institutional-cultural beliefs about public deficits, even in self-conscious official processes of public dialogue, 'listening' and consultation. The typical expert belief – another version of the deficit model (e.g., May 2001) – is that the public craves certainty and zero risk, and mistakenly expects science to deliver it. Since in principle this is an impossible demand, so this line continues, the public mistrusts science when it fails to deliver; but this mistrust is founded on misunderstanding. As I have explained elsewhere (Wynne 2001), this 'mark-two' deficit model is itself founded on scientific-institutional confusion of two qualitatively different kinds of 'uncertainty', combined with misunderstanding of the basis of public concern and mistrust here (Marris et al. 2001). The typical public's concern over uncertainty is about ignorance – unanticipated and unknown consequences – not known uncertainties. Yet the authorities' repeated and exclusive reference to risk assessment as a response to public resistance in effect denies this endemic state of ignorance, because it can only refer to known uncertainties (and, strictly, only to known possible effects with known probabilities). I suggest that contrary to the 'public deficit' institutional belief, the public's mistrust reflects its continual experience of scientific denial of ignorance and of the limits of scientific prediction and control, which is the inevitable effect of the exclusive risk discourse response to public expressions of concern.

I give just one example here, from a much larger sample. In 1999 the UK government conducted a public consultation on the biosciences, supported and facilitated by the government Office of Science and Technology (OST). The exercise (see Irwin 2001a) involved a coordinated series of workshops, structured focus group discussions, a more quantitative survey of members of the public, and an advisory group of academic experts and biosciences specialist stakeholders working with the officials responsible. In the preparation of background scientific information for the qualitative public fieldwork events, an advisory group member suggested that the disputed and uncertain nature of much of the scientific knowledge in play in the GM foods crops area must be communicated. The OST official responded as indicated in the minutes of the meeting:

> [The OST official] accepted that scientific uncertainty is an important issue but stated that the very limited amount of scientific information being offered and its basic nature meant that to describe it as being uncertain would in fact be more confusing for participants. A compromise was suggested whereby the moderators explained how the factual material had been produced and who had played a part in its development. (OST 1999)

This exchange underlines the official's routine assumption that the public has no independent perspective on scientific information in the public domain, nor on its qualities of relevance, reliability, disputedness, fallibility and correction, and of its possible contradiction by other, independently noted evidence. He was imposing the assumption that because the public does not show great knowledge of the scientific content of GM issues, it has no independent means of knowledge of its uncertainties, whether or not these are officially acknowledged. Nor is it believed to have any ability to give its own meaning to these disagreements and uncertainties, but is assumed to be naturally dependent on expert institutions for this interpretive agency.

Yet all the available research on public uptake of science emphasizes how active people are in assessing (correctly or not is beside the point for the present) the credibility and trustworthiness of scientific assertions and their authors, and in putting this into their own independently negotiated and grounded frames of meaning (Irwin and Michael 2003; Irwin and Wynne 1996). To say, without any interest in finding out, that people would not know that scientific knowledge is uncertain and that it would be confusing to tell them so is to impose a particular model of the public or the citizen and her innate (lack of) agency and capacity – as well as being a self-defeating means of trying to structure methods of picking up public perceptions and attitudes.

This is a vivid example of institutional methods of public observation, 'consultation' and 'listening' being structured by tacit assumptions concerning the human citizen which, instead of being identified and tested, are projected into the structuring of observations, conclusions and further commitments. It appears as if these have been scientifically justified by the original observations, and by the existence of an independent expert advisory committee, when that committee's advice has been arbitrarily rejected.

Thus, the idea that even qualitative processes of 'public listening', dialogue or engagement are authentic listening, with an open mind, is exposed to be deeply problematic. As has been suggested in scattered anthropological and philosophical work, genuinely to hear what the 'other' is trying to express, in interpersonal or institutional processes, requires first meeting the demanding condition that one's own 'self' be also in question (understanding the 'other' is almost the defining disciplinary preoccupation of anthropology: de Certeau 1991; Cohen 1994; Dewey 1927; Shotter 1993; Taylor 1992; Williams 1973). No such openness or readiness for self-reflexivity is evident of the dominant institutional culture of science in the kinds of public issue we are dealing with. Instead, and with dogmatic insistence, unspoken internal institutional insecurities are externally projected in models of the 'public' and the 'public world' (for example, claims of media and non-governmental organization misinformation of those publics) as scapegoats for these institutional problems of public mistrust and resistance to 'science'. Thus enmeshed in this culture, powerful institutions of science and policy tend simply to circulate in their own self-perpetuating myths, including myths of the 'public' and of their own openness to them.

This same fundamental problem can be seen in recent science studies discussion of the so-called 'third wave' of science studies of Harry Collins and Rob Evans (2002, 2003), designed deliberately to address the same issues of lay participation in (so-called) 'scientific-technical issues'. Collins and Evans lay out the qualifications that non-scientific lay experts would have in order to qualify for being involved with scientists as contributory experts in such propositional deliberations over whether a given technology or policy is risky or not. Yet despite making some very valuable observations about what is involved, they confine the issues utterly to questions of a propositional sort, neglecting to recognize that questions of meaning are also always at stake in such issues, as well as questions of artificial framing of 'the' public issue as if it were indeed a discrete isolated factor, when it never is in practice.

This quite typical and taken-for-granted framing of even the conceptual issues for improving science–public relationships as if confined to questions about the grounds of legitimacy and authority in propositional questions reinforces the mistaken idea that this is all that such science-intensive policy issues involve. This in turn reinforces the problematic science-policy institutional culture that I have attempted to identify above, especially since it sequesters and privatizes away from democratic accountability issues of public meanings, and of human ends and purposes that drive science as perhaps the key motor of social change in the modern world. This reinforces the confinement of notions of civic agency and capacity to downstream impacts and consequences, leaving out of democratic imagination influence, and debate the fundamental prior questions about what human purposes and visions are or should be driving the upstream processes of research and innovation.

Conclusions

Through an eclectic but salient set of examples drawn from the developed and developing world, and also from globally interconnected domains involving science, I have tried to identify some problematic dimensions of a dominant modern-world institutional culture of science and policy, especially concerning science itself as presumed author of public meanings, as well as public truths. I have also tried to identify the further, deep resistance of this culture to recognizing its own tacit insecurities and dogmatic commitments, even – or maybe particularly – when celebrating its more public-participation, two-way dialogue and listening adventures. A sociologically informed examination of the forms of representation of the issues that are circulated and imposed points to tacit dimensions of these processes that remain unaccountable to any kind of democratic debate or deliberation. These unseen dimensions are concealed by the privilege given to reified scientific risk discourses, whose constructed and contingent character is systematically misunderstood and misread instead as purely innocent object representation, untouched by any performative, normatively potent models of the human, which are, I argue, embodied and projected by them. These public risk discourses thus act inadvertently as Trojan horses, imposing presumed standard meanings on people, and thereby also imposing inadequate models of themselves as human subjects and citizens, and the natural meanings they should hold. They are also projected as having no capacity to articulate and negotiate collectively their own autonomous public meanings and issue definitions or frames.

Analysis of public scientific discourses (often phrased in terms of 'risk') and science–public engagement processes needs to address more forthrightly the implicit meanings that are being presumptively imposed through this ostensibly objective, rational process. In explicating and problematizing such public meanings and interpretation of dialogue processes as presumed by dominant institutions, we also need therein to identify, and hold to account, the normative models of the 'citizen' (as well as the hidden human aims and visions driving scientific work), which such risk discourses project (and obscure).

Globalization processes extend the networks and arenas over which such processes of tacit 'negotiation' or imposition can occur, and render more problematic even than before the comforting but false idea that if these tacit models were so incorrect they would be manifestly contradicted by public responses, and corrected appropriately. Would that human life were so direct and simple – although it can indeed be argued that these inadequate models of the human subject and the authoritarian ways in which they are imposed are receiving just such repeated and growing, but oblique and contextually diverse, forms of public repudiation, globally as well as more locally (de Sousa Santos 2003).

As we examine the increasing number and density of such globalized discourses and related interactions (again in a subtly perverse retroactive force countering the deliberate and sometimes self-congratulatory flood of participatory moves to engage publics with science), framing the meanings involved as ones of risk or science imposes in a quite undemocratic way issue framings and meanings, and corresponding citizen models, which have enjoyed no such democratic accountability and negotiation. It may well be that the more global and cross-cultural these contexts and processes

81

become, the more reductionist and less responsive to diverse frames of meaning or issue definition such institutional processes are capable of becoming. This is a question that needs to be insistently and carefully addressed in practice. Retrieval of authentic democratic potentials with a legitimate science requires this as a minimum condition.

Note

1 Although the language of 'upstream' public engagement is nowadays repeated ubiquitously by policy bodies (e.g., Royal Society 2004; D71/Treasury 2004), it is still enmeshed within the profoundly problematic assumption that it is all about 'better prediction of impacts', when lack of predictive power is just the issue.

2 Here I am reminded of Scott's (1990) work on the autonomous worlds of meaning subversively constructed and enacted by peasant farmers under dictatorial regimes in South-East Asia, but which operate apparently undetected 'under the radar' of the alien overt political culture of the dominant regime.

6 | Knowledge, justice and democracy

SHIV VISVANATHAN

The Norwegian sociologist Johan Galtung once talked of a painting that hung in the ante-room of the late Ghanaian leader Kwame Nkrumah. It was a giant picture, inevitably of Nkrumah himself, struggling loose from his chains. There is thunder and lightning in the air and in one corner of the picture are three men, three white men. The first is the capitalist, and he carries a briefcase. The second figure is a missionary, and he clutches a Bible. There is a third figure in the remotest corner of the picture. He is holding a book whose title can be barely discerned. It is entitled *African Political Systems*, and this third figure is the scientist as colonial anthropologist.

The iconography of the picture used to fascinate me. It represented the power and fury of nationalism battling against the depredations of capitalism, missionizing religion and colonial science. I would begin my introductory classes in political sociology with a discussion of this picture. Yet looking back, it appears mildewed, embarrassing and outdated. Nationalism, which was a liberating movement, has graduated into the national security state, which is often genocidal. Development, which was meant to create justice and equality, has virtually become a war by other means against marginals, tribals and peasants in the Third World. Science, which was seen as a magic wand against poverty, has behaved counter-intuitively. Modern democracy appeared to be a social contract between science and the nation-state to guarantee security and development. It is this new social contract between science, development and the nation-state which creates the other science wars that few philosophers talk about. One needs the passionate scholarship of Ivan Illich to grasp it (Illich 1992). Unfortunately the story of the science wars is read today as a trumpet sound from *Social Text*, which has brought down the Jericho of social science. If positivism was a quarrel between two university dons, Alan Sokal's (1996) article could be considered a superb joke, the work of an almost Jungian prankster. One can add one's laughter and drink to it, even dine out on the story. If it is a spoof on science as a *system*, it is welcome. But the same joke sounds poor when seen from the life-world of a tribal, a marginal or a slum. Jokes from the system are not equivalent to laughter in a life-world. If the trickster in Sokal is ready to perform a pilgrimage to the life-world, a conversation of a different sort could begin. These are notes from one such journey.

I wrote the original jottings for this chapter for economists and activists talking about sustainable development from a World Bank perspective. I remember that at that time we had made a set of pleas, four in all. We had requested that:

- Human rights teams (or at least an ombudsman for each technology) be attached to every development project.
- An audit of each development effort be provided in the language and categories of the people involved or affected. Quality of Life (QOL) indicators are adequate but one needs to experience them in the vernacular of a people. The idea of the good life needs its own idiom of rumour and gossip.
- The scientific epistemology of the project be understood in terms of local theories of knowledge. It was a hint that empowerment in terms of a people's voice alone was inadequate. A people's epistemology is as central as people's participation in any discourse on democracy.
- One needs some form of insurance, of security against development projects.

Of course, we realized that our pleas were part futile, part utopian, a playful wager against the odds. So we finally suggested, as a Sokalian joke, that a wailing wall should be instituted in the World Bank office so that we could mourn or grieve together in the aftermath of some projects. No doubt pathologists' reports are scientific, but one also needs the catharsis of mourning rituals. One mourns over the body of a friend, one performs an autopsy on a corpse (Romanyshyn 1989).

How do the science wars look from the history of marginality in the Third World? This is not to set the ethnocentrism of the Anglo-Saxon world against the parochialism of the Third World. But one has to realize that epistemology is not a remote, exotic term. It determines life chances. Science as development, plan, experiment, pedagogy determines the life chances of a variety of people. Here epistemology is politics. The positivist–anti-positivist wars need a larger theatre. It is from such a site that one must issue an invitation to a different science war. Many readings see fundamentalism and science as incommensurable words without realizing that the spectre haunting India is a variant of techno-fundamentalism, which hybridizes science with the most bloodthirsty communalism. These notes are one set of reflections on the other science wars. But to understand this we must create a certain relation of map to territory, particularly as regards science and democracy in discussion of issues such as development.

In attempting to understand science, development and technology, one feels the same sense of horror and surprise that Hannah Arendt did when she was reporting on the Eichmann trial in Jerusalem (Arendt 1963). Arendt found it difficult to reconcile the sheer ordinariness of the man with the enormity of his crimes. To attempt to do so she formulated the idea of the banality of evil, the idea that violence does not require evil, all it requires is normalcy, bureaucratic expertise and a clerical project (see also Ravetz, this book). The scientific equivalent of a project is a research programme. The scientist in pursuit of a normal science is also capable of radical evil.

The works of Ivan Illich, Vandana Shiva, Ashish Nandy or Boaventura Santos are challenges to the normal science of today (see Nandy 1980; Shiva 1989; Santos 1992; Illich 1992). What they introduce is both resistance and the carnivalesque, suggesting that a science that diversifies its paradigms attempts to minimize the hegemony of one of them. For instance, Boaventura Santos's seminal essay is not only an exercise in intellectual hospitality, but also a suggestion that it is not good fences which make good neighbours but good conversation and concepts, which are disciplined trespassers (Santos 1992). Santos's suggestion is that the flow of concepts across the social and natural sciences has rendered the demon between them a creative gate-keeper. In fact, it has created a powerful hybridity of social science concepts such as complexity, uncertainty, risk, and populations seeding the sciences to create a domain that challenges the standard hierarchy that Thomas Kuhn and every modern university impose on the natural sciences, social sciences and humanities. Santos's work is still the work of a scholar talking to other scholars in a research community. But there is a wider audience, and in fact another world of participants, that gives it a different meaning. To enter this world, we have to understand the civics of the modern world, whose political core is the idea of the transfer of technology.

The civics of the transfer of technology (TOT)

The idea of technology transfer is one of the most quotidian ideas of governance regarding technology. It nestles peacefully in World Bank reports, Population Council monographs and non-governmental organization (NGO) project reports. In an ordinary sense it captures the hegemony and violence of everyday life in a policy world. John Maynard Keynes claimed years ago that behind every dictator and his policies is a book or a philosopher that the tyrant had read years earlier. Arendt (1963) adds that behind every technocrat and a tyrant is the banality of a project. How have grass-roots movements as philosophers of science attempted to counter them at the levels of knowledge and justice? One must emphasize that, particularly in India, the critique of science arose not in universities but from human rights activists, ecologists and feminists fighting a battle against the fundamentalism of official science represented by technology transfer (Visvanathan 2002).

The innovation chain as a structured sequence is an attempt to link science, technology and society through the sequences of invention, innovation and development (or diffusion). To quote textbook officialese, invention represents the creation of a scientific idea and its initial visualization as a technological product; innovation the upscaling and commercialization of an idea; and diffusion its eventual absorption or distribution into the wider society. The idea of innovation is not only a research management discourse but one about development and democracy. In a geographical sense, science originates at the centre and development occurs at the periphery. It is also a technological vision of democracy, where the science is legitimized by experts but consumed by citizens. Participation, local materials and visions appear during the later phases of the innovation chain. The civics of TOT represent a policy map, a model of hegemony, a vision of knowledge and a metaphor for democracy. Science and democracy play out their repertoire of possibilities within an innovation chain. There is a sense of pre-empted futures here because in official visions the alternative to development is not alternative development, but museumization and marginalization.

In terms of a grass-roots critique, the model of technology transfer can be read from two perspectives. The first is dominated by the history and philosophy of science and is basically an internalist historiography, where we wrestle with Kuhn, Popper or Lakatos. Supplementing them within the same frame is the sociology or political economy of science, which emphasizes issues of professionalism, defence pressures or the role of multinationals. But we rarely find a book that moves from the creativity of the science to the studies of innovation and development dominated by science policy experts, economists of development or historians of technology. There is a tacit division of labour here that we must ignore. One can't see the first as creativity and the second as productivity. As Steve Fuller demonstrates, behind every Thomas Kuhn is a James Conant – Kuhn only transformed and banalized into science what were rules of thumb for cold war politics and strategy (Fuller 2000). Rules of hygiene prevent an understanding of the connection between the two. Fuller showed that the works of these science politicians made science safe *for* and *from* democracy. This becomes more apparent in a pedagogic text or transfer of technology model. In these models science is still a 'club'-driven exercise. What is democratized is not the critique of science and technology but the consumption or distribution of science.

The first thing grass-roots groups in India did was to merge the two empires of knowledge. They also helped provide a democratic framework for science by insisting on and challenging the fundamental oppositions between expert and lay or science and the mob and between science and ethnoscience, read either as local knowledge or dismissed as folklore or superstition. The science movements performed a brilliant manoeuvre. They took the science wars across the innovation chain, playfully tweaking not only the hierarchies of knowledge within science but the boundary management between science and other knowledges. They insisted that science was a new social science and challenged the dualism of observer and observed in profound ways. In the following section we shall explore the critique of science presented by the science movements.

A grass-roots critique of science

Science in India began as a positivist celebration wherein Indian scientists such as Meghnad Saha literally dreamt of a society based on the scientific method (Visvanathan 1984). India was a society as proud of its sample surveys and its science policy as it was of its flag. A society that dreamt of its laboratories and dams as the new temples of modern India witnessed the fact that the sacrilege began with science. We faced a set of science projects that were difficult to understand within a positivist science or the old dualism between good science/bad science policy. We had to face the following facts:

1. Our dams had produced not only energy but an ethnicity of over 40 million refugees. One needs a common base to audit development and displacement within the same discourse (Parsuraman and Unnikrishnan 2000).
2. Our scientific Forest Acts threatened both animals and people, creating a debate between scientific and social forestry threatening one-seventh of our population.
3. The Bhopal gas tragedy created thousands of victims who were subject to the scientific gaze but received neither compensation nor healing.
4. The Green Revolution produced the paradox of an official India self-sufficient in food while increasing the salinity of our soils and decreasing the diversity of our agriculture (Shiva 1989).
5. The only dictatorship India had was between 1975 and 1977 and it was justified in terms of scientific metaphors that legitimitized compulsory sterilization in family planning and forced demolitions in the name of scientific urban planning.
6. India today is a nuclear state where science has driven the move towards nuclearization. What is troubling is not just nuclearization but the terms of discourse within which scientific debates are carried out.

The question the grass-roots movements in science had to face as a philosophical and political conundrum was whether the above crises were because of bad science, bad politics and bad technology or was the problem also inherent in the logic of science and technology. This political drama in what I called the politics of knowledge took place at three levels.

- What are the rules for a scientific controversy in a democracy that includes tribals, marginal fishing groups, shifting cultivators, slums, industrial refugees and a middle class demographically the size of Europe? How does one make decisions about science and technology in a society that is undergoing the first, second and third industrial revolutions simultaneously?
- How does one frame an interaction between science and democracy which looks systematically at the 'scientization' of democracy and the 'democratization' of science? How does one phenomenologically bracket them so that one can re-examine these taken-for-granted worlds?
- How does one create a framework of controversy which neither economizes science by instrumentalizing it or reduces it to a battle between scientific fundamentalism (positivism and reductionism) and religious fundamentalism?
- What concepts do we need which go beyond rights, cost–benefit, objectivity and efficiency? What one hopes to present is the framework and the repertoire of tactics and concepts generated.

One realizes, of course, that a wide variety of movements is grouped under the same rubric here, but it is important to capture the unity of this great parliament of science whereby civil society – particularly grass-roots groups and dissenting academics – built a more democratic framework for science. What emerges is not only a great exercise in democratic theory, but also a contribution to the philosophy and history of science.

The initial critical moves emphasized the latter half of the innovation chain. The first major critiques came both from the Bernalians within the state and from left-leaning movements such as the Kerala Sastra Sahitya Parishad (KSSP)[1] and the Delhi Science Forum. Their dream of democracy was still diffusionist. It was a dream of taking science to the villages. What was invented was the idea of the scientific temper, a pedagogic vision that a scientific world-view could be induced in a people. Unfortunately the radical scientist often visualized the scientific temper as an intellectual vaccine that could eliminate superstition, magic and religious fundamentalism. The left-leaning movements carried this same scientific view through science quizzes celebrating Newton, Bernal and Darwin. Here civil society and the progressive state shared a common vision of a positivist science. But in the later debates there came a split between the science policy of the state and the critiques of science by civil society. It was a science war, which emphasized that the citizenship provided by the new social contract was inadequate because it was a citizenship based on an industrial premise, which saw the citizen as a consumer and not an inventor of knowledge. It also realized that both science in India and the Indian constitution were disembedded knowledges.

The critique of science began as a human rights problem because development projects either marginalized or cannibalized the culture of tribes, slums or the peasantry. The standard notion of human rights did not work because, while it was adequate at the level of the individual, it was unavailable at the level of the group. Second, what one needed was a science that realized that nature was not just an object of an experiment or a resource but part of a way of life. As Tom Kocherry, leader of the Kerala Fishers Forum, claimed: 'Seventy per cent of India depends on nature for its livelihood.' Nature was thus not only a mode of production but a mode of thought. The movements realized that there were few life-affirming notions of nature within science. The concept of wilderness used in American ecology was inadequate because for the American the wilderness was an unpopulated monument. One needed something beyond the American dialectic of wilderness and frontier or the British obsession with gardens. The world-view of the Bishnois[2] or the Chipko[3] movement came from their religious cosmology. It was not anti-science but a critique only of a statist science, which saw the pulp and paper industry as a more eligible citizen than the tribes foraging for food and medicines. In the new model of development as an enclosure movement not only were tribals and marginal peasants displaced, they were rendered illegal. What was destroyed was not only the forest but a common body of knowledge about trees, fodder, forest produce, seeds, medicines, building. This was not merely a resource pool but a way of life that sustained a way of knowledge (see also Wynne, this book).

The movements were confronted with two facts. First, the idea of rights was adequate for torture but helpless against science-induced displacement, obsolescence or even genocide. Second, they realized that in the battle called development the idea of nature itself had changed. It was not just farm, fish and fowl, it was also hybridized with technology. The citizen lives simultaneously in a natural, technological, biotechnological and information environment (Whiteside 2002). One had to confront these different hybridities simultaneously. One needs not only a new ethic for nature in science but a new ethic of technology. They also sensed the iatrogenic nature of science policy, created particularly by the reductionist nature of scientific expertise. But the answer was not Luddism. The modern

Luddite cannot smash the abstract machine, only rework the classifications behind abstract thought. S/he must become futurologist, epistemologist and constitutionalist, and must also realize that the new politics of science is created by dissenting imaginations within and alternative imaginations without. A critique of science as an ongoing exercise cannot be located in fundamentalisms, only in competing and reciprocal criticalities. For every Shiva or Medha Patkar there is a Chipko and a Narmada movement. Further, there is no one construction of Chipko, Narmada or Balliapal, any more than there can be one master narrative of science. The power of the movements lay in the fact that they realized that politics is not just a protest against a dam or a forest bill. It must extend a challenge to official narratives of science and to the epistemologies that underlie it. Or, to put it bluntly, how do non-violent movements search for a non-violent science?

The movements realized that the politics of time was crucial at three levels of science: first, the politics of the history of science; second, the politics of memory; and finally the politics of multiple time.

The history of science has always constructed itself as a rational, cumulative, continuous exercise. Science as an exoteric internalist narrative constructs itself in linear and progressive time. Science is conducted in victorious time, which has no place for defeated knowledges. While science deals with a diversity of times – mechanical, historical, evolutionary and quantum (nanosecond) – its own narratives are constructed in the impoverished time of unilinear narratives. For the movements, science fails as a narrative and as an act of storytelling, and yet they realize that it is the very unilinearity of time which provides its cognitive power. As Kuhn (1970) remarked, the textbook as a reflection of a cognitive regime rewrites histories where defeated or alternative hypotheses have little place.

The politics of memory is a close corollary to the first because the progressive rhetoric of science is an amnesiacal one. It museumizes other forms of knowledge in the name of progress. It also renders obsolescent ways of life, which are abandoned because of the changing nature of technology. The innovations of science take place in standardized time. Science understands the grammar of progress but not the logic of obsolescence as a lived world. The paradigm as a monoparadigmatic space comes with an indifference about certain forms of time. Within the innovation chain, Socrates becomes a Schumpeterean idiot.

Democracy needs a multiplicity of times. A tribesperson involved in shifting cultivation operates in a world of over twenty different kinds of time, which emanates from the way s/he deals with soil, seed, seasons, rituals, fast, feast, rest, work, domestic and communal space. Farmers, women, patients and tribespeople live in a variety of times, which they need access to and which science denies them. It is within this context that ecology is as vital to science as quantum physics. What ecology smuggles into science is a notion of memory as a thesaurus of times. What the movements emphasized is that a democracy based on standard factory time is literally an oxymoron. At this point one must emphasize the difference and overlap between the different politics of memory. Ian Hacking talks of three forms of Foucaultian politics (Hacking 1995). The first dealt with the politics of the body, the second with the politics of populations. Hacking adds that the third form of hegemony is the politics of memory as an act of scientization. But the politics of the second idea of memory deals with a liberation from history as the only form of memory with a plurality of times. The trouble with the official idea of sustainability is that it lacks such a repertoire of times.

Once the framework of multiple time is established, the abstractness of science is challenged. Science, as the movements and the dissenting academics suggest, is not merely an object of production created through the optical gaze of the Enlightenment but a subject of consumption and validation. The tacit division of labour between an expert who produces knowledge and a citizen who consumes it has to be rendered less asymmetrical by understanding the citizen as a person of knowledge. The worker, the peasant and the craftsman are all citizens of knowledge about science. This understanding cannot be devalued as 'ethnoscience' while expert understanding is 'philosophy of science'. Such a hierarchy or devaluation creates the possibility of the museumization or appropriation of these other knowledges. Strangely, even at a time when science is appropriating and patenting peasant knowledges, there is no epistemic acknowledgement of their status. Science begins a form of strip mining, where knowledge about local drugs, therapeutics, soils and seeds is abstracted without considering the philosophies they are embedded in.

Beyond participation: the challenge of cognitive justice

Given the tendency of science and technological projects towards displacement, obsolescence and erasure, the movements believe that the externalist idea of community involvement, participation and use of local materials is not enough. These are externalist measures. Even the subaltern emphasis on 'voice' is a trifle sentimental. These become mere epicycles that the scientific panopticon throws out to humanize itself. They do not touch the normal science of a discipline. The movements understand that participation does not constitute an epistemic challenge. It can merely add to the popularization of science or to an increasing awareness about decision-making. But the politics of an epistemic challenge requires a different set of constitutional or legislative guarantees. Probably the best way to explain it is by relating an anecdote.

A few months back, representatives of what are now called 'denotified' tribes – tribes once classified as criminal by the British – came to meet us. These tribes, which are over a few million strong, face a devastating medical situation: sickle cell anaemia, a condition of which they have little understanding. They also face mental trauma from the everydayness of police torture and harassment. The community goes to the government primary health centres and to the herbal doctors. Their representatives had come with a suggestion. What they wanted was a dialogue, a seminar wherein patients, victims, medical practitioners of various persuasions, public health specialists, psychiatrists and human rights activists met and listened to their testimonies of health, illness and well-being. What they hoped would emerge from it was a new kind of health policy which they would present to the local legislature. They wanted a dialogic health policy which saw health and development together: not in the language of expertise but in terms of a new notion of health politics.

What they wanted was not just participation. They wanted *presence* of two kinds, participation and *cognitive representation*. They wished that, when a policy was decided, the tribal doctor and the Western health expert were both present and that the policy should represent the language of this dialogue. Such a presence goes beyond participation and ethnoscience to cognitive empowerment. The political economy and ecology of the tribal situation demand access to a variety of medical systems. Plurality is necessary for true access to a system because one cannot have choice without alternatives. What one needs is the idea of cognitive justice: the constitutional right of different systems of knowledge to exist as part of dialogue and debate. The movement's critiques of science and technology thus realized that the challenge to the expertises of technology required a stronger framework of participation. The idea of participation fundamentally accepts the experts' definition of knowledge. It seeks only to modify or soften it. It seeks a blend of expert knowledge and ethnoscience. But it is a world where expert knowledge is presented as high theory and the layperson's ideas as a pot-pourri of practices, local ideas and raw material. There is no principle of equivalence. Cognitive justice, however, recognizes the plurality of knowledge systems. It also recognizes the relation between knowledge and livelihood and lifestyle. It is in this context that it holds that policy must not be articulated within one monochromatic frame of knowledge but within an existential plurality of them. For example, a medical policy in India should be formulated recognizing the presence of a variety of medical systems and defining a patient as one open to this medical body of knowledge and its ideas of pain, healing, suffering, sickness and death. Cognitive justice goes beyond voice or resistance to recognizing constitutionally the body of knowledge within which an individual is embedded.

The idea of cognitive justice suggests that there is a link between survival and forms of knowledge. It includes not only the rights of dissenting scientists within a dominant paradigm, but also the rights of alternative epistemologies and alternative sciences. The debate on alternative sciences cannot be exhausted by Lysenkoism and the racialism of Nazi science. Alternative sciences existed long before as traditional agriculture or alternative medical systems. A plea for cognitive justice also establishes the understanding that democracy within knowledge is crucial. The opposition of expert and layperson disguises to a certain extent the opposition between science and alternative sciences. One needs instead a parliament of epistemic debates, but also the ecologies that would let these forms of knowledge survive and thrive not in a preservationist sense but as active practices. The idea of cognitive justice thus visualizes a body of knowledge that citizens, especially in subsistence cultures, have access to as consumers, critics, practitioners and philosophers. As a tactic it renders irrelevant the hierarchical contempt implicit in the notion of ethnoscience as a lesser life form or model of being.

In search of plural visions

What the movements and their critique of science sought was not antiscience but a plural vision that allowed for both the wisdom of normal science and the vision of the eccentric, the dissenter, the marginal, the vulnerable and alternative world-views. The playfulness, the new concepts and new reciprocity between science and social worlds created through novelty by combination, was extended by grass-roots politics and philosophers to a wider domain. They forced the democratic imagination to contend with science by inventing new methodologies beyond boy scout calls for participation and empowerment (see Part Four). Programmes for open societies offer science as an image and model for democracy but they do little to add to the democratization of science or its imagination. A science that seeks only consumers' or citizens' approval is a disguised demagoguery that will work against the grass-roots innovators.

Notes

1 The Kerala Sastra Sahitya Parishad (the Kerala literary and scientific association) was a forum established by Malyali science writers. It is today a movement with over 40,000 members dedicated to the popularization of science and to utilizing science for progressive ends.

2 The Bishnois are followers of the fifteenth-century saint Guru Jambeshwar, who instructed his followers to protect plant and animal life. A cattle-rearing and agricultural community, the Bishnois do not allow hunting or felling on their land.

3 The Chipko movement arose as a protest against logging abuses in the state of Uttar Pradesh in India. The word 'chipko' literally means 'embrace'. The movement's name derives from the non-violent practice of women who hugged trees, interposing themselves between the tree and the contractors.

THREE | **Citizens engaging with science**

Commentary

MELISSA LEACH, IAN SCOONES AND
BRIAN WYNNE

This section presents a series of cases that draw on and extend the themes raised in the last section. They illustrate interactions between publics and science in a variety of settings, raising questions about forms of knowledge, epistemology and expertise. These cases show public engagements with science to be bound up with material struggles for health and livelihoods, and social solidarities that emerge to address these, whether among patient groups in the UK, labour unions in India or HIV/AIDS activists in South Africa. The cases consider how contemporary configurations of the state, civil society, the private sector and international organizations, as well as emergent coalitions and alliances that cross-cut these categories and distinctions, shape the possibilities of different types of citizen engagement.

Richard Tutton, Anne Kerr and Sarah Cunningham-Burley's chapter, through an examination of a focus group working on gene patenting in the UK, shows how perspectives brought to public debates about science and technology reflect different people's lived or imaginary perspectives. This is true for both 'publics' and 'experts'. Tutton et al., however, show the necessity of deconstructing such categories, demonstrating them to be contextual, performed and contingent as people seek to position themselves and each other in ways that might shift even in the course of a conversation. Particular ideas of citizenship or non-citizenship are created through these discussions. There are limits to this negotiability, however, as, in order to create meaningful alliances, people latch on to particular discourses or framings; for example, a company being an exemplar of 'good practice' or a pariah. This is an illustration of a broader pattern where, in order to create political solidarities, multiple subject positions and perspectives must coalesce around a particular discourse in order to press claims.

Engagements between publics and science involve complex forms of (often temporary) coalition, alliance and hybrid organization between actors of different kinds. This is illustrated by Steven Robins in his discussion of the alliances that formed around the 'dissident science' camp, arguing against a singular viral cause of AIDS, and the Treatment Action

Campaign (TAC) position, fighting for access to anti-retroviral drugs in HIV/AIDS treatment in South Africa. Robins's chapter also shows how public science engagements interrelate with, and can become coloured by, historically embedded cultural and political frames of meaning, in this case the interpretation of AIDS through racialized lenses linked to South Africa's apartheid and post-apartheid history. In this context, TAC has adopted a very particular, and effective, campaigning discourse that has foregrounded treatment regimes and access to drugs, and has backgrounded the well-recognized complexities of AIDS causation. As TAC activism shows, emergent solidarities straddle local, national and global spaces, perhaps, as Robins suggests, constituting a form of 'globalization from below'.

Other chapters similarly address the processes and terms by which public science policy engagements proceed, drawing attention to a variety of dimensions and scales. Thus Dr Murlidhar V.'s chapter on occupational health in India illustrates the role of a non-governmental organization (NGO), in alliance with labour unions, in forging a connection between the previously quite autonomous life-worlds of workers and medical scientists, struggling to get the former recognized by the latter. The terms of this engagement are, however, those of medical science, as are their mechanisms and means of legitimacy – such as publications in scientific journals and training workers to use measuring instruments. This is an example of 'citizen science' in the classic and relatively restricted sense of equipping publics with the ability to engage with science on its own terms. Nevertheless, in facilitating access to medical science for workers, it offers opportunities for treatment, compensation claims and improvement in working conditions. These feed positively into other dimensions of citizenship, including the claiming of political and economic rights. This illustrates a more general point – that public engagements with science can have wider and unanticipated effects on other dimensions of empowerment and citizenship. Potentially, such dimensions could also feed back into a reflexive capacity and an epistemic awareness, and so claims for 'cognitive justice' around other issues.

As Kees Jansen and Esther Roquas show, many of these context-specific understandings of issues are occluded through processes of internationalized science. Looking at the particular case of biotechnology regulation, they examine how international epistemic communities, particularly as propagated through international networks and committees of scientific advisers, construct and impose internationalized forms of 'cognitive consensus' and notions of 'best practice', whether around risk assessment or instrumentalized forms of participation. They draw attention to the inequalities in these international forums and the frequent under-

98

representation of developing-country perspectives. These internationalized perspectives are often detached from locally contextualized experiences and complexities, yet they become imposed on them via national regulatory frameworks that are expected to implement them. They characterize this process and the problems it causes as 'absentee expertise'. With their focus on Latin America, they show how this arises in places where there is limited national scientific capacity.

While globalization may be promoting and giving power to such international epistemic communities, their effects in particular countries are inevitably mediated by the nature of states, bureaucracies and society. This is illustrated clearly in James Keeley's chapter, which examines the relationship between international discourses concerning biotechnology and the modernizing developmental projects of the Chinese state. Keeley's account echoes the familiar observation that significant cultural and social issues are seamlessly translated into scientific discourses. In this case, we see the state's overall commitment to modernization as a socio-historical project being manifested in discourses around science, risk and nature. The chapter discusses how a pro-genetic modification (GM) discourse, propagated by alliances between private sector actors and international organizations, has been partially taken on, but also in parts subverted and challenged, by actors within China. He also locates the construction of citizenship in this context, showing how a state collectivist notion of the Chinese citizen is being challenged by more liberal, individualist, market- and consumer-oriented perspectives.

Considering citizenship in terms of mobilization around highway construction in Brazil, Angela Alonso and Valeriano Costa's chapter focuses on the political conditions for such mobilization. The chapter reminds us of the importance of social profiles, social and political interests, membership of and engagement with forms of association and access to formal institutions in effecting patterns of mobilization. These structural political dimensions interplay with the more cognitive, discursive dimensions, which are given more emphasis in other cases, in shaping the way public engagements with science play out.

Sheila Jasanoff starts from these important political questions, but moves on to a more explicitly discursive analysis, asking, for example, what implicit political subjects are inhabiting the definitions and framings of issues. She shows how, in the case of Golden Rice biotechnology, it is framed as a universal solution, 'a view from everywhere'. Yet this serves also to erase particular forms of political subject or citizen in favour of a mass representation, skipping over lived experiences and erasing particular political constellations that might articulate these lived experiences and alternative possibilities. Her discussion of this case echoes Brian Wynne's argument about technical discourses embodying implicit assumptions about the human subject and social relations. As Jasanoff suggests, this raises major questions about the avenues through which alternative views of what a technological society might look like can be expressed.

One such avenue is discussed in Paul Richards's chapter, where he makes the case that discussions about biotechnology and plant breeding need to be embedded in international human rights discourses concerning the right to food. Richards shows how institutionalized science – increasingly a private-sector-led version – embodies a particular construction of farmers and the needy poor, yet there exist a variety of other technology needs that may be more appropriate responses. By shifting the frame from one focused on the risk of starvation to one of rights and cognitive justice, a different perspective on agricultural/food technology priorities opens up; one that can be more attentive to the rationalities and agendas of poor farmers' own agricultural innovations. These agendas also embody alternative political and societal agendas: as Richards suggests, local ideas about food security and seed exchange reinforce notions of solidarity and rights – in effect, citizenship. As he puts it, 'local seed systems do not just yield food; they also "grow" communities'.

7 | Myriad stories: constructing expertise and citizenship in discussions of the new genetics

RICHARD TUTTON, ANNE KERR AND
SARAH CUNNINGHAM-BURLEY

Introduction

In this chapter, we explore the ways in which people in the UK discussed the patenting of genes in a series of focus group conversations. We consider in particular people's discussion of the case of Myriad Genetics, a US company that holds patents on BRCA1 and BRCA2, two genes involved in the hereditary forms of breast and ovarian cancer. The Myriad case was a vignette in our study of the ways in which people position themselves and others when talking about access to genetic information, particularly the issues of ownership and regulation.[1] We introduced this case to the focus groups to engender discussion about the implications of patenting for genetic testing. We are interested in the ways in which people took on the roles of 'expert' or 'citizen', explicitly or implicitly, when they considered these issues, and what types of knowledge-claims and moral judgements these positions involved. The discussions about Myriad covered concerns about competition within science and medicine, the accuracy of different types of genetic tests, the globalization of genetic information and the relationships between multinational firms, national governments, scientific and health professionals, public healthcare, patients and consumers. These wider issues of commercialization and the public/private interface surfaced at different points in the focus group discussions, and responses to these embraced moral, political and economic arguments. What people bring to these debates, and the extent to which they are heard or can influence policy, depends on constructions of expertise and citizenship and the different knowledges, experiences and subjectivities implicated in such roles.

After providing some background to the Myriad case we discuss the focus group methodology that we employed, before moving on to analyse the different ways in which groups discussed Myriad. The analysis provides an outline of the different ways in which groups, and sometimes individuals, came to different or similar positions; reflection about the ways in which knowledge-claims and moral values were involved; and discusses the reasons why particular groups or individuals may have framed their accounts in these ways. We identified two main ways in which Myriad was constructed in these discussions: as an exemplar and as a pariah – although these should be seen as two sides of the same coin as both interrogate the relationship between Myriad's actions and the role of private enterprise in the realm of genetic research, testing and healthcare. These versions of Myriad are highly flexible and contingent, and can be understood only within the context of these research conversations. Our analysis emphasizes such contingency by examining the construction of expertise and citizenship, and offers an interpretation of why particular groups may settle upon specific subject positions vis-à-vis gene patenting and Myriad's activities. We deliberately do not attempt to reach a conclusion about what the majority of groups thought ought to happen with respect to the enforcement of the Myriad patent in the UK, or about the regulation of gene patenting more generally. Indeed, we explicitly reject such an analytical construct because it would be too simplistic, given that people's accounts of these issues are neither static nor resolute. We also avoid categorizing groups according to types such as 'layperson' or 'professional', and comparing their views within this framework, as this involves fixed notions of expertise and laity that do not do justice to the range of authority claims involved in the discussions.

We end the chapter by reflecting upon the implications of our analysis for exercises in public consultation and professional–public dialogue about genetics. We argue that normative theories of expertise (see Collins and Evans 2002) or ideal models of citizen participation, such as citizens' juries, involve setting up artificial boundaries between citizenship and expertise, and between the knowledge-claims and moral values on which they are based – boundaries that are forever changing in discursive practice. Analysts and participants alike need to pay more attention to the structure and function of 'authority claims' in these types of public–professional dialogue, in order to answer the questions as to why they are being made, by whom, in what context and to what effect.

A Myriad story

The US-based company, Myriad Genetics, holds international patents on BRCA1 and BRCA2, two genes involved in hereditary forms of breast and ovarian cancer (Dalpé et al. 2003). There has been marked opposition to these patents in several European countries and Canadian provinces on the grounds that they are too broad, with the effect of placing Myriad in a monopolistic position in relation to BRCA testing (Clement 2002; European Parliament 2001; Henley 2001; Wadman 2001; Whestphal 2002). Opponents of the patents argue that they could stifle the invention of alternative diagnostic techniques and limit patient access to the tests, especially in public healthcare systems, since there is no check on what Myriad can charge. They have also expressed concern about the company's policy that tests requiring full sequencing of the BRCA genes be sent to their laboratories for completion (Rimmer 2003). This raises the prospect of Myriad being able to construct a large proprietary database to reinforce its dominance in this and perhaps other areas of clinical research. Opposition to the Myriad patents has culminated in a legal challenge by the Institut Curie in France and other research agencies in Belgium and the Netherlands, supported by their respective national governments (Henley 2001; Rimmer 2003). Myriad has responded to these criticisms by arguing that patents allow them to protect their investment in this costly area, and to provide tests of the highest quality (Rimmer 2003). In Britain, Myriad originally signed a licensing agreement with a British company, Rosgen, to conduct BRCA tests for private healthcare patients, but this company has since gone into liquidation. Negotiations with the Department of Health about the provision of BRCA1 testing for National Health Service (NHS) patients are ongoing (Meek 2000a, 2000b). In the meantime, NHS laboratories continue to perform their own in-house tests without payment of royalties to Myriad (Nuffield Council on Bioethics 2002).

Focus group methodology

We convened a range of discussion groups as part of our research into expertise and citizenship in terms of the new genetics. These can be broadly termed focus groups because we, as the researchers, moderated each group and emphasized interaction between group members rather than between individual participants and ourselves. In this chapter, we present data from eleven groups: genetic counsellors; members of a support group for people affected by cancer; members of a government advisory commission on genetics; school pupils; members of an umbrella organization for people affected by genetic conditions; refugees; members of a Friends Meeting House; members of campaign groups concerned with genetics; university scientists; clinical geneticists/genetic nurses; and actuaries with an interest in genetics. With the exception of the members of the umbrella organization for people affected by genetic conditions, the people in these groups already knew each other. Some, such as the clinical geneticists, actuaries and policy advisers, worked together closely. Others met regularly in religious (Friends Meeting House group), educational (school group) or conference (counsellors) environments. Most of these groups involved around four people. Only two people turned up to the group for members of the umbrella organization for people affected by genetic conditions. We have still called this a focus group, however, because the same format was used and the two participants discussed issues with each other rather than responding in turn to a question from the moderator.

The groups discussed a range of topics, beginning with their views on who influences the direction of genetic research and services, moving on to the Myriad case discussed here, then on to a vignette about UK Biobank, and ending with discussion about public involvement in genetic decision-making more broadly. Detailed reading of the transcripts evoked several avenues of analysis that we are pursuing in the study, including: the dynamics of expertise; appeals to public goods and virtues; commercialization; constructions of patients, publics, government and professionals; and notions of health and disease. We have coded the material using the Atlas Ti software package. Accounts of patenting in general and Myriad in particular were then extracted and reanalysed more closely, generating a series of additional codes concerning the representation of Myriad, the dynamics of agreement and disagreement within the groups, and the negotiation of professional, material, moral and political boundaries in discussions about the rights and wrongs of gene patenting.

Our analysis takes seriously the way in which participants actively construct meaning and subject positions in the course of their discussion, rather than expressing fixed views or speaking from static subject positions (Holstein and Gubrium 1995). In selecting a range of groups, we have tried to move this method on from its close relationship to accessing the views of consumers or laypeople as opposed to 'professionals'. The implicit hierarchy involved in choice of method (focus groups for 'laypeople', interviews for 'professionals') reinforces the tendency to value professional views more highly, or at least to keep 'lay' views in their place (Cunningham-Burley et al. 1999; Wilkinson 1998). Following Williams et al. (2002), we therefore adopted a more symmetrical approach to so-called professionals and laypeople, allowing them both to express ambiguity and ambivalence through the course of a discussion. We note that, in the course of these discussions, people shifted positions and spoke from a variety of different lived or imagined perspectives, which affects both what they said and how it could be understood. Participants constructed meaning through shared conversation: they mutually negotiated their authority and positioning as 'expert', 'patient', 'citizen' or 'member of the public' as the conversation progressed.

We now go on to explore participants' accounts of the Myriad case, or 'Myriad stories', in the context of these group dynamics. Participants position themselves, others in the group and absent third parties through these stories, using a variety of discursive techniques: anecdotes about personal experience, analogies, claims to knowledge, moral arguments and appeals to norms and standards of professional and business practice. Their accounts are likely to be dependent upon their reasons for participating in the group, and their interpretations of what the moderator and research team wanted from them, as well as their relationships with each other and outside parties. This last point is especially true for some of the groups with more of a stake in the 'public' culture of genetics. The campaign group members, clinical geneticists and the policy advisers all voiced concerns, directly or in a muted fashion, about the impact their views might have upon their status with respect to the organizations of which they were a part. Our analysis does not shy away from providing such interpretations of their talk, drawing out inferences about power, expertise and citizenship.

Myriad stories – from exemplar to pariah

Myriad figured as an exemplar of the activities and characteristics of the commercial sector in the majority of the groups we convened, particularly with respect to the impact of commercialization on public healthcare and issues related to the use and storage of genetic information by commercial organizations. As an exemplar, Myriad stories could legitimize, or more often confront, the thorny issues of profit, public good, scientific progress and healthcare systems. Myriad thus became a 'jumping-off point' for critical discussion of capitalism in many of the groups, after initial discussion had considered the range of interests involved in genetics and genetic research. This occurred whether the participants had prior knowledge of the Myriad case or not. In fact, only one group, the actuaries, did not engage with the Myriad discussions. Participants from the support group for people affected by cancer talked about Myriad as a typical example of the way in which companies strove to achieve positions of dominance in markets. One participant was particularly vociferous, returning to this issue at several points and making remarks such as: 'That American example you gave, it's not just to do with genetics or anything like that, it's in every aspect of life, and business especially' (02 DS).

The group exchanged stories about different kinds of monopolies in both private and public industries, drawing on their knowledge about well-publicized cases such as that of Microsoft. The Myriad vignette enabled this group of participants to express wider concerns about the behaviour of commercial companies and the role of government in modifying this behaviour, although their prognosis was far from optimistic. This formed part of a wider discussion, in which the group expressed frustration and a sense of alienation from the medical professionals and institutions involved in cancer research and care on a number of occasions. They characterized themselves as being 'outsiders', unable to influence the 'powers that be'.

The small group from the umbrella organization for people affected by genetic conditions also used the Myriad example to discuss wider concerns about the commercial setting, particularly in relation to the privacy of genetic information. In relation to Myriad's requirement that their labs carry out full sequence tests, one participant felt that people simply would not like their samples to travel so far. She was concerned about the lack of control and voiced doubts about what Myriad might do with so much information from patients. Both participants had some direct knowledge and experience of involvement in research, and argued that Myriad's behaviour could be read as abusing the good faith of such involvement. They positioned themselves as patients with little power rather than as consumers or citizens, but tended to ally themselves with medical science. For this group, Myriad raised concerns about the nature and extent of the private sector's involvement in research.

The group of refugees also cast Myriad as an exemplar of capitalism, but within the context of a shared sense of being under surveillance by government and business. Their conversation was characterized by notions of power and dominance, a narrative that carried through into the Myriad discussion. For this group, Myriad was typical of the way in which all companies sought to control individuals by gaining knowledge about them. This group also expressed concerns about how science had been corrupted or at least pressed into service by commerce for its own ends over the last few decades; building on the Myriad vignette to express a general unease about the political and economic context of science in the present and future. Rather than being active citizens, this group positioned themselves as outside the mainstream and relatively powerless.

The members of a Friends Meeting House expressed similar concerns, although their discussion positioned them as a significant moral community rather than as alienated or downtrodden outsiders. This community also involved differentiation in the form of various participants' claims to authority on the grounds of their technical or scientific experiences. This resulted in a wide-ranging discussion, and a series of stories about patents on other inventions, for example cat's-eyes. One particularly dominant participant with a scientific background said this patent was of financial benefit to the inventor but that it stifled further innovation and compromised road safety. Another participant told a story about the pollution of science by commerce, a situation that he contrasted with a past in which the free exchange of information and ideas was possible. Similar stories surfaced in some of the other groups. The first participant then told another, more emotionally and politically loaded story about the development of the AIDS treatment: 'People are saying about some firm developing an anti-AIDS drug who, because they have a patent on it, can make the price of the drug beyond the reach of the countries in Africa where it's actually needed. Now that's … that's morally disgusting' (06 BR). The various stories told in this group served to demonstrate the participants' knowledge and understanding of such events, based on their professional backgrounds and religious convictions: they involve moral positioning and constructing businesses as exploitative when they protect their commercial interests by using patents that have a detrimental effect on scientific freedom and public health.

The school students positioned themselves as relatively unaffected by the issue of Myriad and genetic patenting. For them, the discussion was more of an opportunity to explore and debate different ideas, drawing on their knowledge gained from involvement in debating events or work experience placements. They seemed to see themselves as active citizens in waiting – young people with something to contribute to these debates in the future. The participants shifted positions on specific issues: taking, modifying and then abandoning different viewpoints in the light of others' comments. Despite individual participants expressing some unease, the group as a whole came to a shared position that commerce was the norm in British society, and that commercial involvement in the development of genetic tests or therapeutics was perfectly legitimate. For them, Myriad seemed to be an exemplar of normal business practice: it had funded the research, had 'got there first', and so was entitled to make a profit from its product. At the same time, they proposed that the development of genetic tests was more akin to the situation in other industries in which there was significant public interest and which the government through some body might regulate accordingly. One participant imagined: 'A regulator set-up sort of like Oftel … so there'd be somebody regulating them probably from the government, saying you can monopolize the market as long as you don't be ridiculous about it' (05 J).

The genetic counsellors and clinical geneticists/genetic nurses were two groups for whom the Myriad case was especially salient in professional terms. Again, in these groups we saw that the Myriad case precipitated a general discussion about commercialism in the NHS. The clinical group argued forcefully that genetic patenting was undesirable because it exploited patients and others who had provided biological material or personal information to assist the research into the genetic basis of disease. Members of both groups argued that the prospect of companies having a monopoly over particular testing services was detrimental to the existing network of labs in the NHS, leading to a loss of skills and services that could not easily be replaced. In addition, such a monopoly would not lead to better patient care. For example, one participant suggested that commercial testing would increase costs for the NHS, leading to restrictions on the numbers of patients eligible to undergo testing; another that holistic clinical care involved more than just the provision of an accurate test. Some members of these groups constructed clear boundaries between appropriate professional practice and predatory, immoral commercialism, although they did not want these strong views to be 'on the record' in case of repercussions. Others expressed concerns about professionals' ability to maintain such a boundary. Relationships between the public and private spheres in the healthcare sector were described as particularly problematic, and Myriad served as an exemplar of why this was the case. These groups drew on their own professional knowledge and norms of practice to explain and explore the problems of gene patenting. Their expertise, however, did not necessarily enable them to position themselves as powerful players in the difficult world of commercial interests and patient care.

Myriad was also an exemplar for the group of campaigners concerned with the new genetics; it enabled them to invoke a range of campaigning issues in the discussion. On the one hand, Myriad was a story about the problems posed by the whole area of genetic patenting. One participant argued that genetic patenting was quite distinct from other areas of business where patenting was acceptable. She made it clear that the organization she represented had objections specific to genetic patenting and was not opposing the whole of the capitalist system. Her main concern was that restrictive patenting could actually stifle further innovation and research into diagnostics or therapeutics desired by patients and physicians – a point raised in other groups too. This overall support of a regulated free market contrasted with the discussions in the groups of genetic healthcare professionals. Another participant linked Myriad's insistence that their labs do full-sequence testing with wider concerns about confidentiality and security of genetic information. She framed Myriad as a part of current policy discussions about the storage and use of genetic information by different organizations. Participants also tied Myriad into discussion of their 'campaigning credentials', with one participant self-consciously framing his response to the Myriad case in terms of his considerable experience of campaigning against gene patenting. They positioned themselves as knowledgeable commentators on the science of genetics, its ethical and social implications, and public reactions to and understandings of this science. They also stressed their own interest in the public good.

The characterization of Myriad as an exemplar in these groups embraced diverse views of private enterprise and the role of commercialization of genetic-related health technology. All groups referred to morally appropriate entrepreneurial behaviour, with Myriad often castigated as going beyond acceptable practice. Some cited regulation as important and all groups related the Myriad case to wider issues, often considered problems, of the market economy. In contrast, a few groups characterized Myriad as a pariah: although similar issues were discussed relating to the problems that the Myriad case highlighted, these were identified as specific to Myriad rather than relating to the wider economic and political systems of which it is a part. 'Myriad as pariah' was not a fixed position to which everyone in the group subscribed, and the two accounts could coexist in the same discussion.

This complexity is particularly apparent in the group of policy advisers' accounts. They had a long and complicated discussion about the Myriad case and about gene patenting more generally. Like the campaigners, they sometimes positioned gene patenting in relation to the storage of genetic information. At other times, some participants made strong claims that Myriad was a pariah. For example, one particularly dominant member of the group, who claimed a degree of insider knowledge, told a story about a 'good' type of genetic patent, the cystic fibrosis (CF) patent, and contrasted this with the Myriad patents. He described the CF patent as held by an academic group whose licensing arrangements ensure that they receive a 'reasonable return' on their investment as opposed to Myriad's expectations of 'unreasonable return'. The group went on to discuss the benefits of commercial arrangements that exploit knowledge in the public interest. Three members of the group represented Myriad as out of step with the general approach of the industry. As the discussion progressed, the same participant who had introduced the CF analogy reinforced Myriad's aberrant status when he argued that numerous groups contributed to the location and isolation of the BRCA genes. Myriad's financial and technological superiority, rather than intellectual insight or 'brain power', meant it was able to be in a position to claim the patent. These arguments formed part of a broader tendency among this group to position themselves as pragmatic about what governance structures would be effective in this sector. When one participant went on to dismiss the 'no patenting life' argument, however, consensus was no longer evident. One member raised the issue of Myriad's patent on genetic sequences rather than on the technique to identify variations within the sequences, which raised the issue of a distinction between patenting discoveries and inventions. This resulted in a long technical discussion about patent legislation, and the group could not reach agreement about how to define acceptable patenting practices. It also involved considerable negotiation about who had the authority to make particular claims on behalf of the group, and disagreement between two participants about whether or not one of their strong negative comments about American capitalism ought to be 'off the record'.

The group of university-based chemists and biologists also identified Myriad as an aberration. Like the policy advisers, this group positioned themselves as knowledgeable about the governance of scientific research. The Myriad case was not one with which they were very familiar, however. They discussed their own notions of conventional practice, and came to the position that the Myriad case was very much an aberration. In these stories, patent-holders licensed local companies to conduct their tests and received an income by this means. They agreed that Myriad's requirement that they perform the sequencing in Utah was a departure from the norm. These participants expressed a clear interest in a well-governed system that would allow commercial exploitation but not in a way that favoured one company and prevented further innovation. Notwithstanding this clear construction of Myriad as an aberration, one participant did argue that it raised concerns about the workings of the current system and suggested that there was a need to assess whether some kind of 'inbuilt mechanism' of regulation could be developed to balance commercial and public interests. Many groups expressed these concerns, however they characterized Myriad.

Discussion

The 'Myriad stories' had a range of contextual forms and purposes in each of the accounts generated in the focus group discussions. Myriad could be an exemplar of capitalism as a form of exploitation or innovation, and of the working of policy domains such as genetic information or consumer rights. The accounts we have discussed here contributed to constructing participants' status as outsiders from the healthcare system or society as a whole, insiders in professional, campaigning and policy networks, and/or as arbiters/judges of the 'public good'. 'Myriad as a pariah' had a similar role when it worked to construct the professional, campaigning or policy-making credentials of the group or individual concerned.

'Myriad as exemplar' and 'Myriad as pariah' may appear, on first inspection, to be a dichotomy, yet our discussion shows that both of these stories can be used to the same effect. These are not the only stories about Myriad that we have found in the course of the research, but they are one way of getting some analytical purchase on the discourses constructed in these diverse discussions. We recognize that some participants did not find these frameworks useful vehicles for constructing shared or meaningful subject positions. For example, the Myriad case was not easy for the insurance actuaries to discuss. They were unable to agree on whether or not it was possible to patent discoveries, as opposed to inventions. This was not a fruitful topic of discussion for this group, because it did not allow them to share cogent experiences or display what they considered 'relevant' knowledge and insight. They took time to turn the Myriad discussion to a topic with which they were more familiar – academe/industry links – but there was little enthusiasm for pursuing the specific topic of patenting.

Reading these discussions as a means for participants both to establish their individual worth and to make meaningful connections with other participants, we find that expertise and authority are dynamic rather than static entities in this process. We cannot reduce expertise to a particular set or sets of knowledge or occupational positions. Instead, the groups continually negotiated expertise, co-constructing what counted as legitimate types of anecdotes, analogies, 'facts' or generalizations through their discussions. People within the group mobilized certain experiences to bolster the authority of their arguments, but this was open to contestation by other group members. People in groups convened in relation to their professional capacities moved between claims about the accuracy of knowledge and the values of public health or the public good, just as people in groups convened in relation to their 'citizenship' mixed professional and experiential knowledge and values when they made their arguments. Participants moved positions in the course of these discussions, sometimes speaking as 'professionals', sometimes speaking as, or on behalf of, patients, consumers, citizens or 'ordinary members of the public'.

What are the implications of our analysis for professional and public dialogue about genetics, particularly gene patenting? Many of these exercises privilege consensus and mutual respect among 'experts' and 'laypeople' (Dunkerley and Glasner 1998; Irwin 2001a). The ideal formula mixes relevant technical expertise provided by professionals with citizens' sense of common morality, and produces a compromise where risks and benefits are appropriately balanced (Collins and Evans 2002; see also Wynne 2003 for a critique). We would argue that these formulae ignore or seek to eradicate the 'political underbelly' of discussions about the social implications of genetics and the moral values embedded in all subject positions. They do not acknowledge the dynamics of authority, just as they ignore the constructed, achieved character of meaningful facts and moral values. The people who design these models do so to assert their authority and moral worth, as advocates of these public participation exercises, be they promoting or criticizing science. All these exercises are ripe for manipulation because the process of organization codes for certain notions of expertise or legitimate citizenship within the exercise. Although participants may subvert these codes, their control over the official interpretation of the event is limited.

To end this chapter, we want to do a little storytelling ourselves. Imagine that we assembled all our participants into a room to discuss gene-patenting policy. We suggest that they would reach a vague compromise, advocating 'ethical commercialism' whereby companies made reasonable returns and developed innovations in the public interest. We would find, however, that this consensus would not hold up under sustained discussion about the definition of 'reasonable return', 'innovation' or 'public interest', given that all these terms are highly contingent. Only certain individuals or groups would be sufficiently motivated to take this path; for others the Myriad discussion would lack saliency. We expect that, of the groups discussed here, the geneticists, policy advisers and campaigners would dominate, and the patient group would resist such domination with powerful personal stories. The people who took up the detail would do this in part to be helpful to the researchers, and, in part, to assert their authority in the face of what they perceived to be other, less knowledgeable or virtuous parties. The conversation would be less about sorting out a policy for gene patenting than about negotiating authority and status and preserving precarious alliances and interests (particularly when this type of consultation exercise would not translate into actual policy). Participants would form alliances across different subject positions, and construct knowledge/morality hybrids in the process. The discussion would have value beyond the exercise, as it would develop people's rhetorical skills and professional or citizen networks. The actual decision, however, should one be made, would not travel far beyond the context of the discussion unless we took it as our own and mobilized it in the course of establishing our own expertise as sociologists with an interest in policy. For participants and analysts alike, Myriad and gene patenting would be a part of these dynamics of expertise and authority: means to an end, rather than an end in themselves.

We do not mean to suggest that the dynamics of expertise and authority are morally repugnant. Nor do we want to suggest that if we could all become more reflexive about these practices we would evade their influence. Such reflexivity would surely only add yet another layer of claim and counter-claim to an already complex arena. Our aims are rather more modest. Just as we have all learned to question the wisdom of experts, we want to encourage our readers to raise an eyebrow at grand visions of expert–citizen dialogue and engagement, for *many a story they tell* ...

Note

1 This research was funded by the Economic and Social Research Council's Innovative Health Technologies Programme, award reference number L218252059, 1 April 2002–31 March 2004, principal investigators Dr Anne Kerr and Dr Sarah Cunningham-Burley. Codes following quotations refer to the research programme indexing system.

8 | AIDS, science and citizenship after apartheid

STEVEN ROBINS

Introduction: science, race and cultures of colonialism

AIDS statistics in South Africa have unleashed an extraordinary amount of political heat, controversy and contestation, with the government persistently questioning the reliability of these statistics and projections. Matters came to a head in 2001 with the 'leak' to the press of a Medical Research Council (MRC) report that estimated that 'AIDS accounted for about 25% of all deaths in the year 2000 and has become the single biggest cause of death' (Dorrington et al. 2001: 6). The government's initial response to the MRC report was to challenge its findings by claiming that 'violent death', not AIDS, was the single biggest cause of death. This triggered a major controversy which raged in the media, culminating in the government's concerted efforts to 'delay' the release of the MRC report. In addition, government applied considerable pressure to the chairperson of the board of the MRC to institute a 'forensic enquiry' to uncover the source of the press 'leak'. The president of the MRC, Dr William Makgoba, was also subjected to relentless pressure to withdraw the report, with government spokespersons claiming that its findings were 'alarmist' and 'inaccurate'.

One of the possible interpretations of this response from government was that the findings were perceived to imply that the government was not managing the pandemic effectively and that the situation was 'out of control', which could have negative impacts in terms of much-needed overseas investment. Other possible reasons include discomfort with the findings among certain sectors of government and the ruling ANC party, who believed that the report reinforced media and popular beliefs and prejudices that AIDS is a 'black disease' concentrated in the rural areas of the former black 'homelands' of KwaZulu-Natal and Eastern Cape provinces. This racial and geographical 'profiling' of AIDS, it would appear, shaped both state and citizen responses. The questions of race and identity, I argue, lie at the heart of responses to the AIDS pandemic and to AIDS science. The racialized character of these responses was not, however, confined to President Mbeki's inner circle. It has been more widespread.

In December 2002, the Human Science Research Council (HSRC) released a study that questioned popular perceptions about the racial and geographical distribution of AIDS. A large-scale household survey was conducted to determine the HIV prevalence rates in different provinces among races, sexes and geographical locations. In an article entitled 'AIDS survey shatters stereotypes', the *Mail and Guardian* (6 December 2002) reported that 'KwaZulu-Natal has shaken off the tag of having the highest HIV-prevalence rate [and] the Western Cape gets a wake-up call because its HIV prevalence rate of 10.7% is higher than the 8.6% revealed by [the MRC] antenatal survey'.[1] The article also noted: 'a surprising finding is that the Eastern Cape has the lowest prevalence rate (6.6%)'.[2] In contrast to studies that indicated that AIDS prevalence was highest among poor, rural, uneducated black people of the former homelands, the HSRC study found that highly mobile urban people in the informal settlements and townships, as well as the middle classes, were most certainly at risk.

Notwithstanding this challenge to AIDS stereotypes and prejudices, the 'cold facts' of AIDS statistics are likely to continue to produce competing interpretations, including those that construct AIDS as a 'black disease'.[3] It is therefore quite conceivable that African nationalists such as President Mbeki interpreted these statistics as evidence of a long colonial and apartheid legacy of scientific racism. In other words, they were read through the colour-coded lens of colonial histories of discrimination and dispossession. For Mbeki and his 'dissident' supporters, such findings were not the product of neutral, rational and universal scientific inquiry, but were understood as the products of historically constructed and politically driven processes embedded in specific histories of colonialism, apartheid and capitalism.

In South Africa, the dissident debate and the numerous cultural obstacles encountered when implementing AIDS prevention programmes have forced scientists, non-governmental organizations (NGOs), AIDS activists and government to acknowledge and respond to 'local' and 'lay' interpretations of AIDS. These include the blaming of AIDS on witchcraft, as well as a variety of AIDS conspiracies: 'whites' who want to contain black population growth; 'white doctors' who inject patients with AIDS when they go for tests; the CIA and pharmaceutical companies who want to create markets for drugs in Africa; the use of Africans as guinea pigs for scientific experiments with AIDS drugs; beliefs that sex with virgins, including infants, can cure AIDS; and beliefs that anti-retrovirals (ARVs) are dangerously toxic. But perhaps the most daunting problem for AIDS activists and health professionals was the President's initial flirtation with AIDS 'dissident' theories and the implications this had in terms of attempts to establish AIDS treatment programmes. The President's position, along with a plethora of popularly held 'AIDS myths' and the stigma and shame associated with AIDS, contributed to defensive responses and AIDS denial among the general population as well as within the President's inner circle of policy-makers and politicians. What are the implications of all this for contemporary debates on science and citizenship in a globalizing world?

The AIDS pandemic in South Africa raises a number of troubling dilemmas for attempts to democratize science. Given the relative weakness of African states and the extremely thin spread of scientific knowledge and institutions, what can citizen science, popular epidemiology, ethnoscience and indigenous knowledge do to deal with a lethal pandemic such as AIDS? Or would state legitimation of these public knowledges not further undermine already weak scientific institutions and biomedical knowledge regimes? What does citizen science mean in contexts where contestation between the public's and experts' forms of knowledge and science threatens to undermine biomedical scientific authority and AIDS interventions that could potentially save lives? What about contexts where contestation over AIDS science becomes highly politicized because governments are distrustful of the autonomy of the scientific establishment, or where 'indigenous knowledge' and 'local solutions' are reified as part of cultural nationalist ideologies and programmes? What about situations where people's own knowledge and practices result in AIDS denial, violence and oppression; for instance, when the South African AIDS counsellor Gugu Dlamini revealed her HIV-positive status to rural villagers, who responded by killing her for bringing shame and disease to her community?

This chapter explores what notions such as the 'democratization of science' could look like from the epicentre of the worst public health hazard in Africa's history. It focuses on the opportunities and constraints that exist for mediation and negotiation between various experts and publics given this state of emergency. The AIDS pandemic raises particularly difficult questions concerning the role of deliberative and inclusionary processes in scientific domains: Who is to be invited into what forums? What do these deliberative processes mean in contexts where scientific authority is distrusted both by powerful individuals within the state, and by large sections of the public?

By focusing on the responses and strategies of government, AIDS activists and civil society organizations such as Treatment Action Campaign (TAC), it is possible to begin to address some of these questions. A case study investigates TAC's strategies of engagement with scientists, the media, the legal system, NGOs and government, as well as its grass-roots mobilization, AIDS treatment literacy campaigns and AIDS awareness campaigns. It examines the opportunities and limits that framed TAC's interactions within these different spaces.

This investigation of the relations between citizens, scientists and government in the context of the African AIDS pandemic is not merely academic. For example, certain lay knowledges and alternative, fringe scientific perspectives (AIDS dissident science) have translated into support for AIDS myths and conspiracy theories that have, according to AIDS activists and health professionals, had a devastating impact on public health interventions, directly contributing to the loss of tens of thousands of lives. Some AIDS activists blamed dissidents and AIDS denialists within government for failing to provide ARV treatment, and thereby contributing towards AIDS deaths.

While the dissident debate raged on, TAC activists, health professionals and the trade unions took to the streets and the courts in the struggle for AIDS treatment based on citizens' constitutionally enshrined rights to healthcare. Zapiro,[4] the best known of South Africa's political cartoonists, graphically captured this by depicting the President as playing the dissident fiddle while Rome was burning. In the face of relentless criticism of the President's pro-dissident stance, his spokespersons and supporters argued against the guild-like exclusivism of the scientific community and insisted upon the democratic right of the President to participate in debates on AIDS science. AIDS activists and health professionals made the counter-argument that the President's role in the dissident debate was undermining public health institutions and the scientific authority and autonomy of experts, scientists and health professionals. While this case of high-level political interference in the scientific arena may appear extreme and exceptional, it none the less draws attention to more general questions relating to science, politics and citizenship in the twenty-first century.

Lethal solidarities: dissident science and the cultural politics of AIDS

AIDS is a global disease that has devastated communities struggling under the burdens of poverty, inequality, economic crisis and war (Schoepf 2001: 336). AIDS is also an 'epidemic of signification' (Treichler 1999), and responses to it have been unrelentingly moralizing and stigmatizing. In Africa, this 'geography of blame' (Farmer 1992) has contributed towards racist representations of African sexualities as diseased, dangerous, promiscuous and uncontrollable. This, in turn, has triggered defensive reactions that draw on dissident AIDS science, conspiracy theories and AIDS denial among African politicians, officials, intellectuals and journalists.

Representational politics has plagued AIDS debates and interventions in South Africa (Schoepf 2001). These issues have had a profound impact upon the ways in which 'civil society' and 'the state' responded to the pandemic. Virtually every aspect of the pandemic – from AIDS statistics,

to theories about the causal link between HIV and AIDS, to studies on AIDS drug therapy – led to contestation between government on the one side and AIDS activists, scientists, health professionals and the media on the other. Given perceptions that AIDS fuels racist representations of Africans, it was perhaps not surprising that responses from President Mbeki took such a defensive turn.

The AIDS dissident debate in South Africa can be narrated from a variety of angles. It can be told as a story of how a small but powerful policy network was built around President Mbeki, and how this 'inner circle' was able to shape the direction of AIDS policy in South Africa. It is also the story of TAC and a highly organized and globally connected 'community' of scientists, health professionals and civil society organizations who contested this dissident line. By November 2003, after three years of mass mobilization, court cases, civil disobedience campaigns and demonstrations calling for AIDS treatment, the dissidents were on the retreat and ARV treatment was in sight. In August 2003, the Cabinet announced that it had decided to go ahead with a national ARV programme. But how and why did South Africa follow this tortuous path?

It was only in the late 1980s that AIDS in South Africa began to be acknowledged as a serious public health problem. Prior to this it was widely perceived to be a North American 'gay disease', with San Francisco and New York at its epicentre. It took almost a decade for the seriousness of the

AIDS pandemic to filter into the consciousness of South African citizens, the media and policy-makers. By the time of the World AIDS Conference in Durban in July 2000, most South Africans were aware that the country was in the midst of an epidemic of catastrophic proportions.

The 2000 Durban conference also exposed the international AIDS community to the deep rift between mainstream AIDS scientists and government supporters of the AIDS dissidents. Versions of the dissident view were articulated by President Mbeki and senior ANC figures such as the late Parks Mankahlana and Peter Mokaba.[5] In a press statement reported in the *Mail and Guardian* newspaper (19 April 2002) a few months before his death, allegedly from AIDS, Mokaba, the then ANC chief electoral officer, presented the AIDS dissident position in the following terms: 'The story that HIV causes AIDS is being promoted through lies, pseudo-science, violence, terrorism and deception ... We are urged to abandon science and adopt the religion of superstition that HIV exists and that it causes AIDS. We refuse to be agents for using our people as guinea pigs and have a responsibility to defeat the intended genocide and dehumanisation of the African family and society' (cited in Gitay 2002: 2).

This line of argument, which was elaborated in detail by South African and international dissidents, was mercilessly challenged and lampooned by cartoonists and journalists. Its critics also included academics, opposition parties, AIDS activists and health professionals. Yet despite considerable opposition to the dissident view, even within the ruling party, it none the less came to represent the official government position on AIDS. This culminated in President Mbeki's establishment of the President's Select Advisory Panel of AIDS experts, comprising an equal weighting of 'establishment scientists' and AIDS dissidents.

In March 2002, a controversial AIDS dissident document (Anon. 2002) was posted on the ANC website. The full title of the document was *Castro Hlongwane, Caravans, Cats, Geese, Foot & Mouth and Statistics: HIV/AIDS and the Struggle for the Humanisation of the African*. The document was subjected to intense criticism and ridicule from AIDS activists and the media, who portrayed it as an endorsement of President Mbeki's eccentric AIDS 'dissident' views. The document quoted numerous scientific studies and journalistic forays questioning 'mainstream' AIDS science.[6] Throughout, the author(s) referred to the 'omnipotent apparatus' that sought to bring about the dehumanization of the African family and humiliate 'our people' (i.e. Africans). Citing numerous newspaper articles and scientific findings, the document blamed AIDS drugs and pharmaceutical companies for the 'medicalisation of poverty' and for systematically destroying the immune systems of Africans. The document also claimed that 'for the omnipotent

apparatus [which includes the media, the medical establishment and drug companies] the most important thing is the marketing of the anti-retroviral drugs'. It concluded with the following statement:

> No longer will the Africans accept as the unalterable truth that they are a dependent people that emanates from and inhabits a continent shrouded in a terrible darkness of destructive superstition, driven and sustained by ignorance, hunger and underdevelopment, and that is victim to a self-inflicted 'disease' called HIV/AIDS. *For centuries we have carried the burden of the crimes and falsities of 'scientific' Eurocentrism, its dogmas imposed upon our being as brands of a definitive, 'universal' truth. Against this, we have, in struggle, made the statement to which we will remain loyal – that we are human and African!* (Anon. 2002, italics in original)

Although the ANC attempted officially to distance itself from the document in response to fierce criticism from AIDS activists, the media and health professionals, it became evident that the document's focus on the legacies of colonialism, 'underdevelopment', poverty, the Eurocentrism of science and racist representations of Africans as a 'diseased Other' appealed to a small group of African nationalists within the ANC leadership. *Castro Hlongwane* reads as an African nationalist defence of the AIDS dissident position in the face of what its authors claimed was a racist representation of AIDS as a 'black disease' associated with sexual promiscuity and the inability of Africans to control their sexual appetites.

More generally, racist narratives about the sexually promiscuous, pathological and uncontrolled black African fuelled Mokaba and Mbeki's African nationalist response. This may help explain support for their dissident ideas. Just as the dissident view attributed AIDS to African poverty and disease engendered by Western racism, colonial conquest, capitalism and underdevelopment, it also challenged attempts to attribute the African AIDS pandemic to 'dysfunctional' sexualities and family structures.

Rhetoric, rights and relativism: a case of mixed messages and mixed genres

Following two years of confused mixed messages, in 2002 President Mbeki began to distance himself from the dissidents, claiming that public perception of the government's support for the dissidents reflected a 'failure of communication on our side' (*Cape Times*, 25 April 2002). But was this simply 'a failure of communication'?

Gitay (2002: 25) concludes that politicians, who 'lack scientific tools', should not be allowed to base their health policies on rhetoric, but should instead follow the consensus of the health sciences; the experts' translation of the scientific data. To support his conclusion, Gitay quotes approvingly from an article in the *Sunday Independent* of 23 April 2000 which argues that '*HIV/AIDS is not a freedom of speech issue*. It is about scientifically verifiable facts. There are findings that, after testing, an overwhelming number of scientists consider accurate' (emphasis added).

While AIDS activists and the media described the positions of Mbeki and Mokaba as irrational, politically motivated and incompatible with Western science, it would appear that the dissidents were insisting on their democratic right to critique the science establishment. They did this by drawing attention to the alternative science of the dissidents. ANC spokespersons attempted to justify this high-level government intervention by referring to it as an expression of freedom of thought, a matter of rights. They described Mbeki as a latter-day Galileo, burned at the stake by the media for refusing to conform to scientific orthodoxy. Calls for Mbeki to withdraw from the debate were described as attempts by the 'scientific guild' to shut down and stifle debate on questionable scientific findings.

Mbeki's spokespersons also described his interventions as an attempt to 'open up' what was perceived to be a narrowly technical, biomedical framing of the AIDS pandemic which ignored conditions of poverty and underdevelopment. Whereas much of this critique of the biomedical paradigm would have sat comfortably with most left-leaning South African AIDS and public health activists, the questioning of the link between the HI virus and AIDS was what went beyond the pale. It was this strand of the dissident critique which was perceived to be discontiguous with Western science. The question remains: Why did President Mbeki's deployment of race and nationalist rhetoric in his challenge to mainstream AIDS science fail to win widespread public support?

AIDS and the limits of 'race talk'

Given the history of South Africa, it is perhaps not surprising that race and cultural identity came to assume such a central place in public discourses on AIDS. By the time AIDS began to take such a visible toll on South Africa, the country had barely surfaced from apartheid, a political system characterized by extreme forms of social and economic inequalities and ideological domination that systematically denigrated and dehumanized black people. As a result of this history, as well as colonial legacies of deep distrust of Western science and modernization policies, President Mbeki was able to make the claim that AIDS was being interpreted through a profoundly racialized (and racist) lens: that African sexualities are 'dysfunctional', and Africans are to blame for their morally irresponsible and destructive sexual behaviour. President Mbeki no doubt felt compelled to challenge these racist readings of black bodies and sexualities, as did many other African nationalists. It would seem that AIDS has become a Rorschach, an ideological screen upon which a range of fears and fantasies have been projected. Mbeki's response suggests that he believes that there is a widespread view that it is the socially irresponsible, excessive and immoral sexual practices of Africans which are the root cause of the spread of the AIDS pandemic: the victim is to blame.

Although HIV/AIDS exists among white, middle-class heterosexual communities throughout the world, the stigma of its early associations with homosexuals, bisexuals, blacks, sex workers and drug users has continued to stick. This troubling genealogy of the disease continues to shape the AIDS debate in South Africa. It explains the intense sense of shame associated with AIDS among many South Africans. It also explains the attraction of dissident AIDS science and nationalist views, especially among young, educated black South Africans. A TAC activist spoke of significant support for Mbeki's dissident views among intellectuals and educated township youth, while in the rural areas she encountered widespread denial and myths. By December 2002, it appeared that while TAC may have won the 'Nevirapine battle',[7] and in the process mobilized thousands of black mothers seeking to ensure the survival of their babies, it had not yet won the war against misinformation, fear, denial, silence and shame.

For those HIV-positive, unemployed and working-class black mothers who joined TAC, cultural nationalist arguments did not resonate with their all-too-real experiences of contracting the virus from HIV-positive men and losing children to AIDS, a tragedy that they believed could be averted through prevention of mother-to-child transmission (PMTCT) programmes. For example, V, a young, black female TAC volunteer, tells the story of how, following the trauma of rape by an uncle who later committed suicide, she was diagnosed with AIDS, hospitalized and told that she 'must wait for my day of death'. V eventually joined TAC and received anti-retroviral therapy treatment (ART). For V, TAC literally saved her life – 'now I can stay alive for a long time. I have my whole life' – and the organization became the family that she lost when she was diagnosed HIV positive – 'Mandla and Zackie[8] are like my brother and father'. V's account of her confrontation with AIDS and the spectre of death suggests why the abstract and ideological language of the cultural nationalist response to AIDS and AIDS science did not resonate for her. It also draws attention to the experiential dimensions of belonging that TAC is able to provide for HIV-positive people who, once they reveal their HIV status, are often exposed to stigma and rejection from their families and communities.

This traumatic experiential dimension of AIDS draws attention to the limits of ideological mobilization in terms of shaping peoples' understanding of their identities and their place in the world; their citizenship. Nationalism or 'imagined communities' cannot easily be conjured up in the absence of experientially based understandings and social realities. How, then, was TAC able to catalyse and mobilize community belonging and civic action in a time of AIDS?

The Treatment Action Campaign

TAC was established on 10 December 1998, International Human Rights Day, when a group of about fifteen people protested on the steps of St George's Cathedral in Cape Town to demand medical treatment for people living with the virus that causes AIDS. By the end of the day, the protesters had collected over a thousand signatures calling on the government to develop a treatment plan for all people living with HIV.[9]

TAC's membership has grown dramatically over the past few years. The rank and file comprises mainly young, urban black Africans with secondary schooling. The organization has also managed to attract health professionals and university students, however. The international face of the organization is Zackie Achmat, a fortysomething Muslim former anti-apartheid and gay activist. He is also a law graduate and an openly HIV-positive person. Until very recently, Achmat had made it known publicly that he refused to take ART until it was available in the public health sector. Other TAC leadership figures include black African men and women who joined TAC as volunteers and moved into leadership positions over time. The majority of the volunteers are young, black African women, many of whom are HIV-positive.

When TAC was founded, it was generally assumed that anti-AIDS drugs were beyond the reach of developing countries, condemning 90 per cent of the world's HIV-positive population to a painful and inevitable death. While TAC's main objective has been to lobby and pressurize the South African government to provide AIDS treatment, it has been forced to address a much wider range of issues. These issues included tackling the global pharmaceutical industry in the media, the courts and the streets; fighting discrimination against HIV-positive people in schools, hospitals and at the workplace; challenging AIDS-dissident science; and taking the government to court for refusing to provide PMTCT treatment programmes in public health facilities. Rather than responding to AIDS from a cultural nationalist perspective, TAC mobilized within working-class black communities and the trade union movement, and used a variety of methods to pressurize the global pharmaceutical industry and the South African government to provide cheap ARV drugs. I argue that this class-based mobilization created the political space for the articulation of radical forms of 'health citizenship' linked to a genuinely progressive project of democratizing science in post-apartheid South Africa.

Soon after its establishment, TAC, together with the South African government, became embroiled in a lengthy legal battle with international pharmaceutical companies over AIDS drug patents and the importation of cheap generics to treat millions of HIV-positive poor people in developing countries. As a result of highly successful global and national media campaigns, TAC managed to convince international public opinion, and the Pharmaceutical Manufacturers Association (PMA), that it was moral and just for drug companies to bring down their prices and allow developing countries to manufacture generics. In the face of international public opinion in favour of TAC, PMA withdrew their case – no doubt influenced by the costs of adverse publicity that corporate greed was responsible for millions of deaths in Africa.

Much of TAC's energy, however, was devoted to more local matters:

mobilizing poor and working-class communities, using the courts to compel the Ministry of Health to provide ARVs at public facilities, and campaigning to protect the autonomy of scientific institutions from government interference. Although grass-roots mobilization was primarily in working-class areas, TAC's organizational structure and support networks crossed race, class, ethnic, occupational and educational lines.

TAC volunteers were involved in AIDS awareness and treatment literacy campaigns. In addition, TAC disseminated reports, scientific studies, website documents[10] and media briefs refuting government claims that ARV treatment was dangerously toxic, ineffective, too costly and could not be implemented owing to infrastructure and logistical problems such as inadequate management structures, lack of trained staff and so on. The organization also came out in strong support of doctors, hospital superintendents, medical researchers and the MRC, who, by virtue of their report findings or provision of ARV treatment, found themselves on the wrong side of government, and subject to high-level political interference and intimidation.

AIDS activism and 'globalization from below'

TAC's mode of activism could be described as 'grass-roots globalization' or 'globalization from below' (see Appadurai 2002a, 2000b). Following the precedent of the divestment campaigns of the anti-apartheid struggle, TAC activism straddled local, national and global spaces in the course of struggles for access to cheaper AIDS drugs. This was done through the courts, the Internet, the media and by networking with South African and international civil society organizations. Widely publicized acts of 'civil disobedience' also provided TAC with visibility within a globally connected post-apartheid public sphere. By concentrating on access to ARVs for working-class and poor people, TAC was participating in a class-based politics that departed significantly from the cultural nationalist/identity politics promoted by the new ruling elite of Mbeki and Mokaba. It was not coincidental that the Congress of South African Trade Unions (COSATU), having lost thousands of workers to the pandemic, readily joined the TAC campaign.

The 'Christopher Moraka Defiance Campaign' was perhaps a defining moment in TAC's pro-poor political mobilization around AIDS. It began in July 2000, after HIV-positive TAC volunteer Christopher Moraka died, suffering from severe thrush. TAC's spokespersons claimed that the drug fluconazole could have eased his pain and prolonged his life, but it was not available on the public health system because it was too expensive. In October 2000, in response to Moraka's death, TAC's Zackie Achmat visited

Thailand, where he bought 5,000 capsules of a cheap generic fluconazole. When TAC announced Achmat's mission in a press conference, the international public outcry against the pharmaceutical giant Pfizer intensified as it became clear how inflated were the prices of name-brand medications. No charges were brought against Achmat, and the drugs were successfully prescribed to South African patients. By March 2001, Pfizer made its drugs available free of charge to state clinics.

This David and Goliath narrative of TAC's successful challenge to the global pharmaceutical giants captured the imagination of the international community and catapulted TAC into the global arena. Preparation for the court case also consolidated TAC's ties with international NGOs such as Oxfam, Médecins sans Frontières, the European Coalition of Positive People, Health Gap and Ralph Nader's Consumer Technology Project in the USA. It seemed that this was indeed a glimpse into what a progressive global civil society could look like.

TAC activists nevertheless stressed that grass-roots mobilization was the key to TAC's successes. This was done through AIDS awareness and treatment literacy campaigns in schools, factories, community centres, churches, shebeens (drinking places), and through door-to-door visits in the black African townships. By far the majority of TAC volunteers were poor and unemployed black African women, many of whom were HIV-positive mothers desperate to gain access to life-saving drugs for themselves and their children.

TAC was also able to rely on support from middle-class business professionals, health professionals, scientists, the media and ordinary South African citizens, and used rights-based provisions in the South African constitution to secure poor people access to AIDS treatment. These legal challenges created the space for the articulation of a radical democratic discourse on health citizenship. TAC's grass-roots mobilization and its legal challenges blurred the boundaries between the street and the courtroom. The Constitutional Court judges could not but be influenced by growing public support for TAC, which achieved extraordinary media visibility and shaped public opinion through sophisticated networking and media imaging. They were able to give passion and political and ethical content to the 'cold letter' of the constitution and the 'cold facts' of AIDS statistics.

Flexible politics for flexible times

In December 2001, TAC's legal representatives argued in the High Court of South Africa that the state had a constitutionally bound obligation to promote access to healthcare, and that this could be extended to AIDS drug treatment.[11] While the thrust of TAC's argument before the High

Court focused on socio-economic rights, and specifically citizens' rights to healthcare, the TAC lawyers raised broader issues relating to questions of scientific authority and expertise. The court was obliged to address the ongoing contestation over the scientific 'truth' about AIDS that raged between TAC, the trade unions and health professionals on the one side, and government and the ANC on the other. By the end of 2003 it looked as if TAC and its allies had won this battle for ARV treatment.

Despite efforts to avoid being perceived as anti-government, TAC's criticism of President Mbeki's support for AIDS dissidents created dilemmas and difficulties. TAC activists were publicly accused by government spokespersons of being 'unpatriotic', 'anti-African' and salespersons for the international pharmaceutical industry. This locally situated cultural politics of race and national identity was addressed through a variety of strategies, including workshops, treatment literacy programmes and public meetings. TAC developed ways of combating what it perceived to be smear campaigns and attacks on its political credibility orchestrated by government spokespersons. It also managed the difficult feat of straddling the grey zones between cooperation with and opposition to government policies. Indeed, TAC's legal and political strategies reveal a clear understanding of the politics of contingency in contrast to an inflexible agonistic politics of binaries: 'us' and 'them'.

TAC avoided being slotted into the 'conservative white camp' through the creative reappropriation of locally embedded political symbols, songs and styles of the anti-apartheid struggle. For example, the Christopher Moraka Defiance Campaign resonated with the historic anti-*dompas* (pass law) defiance campaigns of the apartheid era. By mobilizing township residents, especially working-class and unemployed black women, TAC challenged attempts by certain government officials to whitewash it as 'anti-black'. By bringing the trade union movement on board, TAC also challenged accusations that it was a front for 'white liberals', the drug companies and other 'unpatriotic forces'. By positioning themselves as supporters of the ANC, SACP (South African Communist Party) and COSATU Tripartite Alliance, TAC activists have managed to create a new space for critical engagement with the ANC government. They have also introduced new conceptions of health citizenship that have raised questions about the nature of democracy in South Africa.

TAC's strategic engagement with politics of race and class emerges from the organizational memory of AIDS activists who participated in the United Democratic Front (UDF) in the 1980s. This has expressed itself through songs at marches, demonstrations and funerals, and regular press releases and conferences, website information dissemination, television documentaries and national and international networking. This political style is a sophisticated refashioning of 1980s modes of political activism that draws on the courts, the media and local and transnational advocacy networks, along with grass-roots mobilization and skilful negotiations with business and the state.

Perhaps the most important reason for the successes of TAC's grass-roots mobilization has been its capacity to provide poor and unemployed HIV-positive black South Africans with a biomedical and a psychological lifeline, often in contexts where they experience hostility and rejection from their communities, friends and families. The story of V draws attention to how experiences of AIDS can trump cultural nationalist ideologies and race solidarities. The politics of class, and access to life-saving drugs for poor people, seems to offer an alternative to an elite-driven politics of race and cultural identity.

A provisional conclusion

South Africa's devastating HIV/AIDS statistics, President Mbeki's controversial support for the 'dissidents' and TAC's widely publicized court victories over both the South African government and the multinational pharmaceutical giants thrust the South African AIDS pandemic on to the global stage. Mbeki's 'African nationalist' response to the AIDS pandemic illustrates the workings of a cultural politics of identity that diverted attention from working-class and poor people's struggles for access to life-saving AIDS treatment that is accessible to the middle classes. The responses of African nationalists and dissidents within government and the ruling party clashed with the class-based mobilization of AIDS activists and trade unionists, who insisted that ARVs be made freely available in public health facilities as part of citizens' constitutional rights to healthcare. The case study of these starkly contrasting responses to AIDS draws attention to the potential pitfalls as well as the emancipatory possibilities that exist for democratizing science in a time of AIDS.

TAC's mode of activism captured the imagination of activists throughout the world. Here was the archetypical David and Goliath epic. In their quest for AIDS drugs, a small group of committed AIDS activists were able to build a globally connected social movement – a form of practised citizenship – that successfully 'persuaded' pharmaceutical giants and the South African government to put measures in place for the provision of AIDS treatment.

The AIDS pandemic, and the ways responses to it have unfolded in South Africa, raises important concerns about the social responsibilities and relationships between the state, business and 'civil society'. It has also drawn attention to the role of scientific expertise and trust in expert systems, as well as issues of political and scientific authority and moral legitimacy, and the ways publics relate to these. In addition to the profound confusion and uncertainty experienced by South African publics as a result of President Mbeki's questioning of conventional AIDS science, it has become apparent that people's interpretations of the AIDS pandemic are far more complex and differentiated than either government or TAC originally anticipated.

TAC drew on a rights-based approach as well as grass-roots mobilization in working-class black communities. Its dramatic courtroom victories, along with its innovative forms of mobilization, captured the imagination of activists and citizens in South Africa and abroad. This was a struggle for poor people to gain access to life-saving drugs, but it was also a campaign to assert the right of citizens to scientific knowledge, treatment information and the latest research findings; a post-apartheid expression of health citizenship. It remains to be seen how TAC's successes will translate into an effective national ARV treatment programme, as well as providing a catalyst for the democratization of science in post-apartheid South Africa.

Notes

This chapter would not have been possible without the support and assistance of a number of people, especially Sarah Bologne, Nathan Geffen, Ian Scoones, Melissa Leach, Tobias Hecht, Kees van der Waal, Lyla Mehta, Zackie Achmat and countless TAC activists who have been the inspiration for this research project. I would also like to thank John Gaventa and numerous other participants in the joint School of Government, University of the Western Cape and Institute for Development Studies, Sussex University project on Citizenship, Participation and Accountability. I would also like to thank Jonathan Shapiro for allowing us to use his fantastically insightful HIV/AIDS cartoons. Finally, I would like to thank Lauren Muller for consistent support and encouragement.

1 The Western Cape, historically a 'white' and 'coloured' province, was seen to be the least vulnerable to AIDS prior to the HSRC findings.

2 The HSRC study estimated the overall HIV prevalence in the South African population at 11.4 per cent, or about 4.5 million people. Other estimates put the figure at between 4–7 million.

3 Although the HSRC 2002 AIDS prevalence report found that all races were at risk, Africans had the highest incidence rate with 18.4 per cent. Whites and coloureds were around 6 per cent and Indians 1.8 per cent. The 6 per cent rate for whites was up from 2 per cent in 2000, at a time when the white population was perceived to be eight years behind the prevalence in the African population (Colvin et al. 2000, cited in Marcus 2001).

4 Zapiro's real name is Jonathan Shapiro.

5 It is unclear how far these views were shared within the top echelons of the ANC government. There are nevertheless indications that there was considerable disagreement with Mbeki's stance, even within his Cabinet. The

128

strongest internal criticism came from the ANC's Tripartite Alliance partners, the South African Communist Party (SACP) and the Congress of South African Trade Unions (COSATU).

6 The document also included numerous literary, journalistic and academic citations, ranging from Adam Hochschild's (1998) *King Leopold's Ghost*, Herbert Marcuse's (1970) *Eros and Civilisation*, Paul Farmer's (1993) *AIDS and Accusation*, Angela Davis's (1982) *Women, Race and Class* as well as a smattering of quotes from a diverse group of writers such as Henry Louis Gates, Jr, W. B. Yeats, Mark Twain, Jeffrey Sachs, John le Carré, Yeats, Sun Tzu and many others.

7 Nevirapine is the ARV drug that is given to pregnant mothers as part of a national prevention of mother-to-child transmission programme (PMTCT).

8 Zackie Achmat is the internationally known South African AIDS activist who founded TAC.

9 For a detailed account of the early history of TAC and its campaign for PMTCT programmes, see *Treatment Action: An Overview, 1998–2001*, p. 2, at <www.tac.org.za>.

10 See Herman Wasserman's (2003) excellent chapter on TAC and the potential of the Internet for civil society groups in South Africa.

11 The South African constitution is unique in providing for water and housing (along with healthcare and a clean environment) as basic rights in the Bill of Rights.

9 | Demystifying occupational and environmental health: experiences from India

MURLIDHAR V.

Introduction

In India's industrialized zones, health problems linked to occupational hazards and workplace conditions affect many workers, while others are at risk from industrial accidents and their environmental effects. Workers themselves have accumulated much experiential expertise of such occupational and environmental health issues, interpreted within their own life-worlds. Yet having these perspectives and experiences recognized, and occupational diseases identified and acted upon by government agencies and corporations, has proved a much greater struggle. This chapter documents such struggles, which can be seen as central to the citizenship practices of factory workers. Not only have these struggles brought workers' own knowledge and experiences of occupational risks into the public policy domain, but this has been linked to a variety of rights claims: whether rights to material compensation, to medical treatment or to improved working conditions. These citizenship practices have, moreover, been forged in a context where workers' very survival is at stake, and their motivation for struggle is low.

Workers have not waged these struggles alone. Indeed, the chapter focuses on the key roles played by a set of intermediary actors in brokering and bridging the worlds of affected workers, and of scientific and policy institutions. It is based on ten years' experience of the Occupational Health and Safety Centre (OHSC) and the Environmental and Occupational Health Section of the Society for Participatory Research in Asia (PRIA). The OHSC was formed by unions, workers and activists, medical professionals, safety experts and lawyers in 1988, and has worked consistently since then to help identify and spread information about occupational diseases, and to fight for compensation. Central to this brokering has been interpreting and reframing workers' experiences to fit the concepts and standards of legitimacy of dominant scientific culture, while educating workers to participate in diagnosis and monitoring (Murlidhar et al. 1995). The science of occupational diseases has thus been 'demystified' for workers. In this, the worlds of workers and scientists have been bridged largely in terms of science, rather than those of workers' own ways of being, and a particular model of the scientifically literate citizen has thus been promoted. Yet as the chapter suggests, given the scientific uncertainty and even ignorance surrounding many issues of occupational and environmental health, this has been a process of demystification for scientists too, as through the work of OHSC, and the workers' citizen science that it has supported, new knowledge of and diagnostic precision in occupational and environmental health have emerged.

The chapter begins by outlining the origins and early work of the OHSC in a context of high scientific uncertainty about occupational diseases, official reluctance to acknowledge them and extreme marginalization of factory workers. It then addresses the case of occupational lung diseases, and the process through which the OHSC supported workers' citizenship practices around this issue. The chapter goes on to address, more briefly, a range of further occupational and environmental health issues, where similar brokerage has been undertaken, including occupational noise-induced hearing loss (NIHL), disability assessment more generally, and chemical accidents and pollution, drawing out common themes in the emergent relationships between workers as citizens, scientific institutions and governance.

The origins and early work of the Occupational Health and Safety Centre

The OHSC was formed against the backdrop of several serious setbacks to workers' organizations in the 1980s. An unsuccessful strike by textile workers in Mumbai was followed by the rapid closure of many industries there, with the onslaught of the new economic policy pushed by right-wing governments, and amid forces of economic globalization. Nearly 60 per cent of industries in the Agra Road and the Thane–Belapur Road, one of the largest industrial belts in Asia, were shut down. The poor economic conditions, vulnerability and low morale of workers that ensued provided the context in which the OHSC began its work in diagnosing and monitoring occupational and environmental diseases.

When OHSC started its work, there were many obstacles to recognition of workers' experiences of occupational disease, and to translating such recognition into realized rights to treatment or compensation. Many occupational and environmental health problems are surrounded by uncertainty, making diagnosis difficult. Some of these uncertainties are socio-political, others scientific, and some combine both these aspects. There is frequently uncertainty about the causes and precise sources of a health problem, and about the nature and speed of disease processes – despite the perception that medicine is an exact science. This uncertainty is compounded by the lack of a clear regulatory framework and the lack of understanding among concerned parties about the limited legal regulations.

There were also other major hurdles that obstructed the process of recognizing and claiming for occupational health issues. Doctors were poorly trained in recognizing and diagnosing occupational diseases. The attitudes of both doctors and other relevant professionals to doing so was influenced by a bias among the professional class against blue-collar workers in general. At times, this led to professionals deliberately mis-guiding workers who came to them with occupational and environmental health problems. When studies were carried out on workers, these were not made available to anyone except the select few conducting the study, and so were not open to public scrutiny. Should an occupational disease be identified, workers faced further problems in gaining medical or disability certification. Neither was given readily, while disability certification, which is required for compensation, was frequently not understood by doctors and hence not given to workers. Lawyers, even those whose general stance was pro-worker, tended to have a poor knowledge of progressive laws related to occupational health. Poor training, as well as undermanning and general apathy, also characterized the staff of the Employees' State Insurance (ESI) scheme – a contributory health insurance scheme with large financial re-serves. This led to apathy in using these financial reserves for workers, and in particular for occupational health problems. Finally, all these problems were compounded by information issues, including difficult access to the Internet owing to a shortage of resources, and all information being in Eng-lish (with some Latin and Greek), creating serious difficulties for workers in understanding scientific, legal or insurance issues. These factors, as well as Kafkaesque 'red tape-ism' (procedural delays), daunted even the bravest of workers armed with medical certification forms seeking justice.

In beginning to demystify the process of problem identification and routes to rights-claiming, OHSC's first major work addressed the occu-pational diseases of workers in the underground sewer department of Mumbai, acting together with the municipal workers' union. Later, work in diagnosing occupational diseases, educating activists and fighting for compensation was carried out with many unions and collective groups, such as the All India Trade Union Congress, the oldest workers' union in India, and the major textile workers' union, the Trade Union Solidarity Committee, Mumbai (Murlidhar et al. 1995). OHSC also worked together with citizens' groups, for instance in chemical belts such as Parivarthan in Maharashtra.

I now go on to discuss in detail OHSC's role in the struggle to have occupational lung diseases recognized and compensated.

Lung diseases

OHSC fought the issue of occupational lung disease as part of a larger campaign in India, the National Campaign on Dust-related Lung Diseases, which involved many collectives and unions.

In 1992/93 when the OHSC first thought of working on the occupational diseases of textile workers, the diagnosis of occupational lung diseases was clouded with difficulties. These included a lack of means through which workers' own experiences could be expressed in scientific terms, and problems in identifying and differentiating between different diseases. Byssinosis is a lung disease caused by cotton dust and is widely studied. Yet even the source and mode of the changes in the lungs associated with it are not precisely known, while there are difficulties in differentiating byssinosis from chronic obstructive lung disease. Both diagnosis and cause can be complicated by the effects of smoking. There were also pervasive confusions in interpreting lung function tests and the computerized output of the results, based on prediction equations pre-installed within the machine. OHSC worked to demystify each of these issues, until the first case of byssinosis in Mumbai was diagnosed and compensated in 1994, and the results presented in peer-reviewed literature in 1995 (ibid.; Nemery 1995).

A path-breaking study of this disease of textile workers had been carried out in the city of Mumbai in 1977. The study was presented in international forums, and as a result the Indian government accepted byssinosis as a prevalent occupational disease in India and appropriate legislation was brought into effect. Strangely, however, not a single worker participant was informed about the disease, not even the affected workers who were experiencing byssinosis symptoms, albeit interpreting them in other ways. OHSC began its work on byssinosis in Mumbai in 1994, seventeen years after the above study was published and ten years after byssinosis entered the official list of compensatable diseases. The first draft of our booklet in Marathi was circulated among worker activists for comments before printing. One of the activists said, 'I have seen many workers with similar symptoms and we had suspected occupational causes. But we did not know the legal position. Let us plan a medical check-up in my textile mill.' During the check-up, the workers learnt how to perform lung function tests and how to administer them to others. The participating medical and non-medical professionals did likewise. The report was given to each affected worker and the consolidated report was given to the management and the worker activists.

The hurdles faced in using the findings of this participatory study were stupendous. They included top professionals misleading OHSC researchers into searching the weekly *British Medical Journal* (BMJ) from 1980 for a particular article, when it was actually in the *Journal of the American Medical*

Association (JAMA) (these were the days before the Internet revolution). The social security system for workers, the Employees' State Insurance Scheme (ESIS), also created many hurdles that could be tackled only by collective effort. As a result of this study, the first case of byssinosis was compensated by the ESIS in 1995.

Following this success, OHSC directed its efforts towards reaching out to more affected workers in the city, and at the same time sensitizing the medical and legal fraternity, whose participation and cooperation would ensure a smoother claim process for workers.

In Mumbai, an ESIS support group has taken shape. Three times a week, affected workers (those who suspect that they are suffering from work-related illnesses) converge at the office of the Girni Kamgar Union – affiliated to the oldest union in India, the All India Trade Union Congress (AITUC) – where activists take a detailed history of the affected worker, study the case, perform a lung function test or audiometry (hearing test) as appropriate, and analyse the results. After filtering out those workers who do not show compensatable disease, those who appear deserving are issued with medical certificates. Activists and co-workers help the worker through each and every bureaucratic step until he clears the medical board. Many of the workers helped by the support groups have subsequently joined the support group and continue to help others.

Through such processes, many workers have understood the process of diagnosis and how to seek justice for this crippling occupational disease. In this, they have come to engage as scientifically and legally literate citizens. Through their union, they have set up ESI groups in many parts of India, teaching their co-workers the difficult process of diagnosing occupational lung diseases. They have learned how to handle the lung function test machine, and how to take a good occupational history. They have also learned to guide fellow workers through the process of getting compensation. These worker activists spread the message about the support centre by word of mouth and also by poster campaign. After byssinosis, the first case of occupational asthma was diagnosed and compensated in Mumbai. A number of workers who gained compensation for either of these diseases contributed some of their benefits to the purchase of medical equipment for the future diagnosis of others. Otherwise, their work has been supported by voluntary help from sympathetic doctors and also by non-governmental organizations (NGOs) involved in occupational and environmental health, such as PRIA, New Delhi. Indeed, PRIA held similar diagnostic camps in other textile cities such as Aurangabad, Amritsar and Rajnandgaon, where similar independent support groups have also formed and compensation claims have been settled.

OHSC found that the medical fraternity was equally mystified about byssinosis. This is partly because occupational diseases are given very little emphasis within formal medical training. OHSC therefore made efforts to reach doctors and present to them the medical aspects of diagnosis and interpretation, including how to compare a worker's lung function with appropriate predicted lung function. This is a tricky matter, since lung function machines are produced in developed countries and the predicted values are calibrated according to the expected lung function of Western people. Doctors and professionals needed assistance to substitute an appropriate, ethnically corrected reference point for Indian workers, and OHSC provided the necessary equations for this. Many doctors were also under a faulty impression about the medico-legal aspects of byssinosis, considering that they had to be experts and specialists in order to issue medical certificates for occupational diseases. In fact, there is not a single medical college in India offering a postgraduate course in occupational and environmental medicine.

In 1996, the findings of our byssinosis study were published in a peer-reviewed journal. This is not a necessary condition for compensation, but fulfilling it helped to counter scepticism among medical professionals. Subsequently, teaching faculty and resident doctors from medical colleges, doctors from ESI hospitals, private practitioners and doctors sympathetic to unions were trained in Ahmedabad, Vadodara, Mumbai, Vellore, Amritsar, Gwalior and some parts of interior Maharashtra. In the training sessions of doctors, workers and activists were present and contributed to the programme. Some of the worker activists came to train doctors in medical colleges, where they were addressed as doctors by medical students.

At times, sympathetic lawyers have also been guided by OHSC activists through misconceptions regarding the diagnosis of occupational diseases, the establishment of cause–effect relationships and judging the appropriateness of a claim for compensation. Most lawyers, doctors and even trade unionists believe that for every occupational disease the connection between work and disease has to be proved beyond doubt, as in criminal law. Even the mere existence of the possibility of another cause for the worker's problem disproves that the problem is an occupational disease, they believe. In reality, the law has listed certain diseases to which certain types of worker are vulnerable, and it is clearly stated that unless any other cause is proven, the connection between work and that particular occupational disease is presumed by law. In one case concerning another problem, acid injury causing death, the defence lawyers were sure of victory when they managed to get an OHSC witness to say that 'the injury may have been caused by agents other than acid'. But the court finally ruled in favour of the worker's family, since the contrary had to be proved beyond doubt by the defence. For the worker, it was enough to show possible causal association between acid exposure and his illness.

Finally, PRIA, New Delhi, played a facilitatory role in opening up a dialogue with the higher echelons of the ESI board, and influencing some of them to view the on-the-ground reality of occupational diseases more sympathetically. This, too, was an important component of the demystifying process.

OHSC has also engaged with workers, and helped translate their experiences into terms that are deemed legitimate by scientific and policy institutions, on a number of other issues. Here, I outline briefly how this unfolded for NIHL, for disability assessments more broadly, and for chemical accidents and related environmental pollution.

Noise-induced hearing loss

In the mid-1990s, workers in a chemical factory in Mumbai complained about hearing loss. They suspected that this loss was related to high noise levels near the boilers where they worked. Many sources of mystification surrounded the identification of occupational NIHL at this time, however. These included a prevalent belief among doctors that a person cannot have hearing loss if they understand spoken words, and problems in conducting audiometry. For example, many doctors mistakenly thought that a sound-proof room was necessary for conducting audiometry, and so without such resources did not undertake it. When mass audiometries were conducted by doctors, this was frequently without the all-important bone conduction. Indeed, these Mumbai chemical workers were being checked regularly by a firm specializing in legally necessary medical check-ups of factory workers, yet this firm had never recorded the bone conduction of sound, thus omitting the test that could actually reveal irreversible effects on the nerves responsible for hearing. Diagnosis of NIHL was also clouded by biased assumptions among doctors and lawyers that workers were merely malingering, and indeed by problems of true malingering. By painstakingly working on these and other such problems, OHSC was able to assist in bringing the first Indian case of NIHL to full diagnosis and compensation in 1998 (Murlidhar and Kanhere 1998).

OHSC's approach, again, was to seek to translate workers' experiences into scientific terms, and to educate both worker activists and medical professionals in the specificities of diagnosis and rights claiming. As for lung diseases, workers acquired new scientific skills and became active participants in diagnosis and monitoring, expressing their citizenship in such particular, scientized terms. OHSC began by arranging for a medical check-up of the workers in a public hospital. The doctors involved were informed about the relevant literature regarding the diagnosis of NIHL. A group of worker activists learned, in the hospital lecture room, about the interpretation of audiometry readings. They also learned methods for assessing the resultant disability. We had noticed in our orientation courses that most doctors were ignorant of procedures for assessment of disabilities due to hearing loss. Thus workers themselves took over the role: the group of trained workers actually assessed the disabilities of the affected workers and the 'experts', who were authorized to prepare medical certificates, agreed with their assessment figures.

The ESI support group also does considerable work in this field. The audiometries are carried out by worker activists, the results presented in graphs and the disabilities calculated. Any doubtful case is referred to a teaching hospital for review. If the ESI support group is fully convinced, it then requests a sympathetic doctor to issue a medical certificate. Many cases come to the centre that turn out to be non-occupational diseases, such as middle ear deafness. Such cases are referred for treatment, and although the workers are disappointed at their inability to claim compensation, they are at least listened to patiently, and have the opportunity to discuss the nature of their problem. Nearly 60 per cent of the certified cases from the ESI support group do end up receiving compensation, however, while those who are felt to have a legitimate claim but are rejected by the medical board for compensation are encouraged to fight using persuasive dialogues and legal methods.

Disability assessment

As we saw in the cases of both lung disease and NIHL, in occupational and environmental health (OEH) disability assessment and certification are required by law for compensation purposes. This points to broader issues concerning disability assessment which the OHSC has attempted to tackle, as a cross-cutting issue (Murlidhar et al. 1996).

To seek compensation, the legal requirement is for a worker to have a precise disability certification by the treating doctor. Lacking such certification, thousands of occupationally affected and injured victims suffer. Disability assessment is relatively straightforward in cases of amputations and total deafness and blindness. In the case of lung diseases, hearing loss and complicated injuries without amputations, doctors are asked to evaluate disabilities. Yet legal guidelines to assist this are absent.

From 1992, PRIA supported a five-year participatory process to develop guidelines for disability assessment. This involved doctors from all over India, who together worked to produce what is now the accepted book on

137

the assessment of disability, overcoming many of the lacunae in the only other comprehensive source on the subject, the JAMA guides (Cocchiarella 2001). In the years since the completion of the guide, many injured workers suffering from a variety of disabilities, ranging from impotence to abdominal organ damage, have benefited. Of key importance to the use of the guide, especially in legal claims, is its aura of scientific legitimacy. Despite the reality that there is very little scientific basis for the assessment criteria, popular perception is the exact opposite. To maintain the guide's scientific legitimacy, there is a continuous need to engage the certifying doctors in debate over disability assessment criteria and methods.

While working with doctors to enhance the scientific precision and standardization of disability assessment, OHSC and PRIA have also encountered instances of deliberate mystification driven by political economy. Thus doctors specializing in disability assessments sometimes avoid giving reasons or sources for their judgements. Equally, the Special Medical Boards of the ESIS generally do not provide any reasons. It became clear that assessments by the medical board are made more with a view to reducing the compensation that would have to be paid to affected workers than according to scientific criteria. OHSC has faced such issues directly: the expert doctor sending OHSC in the wrong direction to find criteria for assessment in medical literature I mentioned earlier is one example. Alongside providing a set of 'objective' guidelines against which cases can be assessed, then, it is important for workers, activists, researchers and doctors to work together to expose and challenge these instances of overt mystification.

Chemical accidents and pollution

Industrial accidents in India are a frequent source of health problems both for workers and affected local residents. Accidents in the chemical zone occur very frequently, and some of these are major, such as the Indian Petrochemicals Limited (IPCL) blast in 1990, when sixty people died of burns.

In one of the biggest chemical coastal zones in India, the Konkan, OHSC found that workers and doctors had a variety of assumptions concerning how to treat the victims of chemical accidents. Yet these were frequently not informed by the best available medical science, while many views among both doctors and workers appeared to OHSC as misconceptions: for instance, that milk ought to be given in cases of ammonia exposure, or that there are specific antidotes to almost every chemical.

OHSC therefore decided to bring out a book on chemical accidents, first aid and antidotal treatments for Indian industrial settings, adapted from the standard World Health Organization guidelines (Murlidhar 2002).

OHSC also started to educate doctors and activists in the chemical industrial belts, with the eventual aim of networking all the trained people in the coastal chemical zone. Many local activist groups in the Konkan industrial belt have shown keen interest in this acquisition of medical expertise and scientific citizenship.

Chemical and other industrial accidents also affect local environments and the health of their residents. Members of the local communities that experience such effects directly have both the need and experiential perspectives to identify such problems. In some cases, activist groups in India have worked with communities to assist such identification and to publicize the results. Yet in many cases, their efforts – and ability to gain the attention of scientists and policy-makers – have been limited by inexperience in conducting community health surveys. In some cases, they have asked to conduct such surveys, yet have floundered. This was the case for local activists in a toxic hot spot in Kerala, who were overwhelmed by the methodology of conducting a large community health survey. Although the methodology had been planned by well-meaning academics from India and abroad, it appeared to the activists as unattainable, shrouded in mystique in terms of sampling techniques and statistics, the large number of variables involved and the need to avoid bias. Working with Greenpeace India, the OHSC was able to demystify these issues; for instance, by demonstrating some simple statistical techniques, and discussing how questions of bias and choice of variables need to be dealt with in context and in relation to the specific survey aims. The activists' spirits lifted, and they came to feel in greater control of their work. In this, OHSC and the activists together came to reflect critically on the gap that often exists between scientists and academics – however sympathetic – and grass-roots activists who are linked with local social realities. Instead of setting unreachable standards of 'scientific rigour' that totally derail a programme, OHSC worked with activists to establish a middle-ground approach, which could garner scientific legitimacy while remaining achievable and attuned to its community setting.

Conclusion

The challenges faced by the OHSC and PRIA teams have been great, but as illustrated by the examples in this chapter, they have succeeded in overcoming many of these in order to help workers gain justice in many cities in India. This justice has partly been cognitive, in the sense of establishing the legitimacy of workers' own experiences of occupational health problems among 'expert' scientific institutions. This has involved a process of bridging or translation of workers' own perspectives into the terms of mainstream science. As workers have become adept at using and expressing these scientized perspectives and tools, so this has shaped their citizenship practices. In turn, these achievements of cognitive justice have been linked to material claims and to other forms of citizenship right: to compensation, treatment and justice through the law. In some cases, these were long overdue. In the case of byssinosis, justice delayed by seventeen years must have meant justice denied to scores of deserving textile workers who would have withered away from lung disease and poverty after having been the engine of Mumbai's economy during their youth.

The process of demystification that OHSC and PRIA helped to spearhead involved challenges to established practices and interests among many scientific and policy institutions. In medical research, for instance, it involved challenging experts' practices of keeping findings from affected workers: such experts strongly believe that knowledge ought to be within the reach of only a few, and make special efforts to keep the field of experts narrow. Such mystification restricts access to knowledge even among doctors themselves. It serves vested interests and is a hindrance in the development of citizenship. As long as the affected workers and associated researchers and doctors remain inactive, the situation will be shrouded in mystery.

In post-colonial India, furthermore, language has become one of the mystifying factors. Even for a literate worker, to confirm a suspicion of occupational disease would be an insurmountable task for the simple reason that hardly any information is available in the local language. Language difficulties compound other anxieties in inhibiting workers from expressing their knowledge and experience. We have come across many workers who, out of ignorance or fear of losing their jobs, do not admit to the existence of illness in themselves or do not link it to their work environment. Those who do make the connection frequently merely attempt to treat the symptoms. Their frequent visits to their local doctor (who appears uninformed about the occupational source of the symptoms and the associated legal provisions) may result in some injection and a clutch of colourful tablets, which act at best as a palliative for the symptoms or a placebo, and at worst affect the worker with harmful chemicals. Thus at the micro level there seems to be a cycle of mystification about occupational disease fed mainly by ignorance and fear.

OHSC's efforts in engaging workers in new forms of scientific citizenship in terms of occupational disease have met with reasonable success in Mumbai and other places in India. The ESI support groups, in particular, have achieved remarkable success in the past four years. The ESI has had to deposit nearly 20 million rupees in the bank to provide monthly lifelong compensation to the affected workers in Mumbai, owing solely to the efforts of the support group of worker activists and doctors.

Demystification is most effective when it is a collective process, and if this process also proves productive in realizing rights, this gives impetus to the collective activity. While individuals may make important contributions to the process of demystifying medical and legal knowledge, OHSC found it more fruitful when people from various fields of activity came together to begin a collective process. In other words, positive changes involved the practised engagement of social solidarities linking different groups of citizen workers, doctors, safety experts, lawyers and trade unionists. Lessons having been learned from the considerable successes in demystifying occupational and environmental health in the short span of time since 1992, there is now a need for expansion into further new areas, and for involvement of more sections of society on a larger scale.

10 | Absentee expertise: science advice for biotechnology regulation in developing countries

KEES JANSEN AND ESTHER ROQUAS

Introduction

Uncertainties and potential controversies surround the spread of bio-technology to developing countries. In rather different quarters it has been suggested that developing countries lack the capacity and relevant scientific expertise to develop regulation of biotechnology that addresses issues of biosafety, food safety and property regimes. Contingent upon one's view, the central point of concern is incapacity to control the risks of an unregu-lated spread of, for example, genetically modified organisms (GMOs), or the fear that lack of regulation may exclude developing countries from the potential benefits of new biotechnologies. In this situation of uncertainty and potential controversy, both national and international politicians and regulators turn to experts for advice to assist decision-making. Generating cognitive consensus and codifying this consensus in laws and regulations, standards and guidelines, and definitions of best practice are seen as first steps towards reaching normative consensus about controversial 'techni-cal' issues.

Many international organizations are currently working to increase developing countries' 'capabilities' to regulate biotechnology. Their work involves the modelling of regulations – for example, drafting model bio-safety laws or model intellectual property laws; the development of global regulatory regimes; and the transfer of knowledge about how to regulate and how to train regulators. Much of the required work is carried out by groups of experts, who give scientific advice to decision-makers and support policy processes. International organizations such as the United Nations Environment Programme (UNEP) and the Food and Agriculture Organiza-tion of the United Nations (FAO) set up groups of science advisers to create consensus about best practice, to advise on regulatory frameworks and to build regulatory capacity in developing countries.

The mandate, number of meetings and lifetime of these expert com-mittees in the field of biotechnology regulation vary enormously. Some are *ad hoc* committees (including those that meet only once), while others are standing committees. Their work, however, is never uncontroversial, particularly because science advice operates within the rather problematic area between science and politics. The controversial character comes to the fore in the process of composing expert groups within the United Nations system. Should the composition of advisory groups give weight to geographical representation in the selection of experts (paying due attention to equal participation from developing countries) or should those scientists be selected who have a long record of publications in international journals and whose work has been scrutinized by peer review (which entails a geographical bias)? (See Frosch et al. 2002.)

This chapter explores how the social construction of knowledge and the structuring of inequalities – issues of major concern in the sociology of scientific knowledge and in development studies respectively – underlie this practical question of how to compose expert committees for science advice in the United Nations system. The main focus is on international groups of science advisers that meet to develop biotechnology regulation, especially in the FAO and UNEP. It will be argued that problems of such advisory groups couched in terms of their lack of expertise, or 'missing expertise', obscure problems related to the notion of 'absentee expertise', i.e. expertise which, detached from local contexts, prepares future regulatory frameworks.

Science advice: a third category

The dichotomy between 'scientific expertise/truth' and 'policy/politics' still clouds efforts to understand science advice at the international level. Exemplary is Grundmann's (1996) critique of the concept of 'epistemic communities', introduced to the field of international relations theory by Haas (1989, 1992). For Haas, epistemic communities are nationwide or worldwide groups of professionals that articulate the cause-and-effect relationships associated with complex problems, frame the issues for collective debate and propose specific policies. These experts share common values and believe in the same relationships and tests of their truth.[1] Grundmann questions this concept, particularly the idea that consensus-making is an inherent, non-conflictive characteristic of epistemic communities. Consensual knowledge is not a necessary condition for epistemic communities to exist and work, and, furthermore, Haas's suggestion that through epistemic communities 'reason' may defeat economic interests in policy-making does not hold (Grundmann 1996). Haas and Grundmann, in fact, take ultimately opposed positions regarding epistemic communities. Haas identifies them as similar to scientific research groups, albeit having become involved in a political enterprise. Grundmann, in contrast, denies the centrality of cognitive elements, pointing instead to power relations between resource-mobilizing actors – although this makes it difficult to distinguish epistemic communities from any other form of social group.

The lessons of science studies in the last few decades deny the likelihood that scientists in international expertise networks simply translate technical/scientific arguments into policy advice and regulatory frameworks. It is equally problematic, however, to consider international expertise networks as simply instruments for translating economic interests and hegemonic power. Both Haas and Grundmann to a large extent neglect the complex combinations of internal and external factors and processes that shape the knowledge constructs emerging from scientific advisory committees. An alternative model conceptualizes the epistemic community as a social category constituted by both cognitive dimensions and social shaping, including by political interests. Furthermore, knowledge is clearly not neutral or like a natural thing, waiting out there to be collected by laborious scientists just as bees collect honey, but is socially constructed or shaped. The views and standpoints of epistemic community members have social origins, conditioned by the institutions in which they work as well as wider ideologies and paradigms. The selected and condensed information about biotechnology, genes or risks in expert advice is therefore laden with norms, beliefs and views. In other words, expert advice interweaves both facts and values.

Notably, scientific advisory committees exist not because of their scientific value but because of their political and regulatory value. They legitimize political decisions – since expert recommendations tend to be recognized as neutral, independent statements of truth – and they set standards to foster economic activity and technological innovation. This distinguishes them from the model of the objective and independent scientist, whose only activity is to describe nature and explain natural laws and mechanisms. Unlike ordinary scientific groups, advisory epistemic communities have the specific task of ordering, selecting and filtering information, and of developing system knowledge instead of reductionist scientific knowledge. In contrast to experimental research, which creates closed systems, the epistemic community operates in the open systems of the real, messy world, where the number of contingencies is much larger. Despite uncertainties, unknowns and contrasting perspectives from very different disciplines, standards have to be set, advice has to be given and policies have to be issued. Science advisers have to come up with policy recommendations, and not with proposals for new research or scientifically interesting (but in terms of current policy problems irrelevant) knowledge.

Epistemic communities of science advisers also differ from political groups and policy-making communities with regard to their authority structures, the arguments that count, the discursive styles that are accepted (or not accepted) and the ways in which values and interests are recognized. Formally, at least, it is the latest scientific knowledge which counts, not democracy and interest representation. This 'not-pure-politics' and 'not-pure-science' character makes the epistemic community an institution in itself, which is continuously exploring and balancing the tensions and boundaries between science and policy (see Jasanoff 1990: 76–90; also Irwin et al. 1997 for a critique).

International efforts towards biotechnology regulation: the Food and Agriculture Organization and the United Nations Environment Programme

The FAO and UNEP consider themselves as strategically located to facilitate the safe development of biotechnology for the improvement of agriculture in developing countries (Endo and Boutrif 2002; Fresco 2001). The FAO concerns itself with safe food, secured markets, access to genetic resources and environmental impacts of GMOs, while UNEP is mainly involved in issues of biodiversity and biosafety. The two international organizations mobilize expert knowledge through three major fields of activity: building networks of scientists in order to support training and to promote exchange and updating of knowledge; seeking expert advice for the preparation and application of codes and guidelines that favour, standardize and adapt concepts for risk assessment, handling of specific technologies, research protocols and so on; and developing, in speech and writing, ideological statements about rationalizing technology development.

The participation of developing countries and developing-country experts in the expertise-oriented activities of the FAO and UNEP is a contentious issue. On the one hand, participation in terms of numbers may be limited in key standard-setting committees. An example is the *ad hoc* Intergovernmental Task Force on Foods Derived from Biotechnology. It advises the Codex Alimentarius Commission in terms of developing standards, guidelines or recommendations, as appropriate, for foods derived from biotechnology or traits introduced into foods by biotechnology.[2] To give an impression of its composition, the third session in Japan, 4–8 March 2002, brought together 245 participants from thirty-four countries, four international organizations and fourteen non-governmental organizations (including business associations). From Latin America, only Argentina, Brazil and Mexico sent delegates (two, two and four respectively), while the USA had a delegation of seventeen members, by far the largest apart from the delegation of host country Japan (FAO/WHO 2002). This simple counting of heads suggests that smaller Latin American countries are *de facto*

145

not involved in the drafting of guidelines on how to deal with food derived from genetically modified plants and animals, one of the major food safety issues in the contemporary debates on international trade. Since smaller countries are part of the Codex system, however, they become subject to its established norms, principles and rules. They learn these through training and the development of National Codex Committees, which have to advise their respective governments on how to implement the Codex standards and guidelines. With its earlier work on pesticides (FAO 1990), the FAO has developed experience in training country delegations at the regional level in order to 'translate' the general Code of Conduct into national legislation. The result of such work is generally the creation of a cohort of national experts, who become advocates of the ideas of international agencies as well as brokers in adapting national legislation to international Codex standards (see Haas and McCabe 2001). Hence, very often smaller countries become involved only once already formulated standards and guidelines have to be implemented at the national level.

On the other hand, international organizations' response to the criticism that developing-country participation in standard-setting and decision-making is limited. The roster of experts attached to the Biosafety Clearing House, which is part of the Cartagena Protocol on Biosafety, incorporates 139 experts nominated by African countries, but only sixty-eight from western Europe. The statistics showing abundant developing-country participation are proudly exhibited on its website (http://bch.biodiv.org/doc/BCH-ROSTER-STATS.pdf). The question is, however, whether these developing-country experts – no matter their numbers – are really able to make a difference in the kind of knowledge that the roster puts forward. To answer this question it is necessary to look more closely at some of the activities that international organizations undertake ostensibly to enhance developing-country expertise.

Capacity building One of the most ambitious projects to build capacity for biotechnology regulation in developing countries to date is the UNEP-GEF (Global Environmental Facility) project 'Development of National Biosafety Frameworks'. It intends to assist developing countries to meet the obligations of the Cartagena Protocol on Biosafety, which was signed by more than a hundred countries in 2000 (GEF 2000). The protocol aims to ensure the safe transfer, handling and use of living modified organisms (LMOs) that may have adverse effects on biological diversity or human health; the protocol specifically focuses on transboundary movements of LMOs (Art. 1).[3] The UNEP-GEF project has a budget of US$38.4 million to aid 117 countries in preparing national biosafety frameworks (NBFs); to promote regional collaboration and harmonization of risk assessment procedures and regulatory instruments; and to provide advice and support.

Draft NBFs combine policy and legal instruments, administrative systems, risk assessment procedures, and systems for public participation and information. These drafts are assessed by other expert committees formed by UNEP-GEF, and after approval submitted to national governments for further political approval and implementation. The UNEP-GEF project explicitly states that it is 'country driven' but does not clarify how it pursues this intention. Although it surveys national capacity and pays attention to the role of public participation – required by the protocol – participating countries have to adapt to a pre-set schedule of activities in a series of workshops and to use already developed 'toolkits' or 'how to' guides. These toolkits describe, for example, how to build a project structure, membership of committees, what meetings should look like, how information should be gathered and data processed, and so on. Despite the project's claim to support a country-driven process, the very use of the 'toolkit' language leaves countries little space to arrange alternative ways of complying with the protocol. Notable, for example, is how one of the toolkits addresses the selection of stakeholders. It claims that it does not want to indicate directly who should be considered as stakeholders, yet at the same time lists who they might be.

The UNEF-GEF project seems to be rather ambitious in setting up biosafety regulation in 117 countries with its limited budget (Hodgson 2002). Rethinking such projects should, however, involve not just expanding the resources and fields of activity but also questioning the current form of capacity building, on several counts. First, the subjects for capacity building have been chosen by UNEP-GEF experts in Geneva and not after deliberation among participants, with the danger that only dominant risk discourses on biotechnology issues gain attention. Second, this kind of project seems to focus on 'doing things right' instead of 'doing the right thing'. The emphasis is on doing things along 'toolkit' lines and according to the pre-defined standards of good science, rather than doing things that explore new avenues directly connected to local environments and locally contextualized experience. Third, the project is heavily focused on the technical drafting of an NBF in the shortest space of time possible and within a rigid project structure. This means that broader questions about technological trajectories and desired patterns of agrarian modernization – issues that directly relate to the use of biotechnology and which are of utmost importance to developing countries – cannot be dealt with. Hence, there is no real space for discussions about which types of farmers and which industries will win and which will lose from the introduction of biotechnologies.

Design of standards, guidelines and codes of conduct The modelling of biotechnology regulation in developing countries takes place not only via internationally binding agreements and legal harmonization but also through the setting of universal technical standards. The strategies of the FAO towards the development of the so-called 'codes of conduct' could be interpreted as a rather efficient way to improve, in developing countries, the conditions for safe food, biosafety and safe working environments. Through codes of conduct, relatively few experts are required to address technological risks, since a country does not need to develop its own risk assessment procedures. The codes intend to pay explicit attention to the situation in developing countries. Codes of conduct and the translation of international definitions of best practice may imply a trade-off, however: efficiency, harmonization and standardization incur the risk that new standards, legislation and measures are at odds with the complexities of local situations. Dimensions of risk, or whether an issue is understood in terms of risk at all, may be entirely different in divergent local circumstances. International codes, however, barely acknowledge that what to regulate and how may have to vary for different situations. They do not recognize the heterogeneity of technological trajectories and possible paths of agrarian change. The codes assume standardized behaviour from farmers, treating as exemplars what in reality may be only a small proportion of the producers in developing countries.

The FAO claims that it does not develop national legislation; this is the responsibility of national governments to draft and implement, making use of the standards set in the codes of conduct. But the question is to what extent the weak states of many developing countries are able to invest in developing endogenous policies and enforcing appropriate laws. In practice, developing countries tend to adopt foreign ideas, model laws and international codes of conduct without much discussion of content; at least, as long as no direct interests are being mobilized to oppose such new legislation (Jansen 2000).

Discourses of legitimization Another field of science advice is the construction of authoritative discourses that make the spread of biotechnology acceptable for a wider public, and which legitimize public investment in biotechnology at a time when controversies around it are rife. In papers addressing both scientists and a wider audience, FAO experts show the importance of biotechnology for already identified technology needs. A typical example is Izquierdo and Roca (1998), who point to biotechnology as the key technology for the conservation of genetic resources of underutilized Andean food crops. They call for a concerted effort by public organizations to prevent the biotechnology revolution from bypassing these crops. Such studies create the image of an 'on-rushing future' (Wilde 2000), in which new opportunities should be seized before they evaporate. The international community should jump on the bandwagon of biotechnology development in order to rescue it from one-dimensional private interests, and to refocus it on developing-country needs – mainly to increase agricultural productivity and address the production constraints of resource-poor farmers. FAO thinkers ask for scientific responsibility, i.e. taking seriously the risks of biotechnology and the need for transparency (Fresco 2001). In general, they display a cautious approach to engaging with public opinion and consumer concerns. There is also a tendency to dismiss the societal questioning of biotechnology – and citizen action around it – as a question of image. For example, Izquierdo (2000) of the FAO regional office for Latin America and the Caribbean, writes:

> Some of these achievements [in plant transgenics and genomics] have been acclaimed by end-users whereas other accomplishments, for example, release of genetically modified organisms (GMOs), are being attacked, not only in words but also in deeds, by political activists. Some of these educated middle-class campaigners are expressing in this way their rampant 'eco-paranoia', while others hide their real agenda to manipulate the fashionable ecological movement. This controversy has attracted the attention of non-scientific partisans to each side. There have been negative comments about transgenic plants by a crown prince and contrasting positive comments by a former president, both of whom *may not have the required technical knowledge to assess* the potential of biotechnology for crop improvement. (2000: 7, emphasis added)

Izquierdo basically argues that controversies around transgenic crops, and the jeopardized public image of agricultural products, are confusions that result from a lack of knowledge. In his view, whether people reject biotechnology depends on cultural factors. This is contrasted with acceptance of a positive choice for biotechnology, which is seen as scientific. Hence, experts need to be involved in disseminating the scientific message of the benefits of biotechnology, while listening with patience to the opposing views that result from a lack of knowledge. The citation above is a rather literal version of the 'deficit' model, wherein public opposition to science follows from public ignorance of science and can be 'cured' by removing the 'deficit' in the public's knowledge and understanding (see, e.g., Collins and Evans 2002). The discourse thus produced contains not only technical information about biotechnology but also messages about the superiority of science and the supposed non-ideological and non-partisan character of science, and implicit models of the objecting citizen as driven by non-science, hidden politics, paranoia and ideology. It is remarkable that Izquierdo views 'democratic disagreements' and science as two very different things.

Absentee expertise

Thus the expertise-related activities of two international organizations in the field of biotechnology regulation have a number of limitations. Across these, a core problem is to what extent internationally developed regulatory frameworks 'fit' domestic contexts.

The discussion of 'missing expertise' is a good starting point from which to address this problem. Rajan (2002) originated this concept to argue that after the explosion of the pesticide plant in Bhopal, India, there was a specific problem of state failure to respond immediately and effectively to potential hazards and to devise long-term rehabilitation plans. In explaining this, Rajan highlights the lack of 'ethnographic expertise' as one element of 'missing expertise'. This refers to the ability to gain a contextual and grounded understanding of problematic situations and to understand people's experiences and actions in specific bureaucratic, regulatory and development contexts. Rajan suggests that such expertise may be missing owing to structural divisions in society – gender, class, religion – and the capturing of the legislative and executive powers by a variety of vested interests. Unlike the 'lacking expertise' idea that dominates most reflections on capacity building for biotechnology regulation, Rajan's 'missing expertise' concept draws attention to the kind of expertise that is missing and how it relates to local contexts and the broader political economy of the state and private capital. In this, the technical and the universal are not detached from but linked to the ethnographic and the local.

This notion of missing expertise, however, does not capture sufficiently well the nature of international expertise and of the project of capacity building already in place. So, the main issue is 'What do we have?', instead of 'What do we miss?'. The concept of 'absentee expertise' is analogous to the concept of absentee landlord as used in debates on agrarian change. An absentee landlord is a landowner not resident on the estate from which he or she derives income. Management is generally undertaken through an agent. In some cases, savings, speculation or status are the prime investment objectives for the absentee landlord, rather than regular income from the estate. In 'absentee expertise', it is not ownership of land but ownership of expert knowledge which is the source of power. A key characteristic of absentee expertise is that the expert is operating in a mode detached from local concerns and contexts. When it comes to local management, it is the national regulator who implements standards, guidelines and model laws in terms of national regulation. The national regulator is in this sense only an agent who translates the higher-level directives. Although there is, of course, a certain freedom of agency for national regulators, we consider that the whole construct of international expertise advising on the formulation of biotechnology regulation is also a construct of (hidden) power.

The distancing of the absentee expert in terms of national and local contexts can take two forms. It occurs when an expert from whatever country in the world translates their own views, scientific method, knowledge, values and so on into standards, guidelines and model laws. In ignorance of local contexts, a claimed universal truth may be generated which conflicts with local needs, institutional capacities and political-economic histories. It can also occur when an expert from a developing country enters the cosmopolitan world of international science and becomes a member of a social group whose 'thought style' prioritizes certain disciplines, causal principles, problems and solutions that are not necessarily shared by social actors in the different countries themselves. As with the absentee landlord, absentee expertise does not necessarily lead to bad practices, i.e. bad regulation. But the point here is that the whole social construct has built into it several properties that may, dependent upon other factors, limit the development of a flexible and dynamic form of regulation that builds upon local conditions, needs and prevalent forms of citizenship in developing countries.

Conclusion: absentee expertise as a problem

This chapter emphasizes the 'absentee' character of international expertise in order to highlight the problem of detachment from local situations, and domination by foreign interests and universalistic science, for domestic regulatory frameworks in developing countries. Networks of international expertise are more or less diffuse, more or less enduring social groups/fields, where science and politics intermingle.[4] Because its absentee character tends to hide its role, the importance of this expertise in shaping regulation is often not very well identified. The role of absentee expertise is also hidden because the politics of expertise are generally not very well recognized in conventional models of science and science advice. As absentee expertise becomes more and more important in defining how societies have to approach health and environmental issues, it is important that its hidden roles – and the alternatives to it – are better understood, especially in relation to three critical issues.

Expert formation: adaptive copying versus social learning Currently, the formation of experts basically involves the training of newcomers in how things should be done; for example, what proper risk assessment of transgenics is. The new expert gains his or her expertise from established experts, rather than from locally contextualized experience and knowledge. In such a model, which starts at the top of international scientific consensus, absentee experts define what kind of capacity is needed and what kind of knowledge is lacking. The capacity thus created (for example, by training molecular biologists or others from related disciplines to use biotechnology tools and undertake risk analysis) may be able to apply dominant risk discourses on biotechnology issues which do not go beyond constructing conventional meanings of uncertainties and risks (Wynne 2002). There seems to be little public investment, however, in creating capacity to rethink technological trajectories in agriculture and to democratize innovation processes (for example, through teaching in social constructivism and facilitating social learning). There is little debate on what kind of agricultural modernization is wanted. But, if one assumes that the escape from underdevelopment needs unconventional thinking and authentic research and development, then learning to 'do the right thing' – that is, adaptive copying of international expertise – is quite problematic. The issue here is to what extent developing countries are able to advance expert formation in terms of social learning. The latter implies that expert formation is not steered by adaptive copying and single private interests, but by a democratic choice of certain technological futures. This would need a public arena where the meanings, purposes and limitations of agricultural technological innovation are discussed as an alternative for, or are guiding, the international networks of absentee experts.

Standardization and harmonization versus heterogeneity and complexity
Expert formation by international organizations is driven by the strength of a universalized or universalizing science. Three interlinked processes strengthen the internationalization of expert formation. First, international knowledge transfer is seen as a condition for enlarging expertise in developing countries. Second, transnational firms and the World Trade Organization (WTO) encourage countries to use international standards, guidelines and recommendations, instead of national ones. Third, once started, the internationalization process itself generates a need for harmonization of regulation and multilateral networks. Together, these three processes enforce generally applicable standards and codes of conduct, universal definitions of sound science and good rules, regulations and practices, and harmonization. In the real world, however, national political, economic and social conditions, and specific ecological and technical environments, are very diverse, heterogeneous and complex. One could argue therefore

that much greater plurality in forms of regulation and definitions of best practice is needed. 'Doing things right' emphasizes a universally applicable science and harmonized standards, while 'doing the right thing' emphasizes contextualizing standards and allowing for locally specific regulation and technological trajectories.

Legitimacy of technical decision-making: truth, (constructed) consensus and (imposed) compromise If the role of absentee expertise in shaping the future of developing countries enlarges, the legitimacy of technical decision-making is at stake. The dominant model, assuming an absolute separation between universal sciences and politics, between objective truth and social construction, will be under fire each time specific biotechnology innovations arouse new controversies. The widely shared notion that it makes, or should make, a difference when scientists from developing countries participate in the process of science advice is implicitly a recognition of the social construction of knowledge in international expertise committees. If it were only about universal truths, the social background of the scientist should not make any difference.

In the ideal international expert committees as defined by Haas, scientists and technologists come to a shared consensus by virtue of the knowledge they put forward as scientists and technologists, rather than as members of certain organizations or representatives of certain countries. But in practice, international organizations developing biotechnology regulation can never be sure that the public accepts the science advice because of the universal truth in its cognitive content. For people to put trust in science as an institution, the authoritative image of respectable scientists who, after deliberation, reach a considered consensus has to be created. But how does one arrive at a consensus when divided perspectives exist in terms of the issues at stake (for example, when controversies between experts and counter-experts concerning the safety of transgenic crops inflame the passions of the public)? Scientific consensus may not be reached or may be difficult to reach precisely because of existing uncertainties, or because of disciplinary or experiential divisions among the scientists involved. Before giving concerted advice, not only has knowledge to be collected and attuned, but new knowledge has to be constructed. This is a gradual, and often rather hidden, process in which certain forms of knowledge are made dominant while other knowledge is rendered irrelevant. The concerted advice, the consensus, is thus a result of, and produces, power relations between forms of knowledge. The legitimacy of absentee experts depends on successful consensus construction.

Issues of power, however, may be more dramatic and directly experienced

153

than this latent construction of dominant knowledge, language and symbols. Hegemonic power play often raises concerns about the composition of international expert committees. But the issue of participation extends well beyond membership numbers to questions about how power is being exercised. Economic interests and the use of hegemonic power may work together with ascribed scientific status to shape biotechnology regulation. But it is rarely the case that the work of an expert committee in developing biotechnology regulation is a direct result of hegemonic international relations, international trade/political economy or similar external forces; more often, the process through which one view or principle becomes dominant is rather much more complex. Imposed compromise, in any case, may challenge the legitimacy of international science advice in the long term.

This issue of legitimacy, consensus-making and imposing compromise in the world of absentee expertise is not only of academic or theoretical interest. It underlies the problems that international organizations face when organizing science advice. It is also central to finding alternatives for a technocratic approach to policy advice, as well as to an over-politicization of international science advice that reduces it to interest representation. More empirical research on absentee expertise could unravel how consensus-building or the construction of dominance takes place in situations of unequal participation, and in so doing perhaps point to ways in which more grounded, locally contextualized forms of expertise could support emergent practices of citizenship in relation to science.

Notes

1 Haas aims to show that most policy change approaches within the field of international relations theory neglect the possibility that states can learn and that epistemic communities are an important actor, causing shifts in the original goals of policy-makers and introducing new patterns of reasoning.

2 The task force just mentioned is not an epistemic community in its *ideal* form, but already a hybrid, composed of experts *and* decision-makers. Such task forces may turn to consultants or smaller expert working groups for advice on details. In this case the Codex Alimentarius Commission is the decision-making body.

3 The use of the term 'living modified organism' (instead of 'genetically modified organism') was itself a result of intense expert struggle, nicely described as an example of social construction by Gupta (2002).

4 There may be a clear identification with a shared disciplinary background, but other elements that are often seen as basic to community – such as a high degree of personal intimacy, emotional depth, social cohesion and continuity in time – may be very limited or totally absent.

11 | Interrogating China's biotechnology revolution: contesting dominant science policy cultures in the risk society

JAMES KEELEY

Introduction

> Laboratories around the country are aiming their gene guns at pig and goat cells in the hope of developing pharmaceutical proteins and transplantable organs for humans or injecting pollen grains with DNA to produce virus-resistant papayas, potatoes, tobacco and tomatoes. One man is working on cloning the fast-disappearing panda. (Smith 2000)

China has the fourth-largest area sown to genetically modified (GM) crops in the world. It plans to spend over US$500 million annually on agri-biotechnology research by 2004, overtaking the USA. It has developed a host of different GM plants engineered for a range of different traits (Huang et al. 2002a, 2002b; Huang and Wang 2003; Keeley 2003a). China decoded the rice genome largely independent of the West. The country's biotechnology revolution appears to be well on course, leaving other developing countries, not to mention many industrialized nations, in the starting blocks.

An important aspect of China's biotechnology achievements is the way they are manipulated in the global propaganda war enveloping GM crops. China, for the advocates, shows the way forward for developing countries. It understands what the twenty-first-century knowledge economy is about and it shows what can be done if there are no troublesome non-governmental organizations (NGOs) panicking farmers and consumers (see, e.g., Paarlberg 2001). In January 2002, an article documenting China's GM achievements was published in the journal *Science* (Huang et al. 2002a). Publication demonstrated, first, that what is happening in China is taken seriously by the international scientific establishment, and second – as became evident through related e-mail and newspaper discussion – that China is key to the global GM project. It is a winner: it shows that GM is working, and farmers like the products. Critically, it shows that a state can harness the power of biotechnology for developmental ends. As an official from the International Service for Acquisition of Agribiotechnology Applications asserted: 'The Chinese experience amply demonstrates the multifold and significant benefits that appropriate transgenic technology or transgenic crops can deliver to the society and to farmers as a whole.'[1]

This chapter challenges these narratives about genetic engineering in China. It argues that the picture often painted in the global and Chinese media and through corporate information sources is actually a misrepresentation of the Chinese biotechnology story. The argument is made in two stages. The first part of the chapter explores how the Chinese experience differs from what has happened elsewhere. It is argued that biotechnology in China has been effective in achieving a remarkable amount quickly because the state has approached development in a particular way: targeting a priority area and channelling investment to promote rapid technological innovation. This has been assisted by dense networks of hybrid policy-makers, scientists and businesspeople funding, researching, developing, commercializing and regulating technologies.

The Chinese state has a distinctive approach to development that resonates with that of other East Asian states governing the market and delivering rapid industrialization in the 1970s and 1980s (see Blecher and Shue 1996; Duckett 1998; Evans 1995; Kang 2002; Wade 1990; White 1988; World Bank 1993). In this, the state delivers public goods, and allows the private sector to operate in a way that does not undermine this provision. The state shapes markets, and directs and controls capital towards particular policy ends. This model of the state entails a particular vision of the Chinese citizen, in which citizenship is perceived less in terms of claiming and exercising individual rights, as in liberal-democratic traditions, but more in terms of enjoyment of social and economic benefits granted by the state. This idea of citizenship emphasizes the collective more than the individual; the social and economic benefits the state provides are realized only through active engagement in a collective project. Of course, this narrative has been modified as the famous iron rice bowl has cracked and broken, reflected in the encouragement of more entrepreneurial and self-reliant forms of citizenship, and as official narratives of the citizen come to be debated in the media and elsewhere (Anagnost 1997; Barme 1999; Keane 2001; Parris 1999). Biotechnology is part of the vision of the state delivering modernization for its citizens, with the collective benefiting from the development and application of science and technology.

The second part of the chapter explores the way in which 'risk society' debates make this application of the state-governed development model look problematic. Following Beck (1992) and Giddens (1990), many new technologies associated with late modernity, such as the life sciences, create unanticipated and unwanted effects while simultaneously being set to ameliorate other perceived social problems. What these debates identify as risk is inherently embedded in industrialization and modernization, and the risk society is in this sense a new phenomenon demanding new institutional responses, including principally a capacity to act reflexively. For many, given the social nature of risk – who decides what counts as a benefit or cost? how are probabilities assessed? – and the inherent difficulty of managing uncertainty, let alone the embedded social meanings of technological trajectories more broadly, this can be possible only through deliberation between multiple perspectives and values.

The Chinese case is interesting because China has gone about biotechnology as if it were any other aspect of the socialist modernization that it has undertaken so well in the past; in health systems or rural infrastructure, for example. Chinese society and China's place in the world have changed fundamentally, however. China is now highly integrated with the global economy and has an increasingly well-educated and critical citizenry. In relation to biotechnology, this means that the science policy cultures that have delivered change at unprecedented rates are increasingly being challenged. In the past, it appeared possible to some extent to evade doubt, uncertainty and ignorance. Now, suddenly, China has to engage with multifarious articulations of risk and, implicitly, new notions of citizenship. Bureaucrats themselves are embedded in a different global policy, electronic and professional networks (Breslin 2003; Lynch 1999). Diverse risks – from trade shocks to lack of consumer acceptance and unanticipated environmental impacts – have posed fundamental challenges to the state's approach to biotechnology and development. In this respect, the basic sense of coherence, organization and purpose that made Chinese endeavours so effective can paradoxically be a source of weakness.

Given these dynamics, it becomes clear that the embrace of the biotechnology revolution is not as unequivocal as much global discourse suggests, nor is the biotechnology already commercialized in China the indisputable success that its advocates would like to claim. In reality, China presents a much more ambiguous picture, with wider implications for thinking about the potential contribution of biotechnology to development, food security and 'good ways of life' more generally.

China's biotechnology achievements

China's achievements in the biotechnology field have been considerable (Huang and Wang 2003; Keeley 2003a). By far the most important GM crop is *Bt* cotton, which was first approved for commercialization in 1997, with the severe bollworm crisis of the early 1990s still a recent memory. It is now grown over an area of 1.5m hectares (in 2001), which amounts to 35 per cent of the cotton area, in several different provinces.[2] In the northern provinces around the Yellow River, take-up is reckoned to be over 95 per cent (Huang et al. 2003).

Research by agricultural economists at the Centre for Chinese Agricultural Policy has suggested that *Bt* cotton has very clear positive developmental impacts. These include major improvements in production efficiency, positive environmental change and contributions to poverty reduction. Huang et al. (2002b) show that that the cost of producing a kilogram of cotton has reduced by 28 per cent from US$2.23 to $1.61; that yields have increased by about 10 per cent; that where farmers use *Bt* cotton they are US$140 per hectare better off; and that deaths of cotton farmers due to pesticide poisoning (a common occurrence in China) have decreased. These data have aroused considerable international interest and are frequently cited.

China's biotechnology programme is presented as having a developmental focus that distinguishes it strongly from other countries. 'China is accelerating investments in agricultural research and is focusing on commodities that have been ignored in the laboratories of industrialized countries. Small farmers have begun to adopt GE crops when permitted to do so' (Huang et al. 2002a: 674). These authors argue that 'the public dominated research system has given China's researchers a strong incentive to produce crops that increase yields and prevent pest outbreaks' (ibid.: 675). In contrast to industrialized countries, where 45 per cent of the approvals for field trials are for herbicide-tolerant or quality-improved varieties, and only 19 per cent for insect resistance, in China 90 per cent of field trials target insect and disease resistance (ibid.). Furthermore, they argue that 'as *Bt* cotton spreads the social benefits from this crop will easily pay for all of China's past biotechnology expenditures on all crops' (ibid.: 676).

The institutional context for biotechnology science in China

How exactly did the state come to prioritize biotechnology in this way? The Ministry of Science and Technology (MoST) has played the key role, primarily through its flagship technology innovation fund, the 863 National High-Tech Programme. In this, a network of scientists was able to make the case for very large-scale investment in science and technology at a key turning point in recent Chinese history. The programme began in March 1986, after a small group of scientists persuaded Deng Xiaoping that major investment in science and technology research and development was vital if the Four Modernizations[3] were to be realized, and China were not to fall far behind the West:

> China's rush to genetic crops is part of a broader effort to co-opt the new science as China's own before it is dominated by the West, as has occurred with other technologies. The initiative dates from the Reagan-era Strategic Defense Initiative, which poured billions of dollars into high-technology

158

research in the 80's with the goal of building a space-based missile-defense system. Startled by the prospect that America would forever dominate the planet because of its superior technology, Deng Xiaoping called for a Chinese response. A result was the 863 Project ... Beijing called in its top scientists from around the world and set them working on seven broad areas. Genetic engineering was at the top of the list. Since then, the double helix has replaced the atom as the symbol of the modernization drive. (Smith 2000)

For some time, then, a vision of a biotechnology future has been an integral part of China's plans for modernization. The 863 Programme receives substantial coverage through the official media in China. Details of its achievements are only a couple of clicks away on the *People's Daily* home page.

A Chinese scientist (pers. comm., 2002) put the nationalist case very clearly: 'We can't have seeds controlled by the US. It's too dangerous! Control of the seed industry is more dangerous than other weapons. The Chinese government realizes it is easy to control the Chinese seed industry. We are not afraid of US missiles, but we are afraid of this. Imported seed could be very expensive and controlled by a few companies.' One consequence of the large amounts of funding available through 863 is that MoST is a major influence on the research priorities of agricultural research institutes – sometimes to the detriment of non-biotechnology agricultural research.[4]

The state not only guides research, but also plays a major role in the commercialization of technologies. At least one third of the *Bt* cotton in China is marketed by companies that were formed by state research institutes. The most important of these is Biocentury, which markets the varieties with the gene constructs developed by the Biotechnology Research Institute in the Chinese Academy of Agricultural Sciences in Beijing. While this is notionally a private company, it has clearly been fostered in its development at all stages by MoST and the Ministry of Agriculture (MoA), and in the minds of Chinese policy-makers should develop to become an internationally important life sciences company. Even its rivals see this as a possibility. John Killmer, vice -president of Monsanto Far East Ltd in Beijing, comments: 'In less than 10 years, we'll be accessing technology from China' (AgBiotechnologyNet 2000). For the time being, this is still some way off. Even in China, possibly as much as two-thirds of the transgenic cotton is Monsanto varieties. Monsanto is quite constrained by the Chinese state, however, able to operate only through joint ventures and restricted from carrying out breeding programmes.

A closer look at Chinese science policy networks involved in bio-

China's biotechnology revolution

technology reveals how research, development, commercialization and regulation of technology overlap in quite fundamental ways. A brief bio-graphy of Chen Zhangliang illustrates this. Chen is vice-president of Beijing University and Director of the National Laboratory of Genetic Engineering in Beijing. He has been at the heart of the 863 Programme from its earliest days: 'Among the people summoned by Mr. Deng was Chen Zhangliang, who was working in a Monsanto-financed laboratory at the University of St. Louis. He was put in charge of developing transgenic plants other than cotton' (*New York Times*, 10 July 2000). Chen is the youngest-ever professor in China (at the age of twenty-seven), holds a US PhD and is a Global Leader of Tomorrow of the Davos World Economic Forum. He was also respon-sible for developing GM tobacco, the world's first GM crop, which was later withdrawn because of fear that China would lose access to international markets. More recently he has developed transgenic peppers.

In addition to managing the biotechnology component of the 863 Pro-gramme, which channels funding, guides research and supports the com-mercialization of research, Chen is the director of seven listed companies in both Hong Kong and the mainland.[5] Other examples can be given of scientists who are simultaneously company directors, developers of tech-nologies, regulators on the Biosafety Committee and managers of key state research funds (see Keeley 2003b).

One economist (pers. comm., 2002) with close links to Chinese bio-technology policy networks commented: 'Scientists are influential because there are no farmers' organizations and no consumers associations. Zhu Rongji [the Chinese premier] has said that for agricultural policy the MoA has to listen to scientists. Scientists are lobbying to go on with GM, to get more research funding.' Another scientist (pers. comm., 2002) claimed: 'Scientists just want to get more research money. They say something is good and they get more funds, and they get rich, that's all.'

So, given this apparent overlap of interests within the Chinese research and regulatory community, looking at the details of biosafety management problems, how do claims that the Chinese biotechnology revolution is based on sound science with unproblematic benefits look? How does the Chinese state handle uncertainty?

Regulating biotechnology, contesting biosafety

Regulation is regulation, reality is reality. (Biosafety Office official, MoA)

One characteristic of the Chinese state's approach to biotechnology is the way in which it promotes Chinese industry and technology while strategically controlling US business, rather than letting multinational companies dominate as happens in other places. Significantly, it does this not only through 'non-scientific' measures such as trade or intellectual property policies, but also by using ostensibly neutral, 'sound science' biosafety assessment.[6] Keeley (2003b) explores the ways in which province-by-province risk assessments of *Bt* cotton are made. Approvals for entry to new provinces happen in a way that is quite haphazard; while scientific rationales are always presented as the reason for decisions, in fact other factors such as commercial considerations appear to be at work. Hence, Monsanto has found it difficult to move into the key Yellow River province Henan, home of the Chinese Cotton Research Institute. At the same time there has been intense debate about whether *Bt* cotton is suitable for southern Yangtse cotton zone provinces, where gene expression problems, refugia and resistance issues are more prominent. In the end, the Chinese company Biocentury has been granted permission to enter in a limited way, based on its assertion that scientifically its double-gene products have the edge over Monsanto – a claim that is again treated with scepticism by many analysts.

In parallel to such manoeuvring around the risk assessment process, *Bt* cotton seeds are in reality widely sold in provinces for which there is no approval, or where a certain company does not have approval, or involving new transgenic varieties that have not been through any regulatory process at all.

Debates about the effectiveness of and resistance to *Bt* cotton in China have also emerged. These have centred around a group of researchers based in Nanjing, in Jiangsu, a Yangtse province,[7] working in partnership with Greenpeace-Hong Kong. They presented critical research findings at a workshop inaugurated by a key official in the State Environmental Protection Administration (SEPA), and their report received substantial coverage in both the Chinese and international press (see also Xue 2003).

One set of arguments made by the researchers deals with the build-up of pest resistance to *Bt* cotton. They suggest that established models for assessing the development of resistance are unreliable, as resistance may not be a recessive gene as was previously thought but semi-dominant, which changes the selection pressure and has important implications for the speed at which resistance occurs. Over a short-term time frame there may be no evidence at all of resistance developing, but this could suddenly change.[8] Indeed, critics of insect-resistant crops argue that performance can be impressive in the short term, but that it is only a matter of time before pests adapt and the need for new gene constructs becomes necessary. Farmers thus find themselves on a GM treadmill similar to a pesticide treadmill, and end up paying high prices for seeds, while also having to pay for pesticides to cover periods of poor performance. The argument advanced for why Chinese double-gene GK-19 is suitable for the Yangtse and Monsanto's single-gene varieties are not illustrates how more advanced and expensive technologies are needed as the limitations of the first round of GM products become evident.

Critics of China's GM cotton experiment also point to problems with the rise of non-target pests. Xue at the Nanjing Environmental Science Research Institute argues that:

> *Bt* cotton is not effective in controlling many secondary pests ... Field experiments show that the populations of secondary pests such as cotton aphids, cotton spider mites, thrips, lygus bugs, cotton whitefly, cotton leaf hopper and beet army worm increased in *Bt* cotton fields after the target pest – bollworm – had been controlled. Some pests replaced bollworm as primary pests and damaged cotton growth. (Xue 2002: 3)[9]

This implies the need for more pesticides to be used, even if they are no longer targeting bollworms. In turn, this undermines one of the key arguments made to policy-makers about *Bt* cotton, namely that it results in significant savings for farmers through reduced input costs. The data showing very positive economic impacts for farmers may begin to look more complicated when this type of farmer response is picked up. The latest data from Huang et al. raise interesting questions in this respect. They suggest that average numbers of pesticide applications across five provinces have increased from seven in 1999, to nine in 2000, to fourteen in 2001 (2002b).

The point is that the rhetoric about China's biotechnology revolution, namely that it is unequivocally a good thing for poor farmers and that it has only positive environmental impacts, makes sense only when a lot of important assumptions are left out of the picture.

The myth of biosafety regulation as a rational and coherent system dealing with known and manageable risks again looks problematic when assumptions about farming, seed production and distribution systems are brought into the frame.[10] Biosafety systems often assume a manageability that is far from realistic. The Chinese system approves on a province-by-province basis, claiming that the risk is acceptable in one province because of its particular refugium systems and pest complex, but not in another province where these conditions do not hold. In reality, varieties are sold that have no approval and are bred outside the formal system, and farmers buy seed in one province and sell in another.

As a Monsanto representative commented: 'The government knows that it has no capacity, that its rules are inadequate and it can't enforce them.

Of course people are selling GM crops illegally in provinces where it isn't approved' (pers. comm., 2002). This was admitted equally candidly by a senior scientist working on the *Bt* cotton resistance monitoring: 'This year they have small-scale commercialization of *Bt* in the Yangtse river area. But in fact farmers get seed from the black market – it can't be controlled' (ibid.).

The fractious state and new forms of citizenship? Debating the biotechnology vision

China's view is that high-yield and disease resistant crops are the only means of feeding its growing population. (Monsanto 2001: 3)

China is making progress in making democratic and scientific decisions when the outcome concerns the immediate interests of the public. The government has used many methods to listen to people's opinions through public opinion polls, open debates and discussions. Introducing these methods in science policy-making is under discussion. Debates have been organized in newspapers and TV on biotechnology and social and moral principles so that scientists, sociologists and the public can exchange their opinions directly. (*China Daily*, 16 August 2001)

The idea that there is one Chinese view of GM crops promoted by the state acting for Chinese citizens becomes hard to sustain when faced with close scrutiny. In fact, many in China are actually far less gung-ho about GM than dominant narratives suggest. This is reflected in the fact that for several years no new crops have been commercialized, despite several years of field trials and environmental release testing for several different crops. There are various strands to this scepticism. One is the research emerging from ecologists and entomologists outside the main science policy networks. This work enjoys the tacit support of SEPA, which, despite representing China in international biosafety negotiations, has failed so far to play a strong role in biosafety regulation at home. Another strand of doubt links those concerned with trade issues, and the danger that China will lose access to key markets in the European Union and Japan if it commercializes certain GM food crops. Trade disputes with the USA over GM soya imports are an example, influenced by the potential post-World Trade Organization impact on Chinese soybean farmers in the economically marginalized north east.

Doubt is also expressed by bureaucratic regulators within MoA. One official presented himself as having to make scientific arguments about risks associated with commercialization of GM rice to lobbying biotechnology scientists. He commented: 'Rice – we doubt that this will be approved, because China is a centre of biodiversity. Scientists argue "Why don't you approve?" We have been under pressure for two or three years. But we don't give in. Usually we agree with the recommendations [of the risk assessment committee]. Rice is the one case where we don't agree.' Another argued: 'I used to grow sugar cane. I said it is good, it is good, and promoted it, but actually it had some weaknesses that we didn't mention. Scientists working on biotechnology must be the same … Is GM safe? According to today's science we can say that it is safe. But some time later that may not prove to be the case. Biosafety approval doesn't necessarily mean something is safe.' These quotes suggest that despite the importance of scientific bureaucratic networks promoting biotechnology, there is also less homogeneity among policy-makers than is often presented to the outside world.

Critical voices can also be heard in the Chinese media, suggesting that the emerging Chinese middle class could potentially be quite sceptical. A *China Daily* article asks:

> How will the housewives of China, who have so far not encountered GM foods, react to tomatoes labelled as being 'genetically modified'? Most of the scientists [at the symposium] expect a negative reaction from Chinese customers. Part of the reason lies with faulty or inaccurate media coverage in China of GM foods, some of them suggested. They complain that the media have exaggerated the risks, if any, of GM foods and scared off consumers who have little knowledge of GM foods. 'Sometimes, it takes four positive news stories to offset the impact of one negative story,' said one delegate, who requested anonymity. Sometimes, such communication may result in unwanted effects. 'I agree that the public have the right to know the truth about GM foods,' Chen [Zhangliang, as above] said. 'But another truth about human nature is that the more you learn, the less safe you feel.' (16 August 2001)

The notion of a singular Chinese state approach to biotechnology turns out to be quite problematic. From a distance it explains a lot, but in practice it looks fairly contingent, with the assumptions it makes about acting on behalf of citizens – and thus models of citizenship themselves – open to question. Looked at more closely, the state appears to be a series of overlapping and often conflicting networks, embedded in different global networks, and linking into different assumptions about the relation between state and citizen, and the meaning of citizenship. These meanings are multiplied further when the wider social, economic and policy context for GM agriculture in China is considered, including the consolidation of small farms and the creation of larger, 'more efficient' agricultural units, and promotion of rural–urban migration. While the Chinese state's model of biotechnology development constructs the citizen, whether farmer or consumer, in particular ways, this chapter has suggested that these constructs are not likely to be as manageable or as acquiescent as might be hoped – as, for example, recent rural unrest directed at local officials in different parts of China has demonstrated. Such instances underline how the 'risk society' inevitably challenges the science–policy–business nexus of the Chinese state's approach to biotechnology.

Notes

This chapter is based on field research in China, including interviews with government officials, farmers, researchers, research scientists, extensionists, private sector representatives and others during 2000–02. The research is part of the UK Department for International Development (DFID)-funded project 'Agricultural biotechnology policy processes in developing countries', and is informed by work carried out for the United Nations Environment Programme Global Environmental Facility (UNEP-GEF) and DFID on public participation in national biosafety frameworks, and for the Rockefeller Foundation on 'Democratizing Biotechnology'. The Chinese partners in this research have been the China Centre for Agricultural Policy, Chinese Academy of Sciences, Beijing. I have also valued the support and ideas of other colleagues researching biotechnology policy processes at the Institute of Development Studies: Dominic Glover, Peter Newell, Ian Scoones and Tom Wakeford. This research is written up at greater length in Keeley (2003a) and (2003b).

1 Randy Hautea, director of the International Service for the Acquisition of Agribiotech Applications (ISAAA), South-East Asia office (Monsanto 2002a).

2 Cotton is an important crop for China with annual production in the region of 450–500 tonnes, 25 per cent of world production (Mo 2001).

3 Modernization of agriculture, industry, science and technology, and defence. Under the Four Modernizations policy, science would be the route to socialism with Chinese characteristics, not mass movements as in the past.

4 Biotechnology research received 9.2 per cent of the national crop research budget in 1999, an increase from 1.2 per cent in 1986. This compares with levels of between 2 and 5 per cent in other developing countries (Huang et al. 2002a: 675).

5 These produced revenues for Beijing University of US$1.68 billion in 2001; <www.china-future.org/docs/people>.

6 The State Environmental Protection Administration (SEPA) is the leading agency representing China in international negotiations for the Cartagena Protocol on Biosafety, which China is preparing to ratify. SEPA is currently largely excluded from risk assessment decision-making. Officials claim, however, that a Biosafety Law will soon be passed giving them overall responsibility and limiting the role of MoA.

7 The key groups of researchers are at the Environmental Science Research Institute and the Agricultural University.

8 Indeed, according to studies by Shen Jinliang at Nanjing Agricultural

University, susceptibility of bollworm to *Bt* cotton declines by 30 per cent after seventeen generations' continuous selection with a diet of *Bt* cotton leaves. Continued to the fortieth generation, resistance increases 1,000 times (see He et al. 2001; Xue 2002). Other entomologists dispute Shen's findings, arguing that critically no studies yet show clear evidence of resistance in the field.

9 Professor Wu Kongming at the Plant Protection Institute has challenged these data and argued that aphid populations are higher on non-*Bt* control plants. Others would dispute this.

10 These are not the only uncertainties. Other issues that ecologists highlight as potential causes for concern include changes in the diversity indices of pests, which could be associated with further serious, non-linear changes in pest ecologies, possibly requiring new, more intensive management regimes.

12 | Environmental perception and political mobilization in Rio de Janeiro and São Paulo: a comparative analysis

ANGELA ALONSO AND VALERIANO COSTA

This chapter discusses the processes that shape citizen engagement in scientific and technical issues in Brazil, focusing on an environmental case. Such engagements can take the form of movements or 'mobilizations' to resist planned interventions because of their environmental or related social implications. Brazilian sociologists have explained such environmental mobilizations by focusing either on the intentions of environmental actors (Viola and Leis 1995) and the diffusion of particular values, or the construction of perceptions of environmental risk (Fuks 1998; Guivant 1998). Both these approaches offer only partial explanations, however, because they ignore the socio-political dimensions of mobilization, and how particular forms of knowledge become linked with mobilization practices. Thus both fail to address the central problem: what explains mobilization itself? Given a particular technical issue, why does mobilization occur in some instances, yet not in others?

In this chapter, we argue that three sets of issues are important in shaping the conditions for environmental mobilization, and its effectiveness or otherwise: the 'mobilizing structure' available to activists and citizens; the political arrangements with which mobilization interacts; and the social construction of environmental risks, especially the relationship between the knowledge and values of affected actors and the claims made by scientific and technical discourses.

Our arguments are based on the evidence from case studies of efforts to build circular highways, or beltways, in Rio de Janeiro (the Niemeyer project) and São Paulo (the Rodoanel project). Environmental mobilization emerged to block the former successfully, but not the latter. The chapter explores the reasons for these differences.

Our approach

The extent of political activity in any society is extremely varied, both in terms of who engages in it, and over time. As theorists of 'contentious politics' note, social life is riddled with conflicts that occasionally erupt into 'contentious episodes', fluid social mobilizations that involve groups

167

in some particular issue (McAdam et al. 2001; Tarrow 1994). Privileging the dynamic aspect of conflicts, they suggest that an understanding of mobilizations has to take into account the opportunities and threats that actors face, and the mobilizing structures, framing processes and repertoires that they have access to (see Kriesi et al. 1995; Maloney et al. 2000).

We use the shorthand term 'political opportunity structure' (Tarrow 1994: 85) to address the ways in which mobilizations emerge in specific historical conditions, shaped by both structural social hierarchies and long-term state–society relations, and conjunctural issues such as changes in political-institutional patterns amid ongoing political processes. These can give rise to new political opportunities, such as the emergence of possible allies or vulnerabilities in opponents that encourage collective mobilizations. In the first section, we describe the structures of political opportunity that enabled mobilization in Rio de Janeiro, while making it more difficult in São Paulo.

Collective mobilizations typically involve several sorts of participant. First, there are the authorities, usually agents of government; second, activists who become mobilized to challenge authority or make particular claims; and third, the affected social groups – the populations that both the authorities and activists attempt to represent or control. In order to act politically, organization is required, whether through formal associations or informal networks. In the third section, we describe the contrasting 'mobilizing structures' available to citizens in Rio and São Paulo.

In the middle section, we explore the cultural repertoires – socially and historically rooted ways of interpreting reality (Tilly 1993) – that actors draw on in generating their mobilizing structures and constructing their argumentative strategies and collective identities. Drawing on constructivist approaches, we consider the extent to which actors have come to frame dimensions of their social realities as 'environmental problems' in ways that facilitate environmental mobilization (see also Hannigan 1995). Other authors (Hajer 1995; Irwin 2001b) emphasize the central role of scientific and technical discourse in the social construction of environmental issues, and the ways in which actors use science both to legitimize their positions and to garner public support. That state agencies enrol scientific and technical elites in the construction of discourse coalitions in support of the ecological modernization of capitalist societies has been well documented (Beck 1992; Hajer 1995), yet criticized as one-sided (Irwin 2001b). In this chapter, we consider whether and how citizens and activists, too, draw on the discursive support of scientific and technical elites to support their mobilization strategies.

We begin by comparing the political opportunity structures in which the two road-building projects emerged, and go on to consider the socio-economic conditions and knowledges of the people affected. With those elements at hand, we attempt to explain the very different paths of mobilization that emerged in each case.

Political opportunity structures

In Rio de Janeiro and São Paulo in the middle of the 1990s, public authorities launched transportation plans to build large beltways encircling the metropolitan perimeters of the cities. Both projects were justified as necessary to overcome 'saturated' traffic conditions in the cities. Both also carried implications for the natural environment as well as for residents in their immediate vicinities. Segments of the projects, including the widening of the Niemeyer Avenue in Rio de Janeiro and the western stretch of the Rodoanel (literally, 'ring road') in São Paulo, passed through various stages of the process of environmental licensing, and in both cases environmental variables were formally considered in defining the routes. In both cases, then, there was a potential environmental conflict. In theory, both projects would have been able to generate mobilization – either for or against them.

A full understanding of the political process involved in the beltway projects requires closer attention to the formal institutional structures in Rio and São Paulo, and the different political opportunities they implied. In Rio de Janeiro, the municipal government initiated the project. A former urban planner from a centre-right party controlled the municipal executive, while a populist politician from a centre-left party controlled the state executive. This political distance resulted in a lack of coordination and even competition between the two levels.

In São Paulo, in contrast, the state government took the lead on the project. While three levels of government were involved – federal, state and municipal – competition between them did not become important, for particular reasons: a timely political crisis assailed the rightist mayor of São Paulo, charged with corruption, while both the state and federal governments were controlled by representatives of the same party.

The projects drew on different connections with national issues. The Rodoanel project was justified primarily for its regional economic benefits, and only secondarily for its impact on traffic in São Paulo. In contrast, the Niemeyer project was always justified in terms of the benefits it would bring for local traffic. In this context, in Rio the municipal executive led the project in isolation, while in São Paulo the state government transformed the Rodoanel into a strategic project for national development.

There were also different relationships between the political executives and the environmental bureaucracies of the two cities. In São Paulo, these were largely cooperative, while in Rio de Janeiro there was ongoing conflict between the municipal political actors and the state environmental bureaucracy.

There were also contrasting traditions and degrees of organization of environmental activism in the two cities. At the outset of the projects, there was no environmentalist reaction in São Paulo. In Rio, the situation was radically different, with the beltway plans attracting the attention of a range of environmental organizations and, in particular, the Green Party, whose principal location in Brazil is Rio de Janeiro city.

Social profiles of affected people

Differences in income and education levels can strongly condition people's capabilities to mobilize, shaping both incentives and constraints for individuals and social groups to take part in political processes.

In these cases, those who stood to be affected by the two highway projects had strongly contrasting social profiles.[1] In São Paulo, the typical victim of the Rodoanel was a low-income family, with self-constructed housing, a precarious employment situation (53.2 per cent), low levels of formal education (63.3 per cent) and restricted access to markets (88.5 per cent). In contrast, in Rio the Niemeyer project affected an urban and densely populated area. While this included residents of the slum Vidigal, the Niemeyer project most strongly affected the upper middle class of Rio de Janeiro, with high income and consumption profiles, as well as high levels of education (59.5 per cent have intermediate or higher education).

Social constructions of environmental risk

Beyond these socio-economic characteristics, people's perceptions of the environment offer a further important dimension to understanding mobilization. As Hannigan (1995) argues, a pre-condition for mobilization around environmental issues is that people construct important dimensions of their lives as 'environment'.

In a survey, we found that nearly two-thirds of those affected equated 'the environment' with 'nature', in the sense of elements of the world untouched by human action. In contrast, a little more than 15 per cent of the interviewees in the two cities gave the word 'environment' an eminently social definition, encompassing human beings, slums and cities.

The environment does not head the hierarchy of problems for people in either São Paulo or Rio de Janeiro. And when asked directly about 'environmental problems' in their neighbourhoods, 33.7 per cent in São

Paulo and 29.4 per cent in Rio cited unrelated problems. That people do not frame their everyday lives in terms of 'environment' is even more obvious if we consider that about half of those interviewed in São Paulo and a third in Rio, when asked about problems that directly affected their lives, pointed to issues that some might classify as environmental – such as pollution and the lack of urban infrastructure – but they did not name them 'environmental problems'.

Indeed, despite living in an area under construction, interviewees in São Paulo did not 'construct' an environmental problem: 77.6 per cent of them considered the environmental quality of their neighbourhood fair or good. They also expressed modernist values, associating transportation projects with likely socio-economic improvements. In São Paulo, 88.2 per cent believed that the project would bring benefits for the city, 70.4 per cent benefits for the neighbourhood and 65.8 per cent benefits for their family. Eighty-seven per cent indicated the following kinds of benefits: improvements in traffic and security; economic benefits; and even possibilities of environmental improvement in reducing noise and water pollution.

In Rio, what stood out for 23.9 per cent were impacts on lifestyle. Those who considered their neighbourhood a good place to live numbered 88.7 per cent. Rio residents strongly valued the status quo of their neighbourhood life, and in strong contrast with those in São Paulo seemed inclined to identify the social space in which they lived as an 'environment' to be preserved. In Rio, this romanticization of a way of life threatened by processes of change (see Elias 1984) reflects an idyllic construction of the past: 75.7 per cent consider their neighbourhood worse than or with the same problems as ten years ago. In contrast, the people in São Paulo seem to have a much more forward-looking assessment of the Rodoanel.

In all, there was a slightly higher level of 'environmental' preoccupation among those interviewed in Rio compared to São Paulo: 4.2 per cent versus 2.7 per cent. While small, this difference seems to be associated with the socio-economic status and the lifestyle of each group of residents.

Mobilizing structures

Even when people perceive a given dimension of social reality as an 'environmental problem', their access to structures of mobilization shapes whether and how they will react. These mobilizing structures range from people's willingness to participate in collective activities to their effective engagement in associations, their access to formal institutions and their previous experiences with mobilization.

Residents in both sites claimed a strong willingness to participate in collective activities in general. Eighty per cent of those interviewed in

São Paulo and 75.4 per cent of those in Rio de Janeiro claimed that they would mobilize around a local problem, and more still that they would make use of petitions (92 per cent in São Paulo and 70.8 per cent in Rio de Janeiro); meetings (83.5 per cent and 70.8 per cent); and work contributions (77.9 per cent and 45.6 per cent). Even willingness to mobilize around environmental issues appeared high: 48.3 per cent of those from São Paulo and 47.5 per cent from Rio declared that they would carry out volunteer work to help an environmental protection organization, while 49.2 per cent in São Paulo and 48.1 per cent in Rio de Janeiro claimed that they would join an environmental association. On the basis of these potential attitudes, we could expect major environmental mobilization in both São Paulo and Rio around these transportation projects and their effects on people's lifestyles.

But as we move from opinions and values to effective practices, we find that the former do not translate directly into the latter, and a new picture emerges. For instance, when asked about financial contributions to environmental organizations, only 10 per cent in São Paulo and 18 per cent in Rio claimed that they would be inclined to contribute. When asked who should solve a local environmental problem, the majority of interviewees did not feel responsible and instead indicated public authorities such as the mayor and the state governor.

People's prior information about environmental problems, campaigns and institutions also shaped conditions for mobilization – or otherwise. In these respects, residents in Rio performed more strongly: around 40 per cent of Rio interviewees could identify environmental organizations, campaigns or protection measures, compared with just 10 per cent in São Paulo. In Rio, 47.9 per cent of residents could cite programmes to protect the urban environment, whereas in São Paulo most of the interviewees (54.4 per cent) mentioned only campaigns for nature preservation. People in both sites knew about the highway projects themselves: 93.5 per cent in São Paulo and 91.2 per cent in Rio. Fewer knew about the mechanisms through which the decision-making/negotiation process occurs: the public hearing of environmental licensing. In Rio,18.5 per cent of interviewees had heard about this mechanism, compared with only 4 per cent in São Paulo.

Taken together, these data suggest that the group affected by the Niemeyer project had more cognitive resources to construct the project 'impact' as 'environmental risk', implying greater capacity to organize around and express environmental opinions. Cognitive resources mean little, however, without the associative networks and mobilizing experiences that support them. In this respect, it is notable that affected people in both Rio and São Paulo were more inclined to engage in activities related to their neighbourhood or church than to broader, issue-based associative life. Nevertheless, communitarian mobilization is an important indicator of the strength of intra-group links and capacity to resist interventions from outside. In São Paulo, 74.4 per cent of interviewees and in Rio 70.8 per cent participated in communitarian activities. Membership of other associations, while low in both cities, was higher in Rio, where 27.7 per cent of interviewees were members of an association – more than double the figure for São Paulo.

Regarding previous experiences of acting on 'environmental problems', the majority of affected people in both cities had never taken an 'environmental complaint' to any institution or association. Of those who had made complaints, in São Paulo 35 per cent had had their problems solved, compared with 42 per cent in Rio. This may reflect the channels chosen to pursue demands: while those in São Paulo had complained to public authorities – most to the city administration – those in Rio had worked through environmental agencies, the press and civil associations. This in turn reflects social differences. In São Paulo, the majority of citizens neither know of, nor have access to, channels through which to express opinions and complaint other than the state. In Rio, as we have seen, the affected people had higher levels of education and information, linked to greater abilities to express themselves effectively through a variety of channels. Those who have succeeded in their claims are encouraged to use these same channels further for future demands, while experience of unsuccessful claim-making can discourage future participation.

This discussion suggests that there are important differences of lifestyle, perceptions of environmental risk and resources for mobilization between affected people in the two cities. These differences help to explain the different patterns of mobilization in these cases.

The mobilizing process: actors and strategies

In attending now to the dynamics of mobilization, we examine how and to what extent affected residents mobilized in the two cities. This depended on how perceived threats to lifestyle, the social characteristics of affected people and the mobilizing and political opportunity structures interacted. In moving from a focus on affected populations to a focus on the mobilized actors, or activists, we see that they are not necessarily the same. We consider the strategies of those who mobilized both for and against the projects, and how they interacted.

Rodoanel Mobilization in favour of the Rodoanel was carried out by its proponents: the state government and the agency responsible for its execution, Desenvolvimento Rodoviário SA (Dersa). Together, they worked to legitimize the Rodoanel in public opinion. The central justification for the project emphasized its capacity to generate economic development, while the environmental impacts would be minimized through technical solutions.

Dersa followed three main strategies to legitimize the Rodoanel. First, it relied on thorough preparation of documents and specialists. Possible technical problems, environmental impacts and solutions were listed in comprehensive, complex and well-organized documents. Experienced and well-qualified engineers were on hand to defend the project in various forums in the face of possible criticisms.

Second, Dersa engaged in negotiations with local political and economic elites prior to the formal environmental licensing process. It held informal meetings with city council representatives, state legislators, mayors of affected municipalities and members of residents' or business associations. It also mobilized support from scientific and technical elites, especially in areas such as transportation engineering and urban planning. In this way, it was feasible to construct a discourse coalition around the economic rationality, technical efficiency and quality of sophisticated solutions to potential environmental risks which convinced even the technical staff responsible for the environmental licensing. These political negotiations were important for the creation of public legitimacy and for the prevention of possible mobilization against the project. To achieve the latter, Dersa controlled the project's environmental hearings, by calling, organizing and dominating them. This is evident in the numerical dominance of people from the public administration, mostly technicians from environmental and related state agencies and political officials from the state executive, during the hearings. Dersa's concern with the technical legitimization of the project became evident in the practices of the first hearing in the hall of the environmental state agency, which made it appear as an official event of the state government, and a legitimizing 'ritual' for the project.

Dersa's third strategy was to promote the potential benefits of the project aggressively, both to opinion leaders and to the public via advertisements on television, radio, buses and billboards throughout the city. Through this kind of marketing, the Rodoanel was constructed as a revolutionary solution for improving metropolitan traffic.

In contrast with this efficient defence, the Rodoanel project did not attract significant public environmental mobilization. Declarations against it on environmental grounds started to pop up in the media only in January 1998, after the environmental licensing process had ended. When they had the opportunity to express their positions, residents, members of municipal legislatures and leaders of neighbourhood associations did not question the project itself. There was a consensus around the economic rationality and the technical quality of environmental risk control procedures. They limited themselves to asking for clarifications, especially information about compensation for economic losses.

São Paulo's environmental movement did have strong criticisms of the Rodoanel, but did not express them much in public, nor in ways that chimed with the perceptions and experiences of affected residents. In criticizing the project, members of the environmental movement critiqued its road-building orientation within a broadened conception of environment, which included both natural and social problems within the notion of 'quality of life'. This contradicted the definition of the environment in terms of 'untouched nature' predominant among affected residents. The distinction between affected people and mobilized ones thus related, in part, to the cognitive dissonance between them.

Furthermore, the criticisms of the environmental movement made little impact on the project. Disseminated through the media, they generated little response from the scientific and technical community concerned with environmental issues. In contrast, the defenders of the project were constantly in the daily news, defending the technical and economic advantages of the undertaking.

The Niemeyer project The project initially presented in 1997 by the Municipal Secretariat of Transportation called for a widening of the Niemeyer Avenue. During the subsequent environmental impact study, the secretariat's experts concluded that a tunnel linking São Conrado and Leblon would be the best technical alternative. Thus, while the study had been prepared to evaluate the widening of the avenue, its conclusion paradoxically presented a tunnel as the best option. This brief story is a good summary of the differences in the strategic action of the two public agencies in the two cases. In contrast to Dersa's strategies in São Paulo, Rio's Municipal Secretariat of Transportation consolidated neither political nor technical and scientific alliances in favour of the project before announcing it to the larger public. As a result, it had to confront directly not only the environmental movement but also the scientific community, the technical staff of the state agencies in charge of environmental licensing, and members of the state and municipal legislatures.

The few defenders of the Niemeyer project, basically the Secretariat of Transportation of the municipality, its technical staff, some representatives of residents' associations and businesspeople, fell back on technical arguments, emphasizing the need to improve urban planning. Their principal argument was that environmental losses were the price to pay for the social and economic benefits that the traffic improvements would provide.

On the other side, the societal actors opposed to the project developed a series of mobilization strategies. A huge set of actors mobilized in defence of the 'environmental patrimony' of the city, including not just environmental associations but also neighbourhood associations, environmentally oriented politicians, business associations, residents and liberal professionals. Members of scientific institutions and representatives from the Workers' and Green parties, many of them living near the project area, joined the cause. The principal mobilizing actor against the project was the residents' association of Leblon (AmaLeblon), an upper-class neighbourhood that would be affected by the project, and these other actors were progressively enrolled through associative networks.

These opponents drew on various mobilizing structures to delegitimize the Niemeyer project. They participated actively in the hearings, questioning whether the project should proceed. They established coalitions with members of scientific institutions, attracted media attention, produced technical reports, organized demonstrations, petitions and events, distributed pamphlets and held informal conversations in the neighbourhood, in bars and on the beach. The presence of artists and intellectuals in the neighbourhood greatly facilitated their access to the major media that functioned as counter-advertising to the project.

The opponents made two main arguments against the project. The first pointed to its implied 'loss of quality of life', both for society as a whole and for local residents. While the Green Party questioned the broader 'development model' embodied in road-building and its associated environmental degradation, residents' associations argued that their lifestyles were 'threatened' by the project. In this sense, the mobilization against the Niemeyer project took on a defensive tone, an appeal to the maintenance of a threatened lifestyle. Post-materialist arguments were articulated by the mobilized actors, drawing on an idyllic vision of the environment before the acceleration of economic development, as well as a valorization of traditional forms of social life and economic production.

The second argument pointed to the technical deficiencies in the project and its proposed solutions to potential environmental impacts. These technical criticisms were mainly raised by transport engineers who specialized in environmental management. Indeed, these researchers played a central role in the critical analysis of the Niemeyer's environmental impact study. They argued that the project simply postponed the problems of traffic congestion in the area, and that it was conceptually flawed in scientific terms, particularly in relation to the measures chosen to evaluate the environmental impact of the increased car traffic in the affected area.

Mobilization against the project was also carried out at the formal level. The residents' association of Leblon and the business association of Ipanema sent official statements against the project to state and municipal authorities. The state Attorney General called for an inquiry to study possible environmental damage, in conjunction with the formal process of environmental licensing. Activists against the project, members of the Attorney General's office and municipal and state legislators organized and conducted the hearings. The social status and high levels of education of those affected, and their affiliation with political parties and environmental movements, gave the hearings the character of debate, with a massive presence and intense participation by residents. Not only environmentalists but also residents based many of their questions on the scientific and technical arguments against the environmental impact study.

Thus in Rio, while the project had the appealing justification of improving traffic conditions in three large neighbourhoods, the government was largely unsuccessful in disseminating this idea. Environmental mobilization was more successful in defining the Niemeyer project in a negative way, as 'environmentally inappropriate'.

Conclusions: comparing the dynamics of mobilization

Many factors thus worked together to create a successful environmental mobilization in Rio de Janeiro, while working against this in São Paulo. These factors are summarized in Table 12.1.

In São Paulo, the political opportunity structure made the emergence of environmental mobilization more difficult. The Rodoanel project emerged when the municipal and state authorities were in agreement. The state government, which proposed the project, had the political support of the agencies responsible for the licensing and the technical support of a cohesive bureaucracy. In the Niemeyer case, the municipal executive took the initiative without the support of other governmental agencies. The open rivalry between the municipal and state levels of government weakened the project, making the political environment more permeable to oppositional mobilization.

Other relevant differences concerned the perceptions of environmental risk held by affected residents. As we saw, the risks of the Rodoanel were largely not perceived by the affected population, or constructed by the environmental movement as 'environmental'. In Rio, in contrast, the affected area was constructed as the location of a specific, environmentally benign lifestyle by both residents and the environmental movement.

Rio de Janeiro and São Paulo

Table 12.1 Dynamics of environmental conflict

	Niemeyer project	Rodoanel
Political opportunity structure		
	Permeable	Not permeable
	Cooperation between state and municipal authorities	Conflict between state and municipal authorities
	Coalition between technical and scientific elites against the Niemeyer project	Coalition between technical and scientific elites favourable to the Rodoanel project
Profile of affected groups		
Social stratification	Upper and middle classes	Lower social strata
Social perception		
Environmental perception	Nature focus	Nature focus
Perception of environmental risks	Strong; oriented by preservation of a lifestyle	Weak; oriented by economic development
Construction of a technical scientific discourse	Construction of a scientific discourse that rejects the Niemeyer project	Construction of a technical scientific discourse that supports the Rodoanel project
Mobilizing structures:		
Cognitive	High information about environment	Low information about environment
Networks	Associative networks	Communitarian networks
Previous experience of mobilization	Successful	Failed

Mobilizing process		
Mobilized actors	Mobilized actors coincide with affected groups	Mobilized actors are distinct from affected groups
	Civil society (residents' associations, environmental movement with the support of technical and scientific elites) is the main actor	State authorities (state government and state enterprise with the support of technical/scientific elites) are the main actors
Types and efficacy of strategies	Low efficacy of authorities' confrontation strategy	High efficacy of authorities' negotiation and demobilizing strategies
	High efficacy of civil society mobilization	Absence of significant mobilization by civil society
Outcome	Conflict	Consensus/Co-optation

Source: CEBRAP – *Environmental Conflicts Area*, 2002.

Although mobilizing structures were similar in Rio and São Paulo with respect to residents' willingness to mobilize around local problems and environmental issues, patterns of mobilization took different paths. These reflected differences in previous experience of political engagement and access to mobilizing structures; differences connected, in turn, with the socio-economic profiles of the two populations. These differences also meant that in Rio the affected populations and mobilized actors virtually coincided. In São Paulo, by contrast, affected residents (who did not mobilize) and mobilized actors (from the environmental movement) were clearly distinct groups.

The Niemeyer project largely affected upper- and middle-class people with high levels of education, access to the media and to institutions. These people had the cognitive resources to identify the effects of the project as environmental impacts within the same broad framings as those used by scientific elites and environmental movements. In São Paulo, the people affected generally had lower income, consumption and education levels. With restricted access to the media and to formal institutions, they tended not to conceive of their social reality as 'environmental' in the same terms as the political elite's discourses.

There were important differences in the strategies of the authorities in the two cases. First, in both Rio and in São Paulo proponents of the project relied on the same argumentative strategies, emphasizing technical and economic advantages. But while this argument worked in São Paulo, where proponents of the Rodoanel were effective in giving it the positive connotation of progress, it did not work in Rio. Second, the Rio administration made few efforts to create alliances and consolidate technical definitions in favour of the project. Dersa in São Paulo did so concertedly and effectively, and promoted these to the public through an aggressive marketing campaign. Third, the good technical quality of the environmental impact study and report in São Paulo eased the construction of a discourse coalition among qualified members of the scientific and technical associations in the state, which helped legitimize the project. In Rio, the equivalent report suffered from deficiencies and contradictions, hindering both environmental approval and the formation of such a coalition to legitimize the project on scientific and technical grounds. Fourth, in the dynamics of the public hearings, the unity and preparation of the experts in São Paulo contrasted with the indecision and confusion of the technical team in Rio.

In São Paulo, Dersa also drew on a set of 'demobilizing' strategies that made environmental mobilization difficult. By initiating the Rodoanel in a 'degraded' urban area, Dersa made it hard for environmentalists to construct the presence of an 'environmental problem'. This contributed to the timid reaction from the Green Party and environmental movement. Dersa also chose to start the Rodoanel with a section that would affect mainly lower-income strata. Possible mobilizations by this group were cut off before they started by proposals to resettle and compensate affected families. With few mobilizing resources, these groups were quickly 'persuaded' to move. In this way, Dersa managed to neutralize the two actors who would have had reason to mobilize against the project. Thus, manifestations of opposition were few, timid, verbal and had little significant influence on the unfolding of the process. This in turn helped forge the consensus among members of the scientific and technical community around the economic rationality and environmental quality of the project.

In Rio, the main actors came from civil society, with neighbourhood associations, environmentally oriented politicians and business associations particularly active in the Niemeyer case. Forms and habits of associational activity had already been established in this area, and affected residents could thus build their mobilization on an existing organizational base. The neighbourhood association of Leblon was responsible, in partnership with the Green Party, for organizing environmental protests against the Niemeyer project. In contrast, in São Paulo the regions affected by the Rodoanel had associations with much more precarious structures. The absence of previous mobilizing structures increased the cost of mobilization, to the extent that it failed to happen.

It is these differences in political opportunity structure and in access to mobilizing structures which combine with people's varied, socially embedded perceptions of environmental risk to explain the constitution and effectiveness of environmental mobilization in Rio and its absence in São Paulo. In São Paulo, the high efficacy of the authorities' demobilizing strategies, and the absence of significant citizen mobilization, eventually resulted in the environmental licensing of the Rodoanel by 'consensus'. In Rio, by contrast, highly effective citizen mobilization met weak strategies by the authorities concerned, unleashing a set of conflictual processes that eventually thwarted the project and led to it being shelved

Finally, appeals to scientific and technical discourses, and the enrolling of scientific and technical elites into discourse coalitions, were important in both cases – and used variously to disqualify as well as to legitimize the road projects. Thus, while in São Paulo state agencies allied with engineers to use technical discourses in justifying road development, in Rio discourse coalitions linked engineers with other citizens in mobilization against it – and in disqualifying the technical solutions proposed by state agencies. These Brazilian cases thus show citizen mobilization as dependent on a set of factors: the political opportunity structure, the social perception of affected groups, the mobilizing structures and strategies they have access to, as well as technical and scientific expertise mobilized by agents. As it involves contesting the scientific and technical discourses of institutions, effective citizen engagement, too, can depend on the discursive and strategic support of scientific and technical elites.

Note

This chapter was written as part of the activities of the Development Resource Centre, Institute of Development Studies, Sussex. We would like to thank members of this team, especially John Gaventa and Lyla Mehta. We are also grateful to the participants of the seminars in which this material was initially presented: International Society for Third Sector Research (ISTR) Conference, Cape Town, 7–10 July 2002; Institute for Latin American and Iberian Studies/Columbia University/Cebrap – II International Conference, São Paulo, 18–20 March 2002; and 'Science and Citizenship in a Global Context: Challenges from New Technologies Conference', Institute of Development Studies, 12–13 December 2002. The chapter summarizes results of research conducted through an agreement between Cebrap and Ibama between 1998 and 2000, and it was also supported by the Hewlett Foundation. We are grateful for the collaboration of the interns Adriana dos Santos, Karen Weingrüber and Katya Salazar, and especially for the consulting assistance of Leandro Piquet in analysing the quantitative data. We are also grateful for the comments and the translation of the first version of this chapter by Kathryn Hochstetler.

1 Our data here were provided by a survey of affected social groups, with 452 interviews conducted in Rio from 14 to 20 July 2000, and 445 in São Paulo from 7 to 12 July 2000.

13 | 'Let them eat cake': GM foods and the democratic imagination[1]

SHEILA JASANOFF

Prologue

BioVision, Lyons, 26–29 March 1999. A French city long considered a mecca for food enthusiasts hosts a meeting ambitiously billed as a Davos for the life sciences, a place where political leaders, industrialists, pioneering researchers, consumer advocates and environmental groups gather to discuss the future of biotechnology. Contrasts abound. Inside the conference centre, the opening plenary features such luminaries as the Nobel laureate biologist David Baltimore, the newly appointed head of the World Health Organization, Gro Harlem Brundtland, and Europe's research commissioner, Edith Cresson, who concedes nothing in her defiant bearing of the indiscretions that forced the European Commission's extraordinary *en masse* resignation just a week before. Outside, Greenpeace demonstrators mount a protest, controlling visual if not verbal space. Inside, at the generously laden refreshment tables provided by leading biotech firms, a sardonic Eurocrat I have known for years tells me to beware: there may be genetically modified (GM) ingredients in the food, he cautions. Apparently he assumes that a critical academic observer of modern biotechnology must, by that very stance, align herself with the anti-GM forces of the world. In the evening, the distinguished guests are bused to City Hall for the *de rigueur* municipal reception, but their way is barred by fierce-faced radical farmers with trailing banners, demonstrating against GM crops; '*Minotaure sème la mort*', they chant. Freezing in a thin drizzle, the dignitaries wait impatiently until a half-hearted contingent of Lyons' finest arrives to smuggle them in from the cold through an unblockaded side entrance. It is a strangely contentious backdrop for unveiling biotechnology's newly benign image – as dispenser not of questionably safe and marginally useful 'Frankenfoods' to rich Western consumers, but of products that will help nourish the world's poorest and most needy citizens.

'Golden Rice' (Guerinot 2000) in particular – so named because its bioengineered capacity to produce beta-carotene, which converts to vitamin A in the human body, gives the grains a pale carroty hue. This innovation, it is claimed, will help solve the severe problem of infant blindness afflicting hundreds of thousands of malnourished infants throughout the developing

183

world. An Indian scientist puts the case with conviction. In India, he suggests, Golden Rice will easily be assimilated into local food customs that have already made a special place for grain of this colour. Tinted and scented with saffron or turmeric, served at weddings and other celebratory occasions, yellow rice in India is the edible embodiment of the smile of fortune. Now, the gene engineer's prowess can improve on the ancient craft of cooking with spices. Bio-engineered Golden Rice, its colour bred in the grain, is poised to take its place in the sun, perhaps heralding a change of fortune for the beleaguered food biotechnology industry. Or will it?

As we turn to this question, let us keep in mind the complex choreography of the Lyons meeting, with its cross-cutting lines of politics, knowledge and discourse: farmers and environmentalists on the outside, scientists, bureaucrats and academics on the inside – all speaking different languages to be sure, but all joined none the less in a dance of engagement with the same set of issues, expressed through stylized gestures (talks, chants, banners, blockades, receptions ...) that need no translation to be mutually intelligible. There is in Lyons a thick politics of biotechnology, but are the resources for conducting it as widely distributed as the technology's proponents hope their seeds will be one day?

Seeds of controversy

While industry representatives enjoyed the media buzz around Golden Rice, their new 'poster crop' for genetic modification, a substantial backlash was also forming. Vandana Shiva, India's celebrated feminist critic of biotechnology, was one of the counter-movement's most outspoken leaders. In an electronically distributed article in 2000, Shiva labelled Golden Rice a 'hoax' and charged the advocates of the technology with making a slew of false and unfounded claims about it: overstating the rice's nutritional benefits; failing to account for its total impact on individual and family diets; overlooking the logistics of food supply in poor countries; ignoring more traditional sources of vitamin A; threatening rice biodiversity; and establishing corporate monopolies on an essential food grain by patenting each trait of the product, as well as the processes for manufacturing it (Shiva 2000).

Reaction to Shiva's report made it clear that the sponsors of Golden Rice did not dismiss her claims as irresponsible technophobic ranting. Indeed, her analysis called forth a measured response from Gordon Conway, president of the Rockefeller Foundation, an early funder of research on vitamin-enriched rice. Replying to a request for comments from Greenpeace, Conway readily conceded that Golden Rice was not 'the solution to the vitamin A deficiency problem', but rather only a complement to a balanced diet containing other sources of vitamins. He also agreed with Shiva that the media campaign around the product had gone too far, seeming to forget that 'it is a research product that needs considerable further development' (Conway 2001). At the same time, Conway emphasized the central theme from the standpoint of the Rockefeller Foundation: there is no reason not to make rice, a staple of the developing world, into a more nutritious food, and if conventional breeding techniques are not up to that job, then genetic manipulation is surely fair game. No surprises here, given the foundation's long history of involvement in the agricultural applications of the life sciences. In an earlier era, the Rockefeller Foundation had harnessed a nascent molecular biology to lay the basis for the Green Revolution (Kay 1993). Support for engineering micro-nutrients into rice, thereby launching the next agricultural revolution, continues the same policy by other means.

Shiva's attack and Conway's rebuttal touch on several salient themes in contemporary debates about biotechnology – in particular, food safety and security; product promotion and media hype; intellectual property and indigenous knowledge; the role of multinational corporations; and post-colonial power relations among developed and developing nations. Familiar battle lines have been redrawn with reference to the merits and demerits of this particular technological application. The quarrel extends to the desirability for the world of an agriculture built on GM.

The 'case study' aspect of the Shiva–Conway exchange is striking, though not perhaps surprising. Immediate, colourful, consequential and polarizing, the case of Golden Rice understandably captured the attention of biotechnology's critics and defenders. The product became a convenient focal point for long-standing ideological conflicts. As a staple food product of the global South, Golden Rice is a particularly useful resource for symbolic politics: it serves both the narrative of progress and beneficence associated with modern biomedicine and the narrative of appropriation, manipulation and dominance favoured by anti-globalization forces. But narrowing the focus in this way has proved problematic for biotechnology critics in much the same way as the case study method tends to be for social analysts. The particular siphons critical attention away from the general. Deeper theoretical perspectives on what is at stake in the politics of biotechnology – more specifically, what is new and debatable about the politics of engineering *life* – tend to get lost in the noise about the individual application. The issue is posed in reductionist terms, as if whether or not to create a particular product through genetic modification is the most important question.

Of course, the product-specific debate also stands in for older, ongoing battles about progress and development in the Third World. It calls into question a particular framing of vitamin A deficiency as a global problem amenable to technical solutions through the ministrations of science-promoting institutions such as the Rockefeller Foundation. Scientists no less than Third World activists are engaged in self-conscious acts of framing. That much becomes clear from publications such as a 2003 article in *Science*, a premier US journal for the life sciences, in which Conway and his co-author, Gary Toenniessen, set out the case for using modern science to alleviate Africa's food security problems. Ironically, they employ a fictional device embedded within a scientific article to press their argument: a 'case study' of a particular Kenyan woman, 'Mrs. Namurunda', who is not, however, a real person; she 'represents a composite of situations existing in Africa' (Conway and Toenniessen 2003). Nevertheless, her story is told in highly specific terms, complete with charts and numbers showing how her insecure, unproductive farm makes the transition to security and profitability with the aid of science. The counter-vision proposed by Shiva and other Third World actors committed to poverty alleviation centres not on individuals like the fictional Mrs Namurunda but on communities. These analysts would rather rely on networks of local expertise, based on robust traditional knowledges of seeds and health, to address what they see as the foundational causes of regional economic and social disparities. In the work of groups such as Africa's Third World Network, one finds a determined resistance to the modernist, science-promoted vision of progress: one that begins with invention in the labs of wealthy Western nations and then is disseminated by multinational corporations, through mechanisms such as high-input industrial agriculture, to the rest of the waiting world (see Adezde 2004).

The problem for science and democratic theory, however, is more complex than either reading of the Shiva–Conway debate. Neither the focus on a specific product nor the rejection of science-driven visions of progress in favour of traditional agricultures comes to grips with the most salient questions about the political management of biotechnology. How should innovations of global significance in the engineering of life be governed to meet the needs and demands of a global civil society? How should civic capacity to cope with biotechnology's revolutionary potential be created and institutionalized in an unequal, but ever more interdependent, world? How, more generally, can societies that, for now, play little or no part in originating invention in the life sciences nevertheless gain meaningful roles in governing the trajectory of innovation? As yet, these questions remain unasked and largely unanswered.

For all its passion and commitment, the confrontation between Shiva and Conway remains captive to the conventional politics of globalization. In its focus on large structural forces (corporations, foundations, nation-states, intellectual property regimes, malnutrition, poverty, gender), it foregrounds the classical themes of colonial domination and post-colonial critique. It is played out on the cognitive high ground of the reliability, or not, of truth claims about a science-based technology. It is *not*, in the first instance, a debate about what forms of life, both biological and social, should be produced by means of genetic engineering, nor about how the technology should be steered or its uses directed by the global publics for whom its products are allegedly intended. It is *not* a debate about the dynamics of simultaneous technological and social innovation, the associated new politics of uncertainty and ambiguity, or the creative role that global citizens might play in imagining global technological futures.

This chapter seeks to reframe the debate on Golden Rice so as to bring these issues of technological governance to the fore, and it does so by repositioning GM rice within a wider political and cultural critique of biopolitics (see in particular Foucault 1985). Agricultural and food biotechnology, we should bear in mind, is not just a matter of scientists tinkering with the genetic composition of particular crops or animals so as to 'improve' them. It is about reshaping an entire network of production and consumption that addresses the most fundamental of human needs, food and economic subsistence. At one end of this network sits the allegedly sovereign consumer-citizen, presumptively capable of asserting choice in the marketplace of new products; at the other end are corporations and their governmental or private sponsors and patrons, whose upstream production decisions define the parameters of choice, through innovations that reshape the consumer's tastes, diet, bodily functioning, purchasing power and lifestyle options (see Doubleday, forthcoming and Jasanoff 2003b).

Biotechnological product design emerges in this view as a thoroughly political – indeed, *biopolitical* – moment. It produces not only new life forms but new forms of life. It is a trajectory of innovation that has enormous potential to restructure not only the political economy of agriculture but the very conditions in which human life is lived and the terms in which people debate basic notions of progress and betterment. But who is party to these new political formations, and by what means, discursive or institutional, can these parties express their views and values or exert influence?

To address these questions I first probe the history of Golden Rice so as to illuminate how the technology has been framed and who speaks for it; my object is to show how the design of the product embeds understandings of the people and life-worlds it is intended to serve. I then discuss the ongoing democratic critique of biotechnology and the public's role in governing this area of technological change. This inquiry makes it clear that there is an asymmetry in the production and reception of agricultural biotechnology. The 'crisis' that Golden Rice is designed to ameliorate has been cast in global terms; in contrast, the political capacity to resist the dominant framings of technology – more specifically, the democratic imagination that is a central concern of this chapter – remains historically grounded, institutionally and discursively circumscribed, and place-based in significant respects. This lack of symmetry, I suggest, is one reason why projects such as the development of Golden Rice are unfriendly to the flowering of bottom-up engagement in the politics of innovation. I ask in conclusion whether it could be otherwise.

Engineering life, engineering society

Canonical accounts of the birth of biotechnology often cite as a pivotal moment the meeting of Herbert Boyer and Stanley Cohen at a 1972 conference. Boyer's lab at the University of California San Francisco had identified an enzyme that could cut strands of DNA at specific locations, producing strings that could attach themselves to other DNA segments. Cohen's group at Stanford University had developed a means of introducing 'foreign' DNA into bacterial cells by using plasmids (small circular units of DNA) as carriers. Together, their techniques produced a powerful instrument for removing DNA pieces from one organism and introducing them into another. In 1973, Cohen, Boyer and Nobel laureate biologist Paul Berg inserted a gene from an African horned toad into the plasmid SC101 isolated in Cohen's lab, thereby producing the world's first genetically engineered, recombinant DNA (rDNA) organism.

Invention, according to such stories, is a matter of genius and serendipity, of brilliant insights sparked by chance encounters between prepared minds, of science put to use in solving well-defined problems. Critical, too, to conventional histories of rDNA has been the trope of precision. The extracted DNA is snipped from the source organism with enzymes that know precisely where to cut the strands; in turn, the 'sticky' cut ends know exactly how to join together with the corresponding base pairs on another DNA strand. Images of the process often depict the enzymes as scissors. The techniques are clean, impersonal, predictable and – from the standpoint of molecular biology – essentially failsafe. It is so transparently simple in conception that it can be modelled as a children's toy, using coloured plastic 'poppet beads' to represent gene sequences. Why, then, the political hullabaloo over this miraculous technique for redesigning life?

Industrial genetic engineering, to give the shortest answer, is not the same as inventive genetic engineering. It took far more to convert bio-technology into a multi-billion-dollar industry than the lucky discoveries of three California scientists in the years of the Watergate break-in and the Vietnam peace accord. It took law, to begin with. Intellectual property rules formed the ordered environment in which a fortuitous lab experiment could be reconceived as a useful instrument, and permission to replicate it could be licensed to industrial developers. The patent taken out by Cohen and Boyer in 1982 earned Stanford University, one of the patent-holders, some $300 million in revenues.[2] Building an industry also took a different kind of inventiveness from that of university-based bench scientists happily tinkering with DNA and plasmids. It called for a capacity to imagine how the technique of moving around bits of DNA between organisms could be used to alter living things in ways that would produce commodities, pro-mote consumption and make money. That second inventiveness had more to do with manipulating society than manipulating genomes: it was more about social control, in other words, than about controlling unruly nature. It was also the step that created the most obvious opening for politics, for it demanded the reshaping of society to accept biotechnology, just as it reshaped living organisms to meet real or imagined human needs.[3]

Making a saleable product is to create a need. That need may be essential for survival, rooted in human biology. Food, drink, clothing, medication and shelter, for example, are usually regarded as commodities that meet essen-tial needs. Without them we could not sustain life at any level. Yet in today's complex societies, the needs that most products meet are more often *made* than found. Advertising, brand names, store displays and planned obsoles-cence are among the sophisticated means that producers use to awaken in consumers the wish to buy their ever-changing commodities. The objects of desire that glut the markets of affluent societies cater to constructed desires. Even 'essentials' are designed to appeal to tastes that are in no sense natural. Many of us could not 'survive' without our morning coffee, but there is nothing inherent in human nature that requires our coffee to be sold in a dozen different flavours or a half-dozen different formulations, each served in three separate sizes. People did not evolve to need seedless grapes or long-shelf-life milk or apples of uniform redness, size and shape. Household chemicals did not have to be packaged in designer containers that would harmonize with high-tech, stainless-steel kitchens. The demand in each case was generated along with the product itself.[4]

Surely, though, the reader of realist inclination will interject, extreme needs induced by disease and hunger are not constructed. There is a real global AIDS epidemic, killing millions; equally, starvation, vitamin deficiency and infant blindness are not conditions that exist only in the imagination of multinational pharmaceutical or biotechnology companies seeking profitable global markets for their processes and products. We must tread carefully here, for the object of critical interventions into the politics of the life sciences and technologies is not to deny the reality of human misery or the hope that comes from getting on more ingeniously with nature.[5] The purpose is to hold science and industry answerable, with the utmost seriousness, to the fundamental questions of democratic politics – questions that have fallen into disuse through modernity's long commitment to treating science as a realm apart from politics in its ability to cater for society's needs (see Polanyi 1968; Conway and Toenniessen 2003): Who, we may ask, is making the scientific and technological choices that govern lives? On whose behalf? According to whose definitions of the good? With what rights of representation? And in which forums?

We see below that, well before its actual availability in developing-country food markets, Golden Rice is being produced within two discursive regimes that pertain particularly to development: crisis and salvation. In reviewing each regime, it is worth asking who has or does not have a voice in constituting the socio-technical system that Golden Rice at once embodies and elides.

Crisis and charity on a global scale The production of Golden Rice implicated from the first a network of actors that cut across conventional definitions of the local and global.[6] The scientific work was located at the Swiss Federal Institute of Technology (ETH) in Zurich, where Ingo Potrykis and Peter Beyer carried out their path-breaking research from 1991 onwards, with initial funding from the Rockefeller Foundation. In time, their project also attracted support from the European Commission, the International Rice Research Institute (IRRI) and private biotechnology companies including Zeneca Agrochemicals, the plant science division of AstraZeneca. In 1999, AstraZeneca merged with the giant chemical company Novartis to form Syngenta. A Syngenta news release of May 2000 announced that the inventors of Golden Rice had reached an agreement to work with Zeneca and several other public and private concerns 'to enable the delivery of this technology free-of-charge for humanitarian purposes in the developing world' (Syngenta 2000).

Regardless of their position in the network of research and development, all the major players represent their role as responding to a global public health crisis. They cite data from various world organizations to show that millions of people are at risk from vitamin A deficiency, and comparable orders of magnitude will lose their vision or die without dietary relief. For example, Monsanto announces its investment in 'golden' crops, part of 'a sustainable solution to global Vitamin A malnutrition', in the following language: 'According to the World Health Organization, vitamin A deficiency is a global epidemic, with around 250 million people suffering significant illnesses, including impairment of vision, inability to absorb proteins and nutrients, and reduced immune function. Approximately half a million children go blind each year because their diets are deficient in vitamin A' (Monsanto 2000). This is a 'global epidemic' which, by implication, demands solutions on a global scale by world organizations such as the World Health Organization (WHO). It is also an urgent need, requiring expeditious solutions. With 250 million potential beneficiaries, the effort can only be seen as a massive contribution to public welfare.

A May 2001 report from the Council for Biotechnology Information sounds similar notes: 'In fact VAD [Vitamin A deficiency] alone is responsible for at least half a million cases of childhood blindness and a startling one to two million deaths each year. Moreover, UNICEF estimates that some 124 million children around the world are dangerously deficient in Vitamin A. This is this [*sic*] health crisis that triggered the development of Golden Rice' (Council for Biotechnology Information 2001). Once again, the concerns are of global dimension ('around the world'), certified by global institutions (UNICEF), and demanding urgent attention (1–2 million deaths a year) from those in a position to step in with technological solutions.

These and similar texts either explicitly assert or tacitly assume the centrality of science as the instrument of salvation. In their account of Mrs Namurunda's plight, for example, Conway and Toenniessen first position her as a latter-day victim of the kinds of plagues that devastated Egypt before Pharaoh agreed to let the Israelites go free. Mealybugs, weevils, nematodes and fungal diseases blight her crops, while drought reduces her already precarious yield. All this changes when she adopts new disease- and insect-resistant crop strains produced by advanced agricultural research. Mrs Namurunda now makes enough profits to send her children to school and even contemplates exporting her farm products to Western markets. The authors conclude, 'Even problems that are new or were long thought intractable can be solved using modern science' (Conway and Toenniessen 2003). It is hardly surprising, in this light, that the first technical report on Golden Rice in *Science* represented its development as 'the best that agricultural biotechnology has to offer to a world whose population is predicted to reach 7 billion by 2013' (Guerinot 2000). The theme of salvation was sounded again when *Science* published two sequences for the rice genome in 2002. The journal waived the normal rules for depositing the sequence information in the publicly managed GenBank for the corporate researchers from Syngenta, allowing the company to propose specially

191

crafted, more restrictive rules of access. Defending this decision, the editor, Donald Kennedy, said the gains from publication 'will come to a legion of hidden beneficiaries: the rural smallholders in the Third World on whose productivity the nutrition and health of millions of people may depend. Who should make the rules for them?' (Kennedy 2002). The answer, in this case, was evidently *Science*, as the unelected but tacitly acknowledged representative of science writ large.

What is wrong with these benign visions? Is it not appropriate, after all, for supranational agencies such as WHO, UNICEF, the Rockefeller Foundation and Syngenta, not to mention not-for-profit journals such as *Science*, to pool their resources in order to combat evils of global proportions? Why should democratic theorists worry about this development instead of unreservedly applauding it? Ingo Potrykis, the chief scientific architect of Golden Rice, has asked these very questions and robustly defended the Golden Rice project's humanitarian motives. In an open letter to Hope Shand of the anti-biotechnology activist group RAFI in 2000, Potrykis expressed some reservations about the notions of public–private partnership that had forced him and his colleague Peter Beyer to work with commercial partners. At the same time, he defended such arrangements as essential if the product was to fulfil its humanitarian aims by reaching the world's poor. He also criticized university researchers for using the intellectual property rights system to set up more barriers to information sharing and to serving 'the underprivileged' than had been erected by industry (Potrykis 2000).

Despite Potrykis's optimism about his network's motives and strategies, four aspects of the construction of a global scientific gaze on vitamin A deficiency (VAD) leap out as problematic. One is the erasure of identifiable individuals and groups which almost inevitably accompanies the effort to define a global humanitarian need. We see here an analogy to the modernist state's planning vision which James Scott described in *Seeing Like a State* (Scott 1998). In constructing and thereby making more 'legible' a worldwide community of VAD sufferers, the would-be aid givers eliminate local particularities. It no longer matters where individual victims are located, nor what access they have to institutions through which they can assert a meaningful political voice. The beneficiaries become a faceless mass – described by categorical nouns such as 'the urban poor' or 'subsistence farmers' or 'victims of malnutrition' – uprooted from any political, cultural or spatial context. They are *dis*placed in the sense of being rendered placeless.

Second, the move to collectivize the malnutrition problem as being of global proportions also permits the 'solution' to be presented as a universal. Yet we know from thirty years of development research that place is critical both to the shaping of problems and to the effectiveness of solutions. For example, as Amartya Sen showed in his classic study of four great famines (Sen 1982), the supply of grain alone is not enough to predict whether or not people will go hungry in a particular region. Much depends on the socio-economic system through which people are able to exercise their entitlement to food. A decade earlier still, Mahmood Mamdani went to India on behalf of Harvard School of Public Health to see how a contraception programme centring on the distribution of birth control pills was faring on the ground (Mamdani 1972). Getting the pills into women's hands, Mamdani found, was not equivalent to getting them ingested. Many obstacles intervened. Once again local customs and institutions ruled the way the technology was used (or more commonly not used); cultural specificity modified and subverted the universal planner's beneficent, but in this case unhappily parochial, intentions.

A third significant problem is the elision that occurs when the technological innovation of rice bio-engineering is equated *tout court* with 'solving' the problems of hunger, malnutrition and vitamin deficiency. Gordon Conway implicitly recognized this point when he wrote to Greenpeace's Doug Parr that reports of the availability of Golden Rice had been exaggerated: much more studying and testing remained to be done, Conway acknowledged, before one could plausibly claim to have a reliable, standardized product, capable of producing high levels of the desired micro-nutrients, and, not least, effectively delivering them into human bodies. Even then, however, Conway saw only part of the difficulty of developing a working technological system that would connect high-tech Western labs to small family farms worldwide, and carry food from those fields to the mouths and bodies of needy children and hungry adults. In the imagination of actors such as Conway, the promise of science and technology was able to leapfrog (to use a much-loved term in the discourse of development) the very problems of state failure, institutional disarray and economic inequality that are among the root causes of the crisis that 'the science' of agricultural biotechnology seeks to redress. One could almost conclude that the precision that molecular biologists ascribe to the techniques of genetic modification had colonized the minds of development experts, allowing them to forecast a similarly frictionless precision in the introduction of biotechnological inventions into complex social systems.

Fourth, and finally, constructing a global problem implicitly bumps up the space of the political from the national to the supranational level. Yet the rules for civic engagement in this emergent space are far from clear, and the institutions for conducting politics on a global scale are noticeably deficient. In a recent essay, I suggested that, at the turn of the third millennium, the citizens of the world are engaged in a tacit constitutional convention which is, in effect, sorting out fundamental questions about the rights and responsibilities of actors in the realm of global politics (Jasanoff 2003b). These actors include corporations and other multinational agencies (for example, mega-foundations such as Rockefeller and Ford) whose transactions on the world stage have not in the past been held to clear normative standards or subjected to political checks and balances. An important purpose of global constitution-making, I suggested, is to fill this accountability gap, and I looked at ways in which developments in science and technology are forcing people to confront at global levels such issues of constitutional dimension as new definitions of selfhood and identity, new relations between citizenship and consumption, and new links between power and knowledge at global levels.

These, however, are arguably the relatively benign symptoms of a development (the emerging global commitment to norms-making) whose more dubious aspects the case of Golden Rice exemplifies in earnest. For here we have an innovative shift in modes of global agricultural production that is, at best, only loosely coupled to the forms of deliberation and participation that we would hope for in any working constitutional order. Stylized electronic debates between a Vandana Shiva and a Gordon Conway, or an Ingo Potrykis and a RAFI representative, are no substitute for the day-to-day work of parliaments, agencies and courts. Globalization, in this case, appears to entail a loss of definition in the forums and expressive forms of politics on issues that are profoundly political – and no less so because they are at the same time also scientific and technological.

Citizenship and the democratic imagination The global construction of VAD that underpins the case for Golden Rice represents this product as meeting both medical and humanitarian needs on a global scale. These framings claim to speak for millions of the world's most vulnerable people, and they thus carry enormous implications for the distribution of power and authority. When a need is represented in medical terms, not only is the person whose ills are so designated recast in the role of patient, but the care/cure provider is simultaneously cast as the authoritative expert. That expert controls the terms of debate and (a point perhaps insufficiently emphasized) also the resources needed to cure the medicalized condition, in this case the tools of cutting-edge plant biotechnology. Similar observations could be made with respect to humanitarian crises and the role of relief agencies in alleviating misery. Growing awareness that policy framings not only solve problems but allocate power – by dividing the world into categories such as victims and care-givers or lay people and experts – has led commentators on the politics of science and technology to recommend greater democratic scrutiny of framing processes.[7] But the means for securing such critical supervision have yet to be developed in connection with innovations arising from the life sciences.

In technical decision-making as in other policy domains, contemporary publics can hold their governing bodies accountable by formal as well as informal means, but the methods for doing so are constituted largely within the frameworks of national political cultures. Thus, the formal structures of the nation-state help shape the opportunities citizens have for questioning experts, demanding proofs, asserting their own knowledge claims and gaining access to the basis for the state's expert judgements (see Brickman et al. 1985). Supplementing the official processes of public comment and criticism are more deeply rooted traditions of knowledge production and use that condition, in any national context, the kinds of arguments officials tend to offer and citizens to find plausible; for example, seemingly objective, quantitative risk assessment enjoys greater credibility as a decision-making technique in the United States than in most European countries. These patterned ways of public knowing, which I have elsewhere termed civic epistemology (Jasanoff 2005), form an important element of political culture in modern knowledge societies. In turn, the legitimacy of public action depends in part on the capacity of national institutions and policy-makers to discern and cater to the epistemologies of their intended constituencies.

Not only governments but myriad other institutions both reflect and reinforce a nation's civic epistemology. Thus, in the legalistic culture of the United States, inquiries of all kinds, both official and unofficial, routinely adopt adversarial styles of fact-finding, exemplifying a deep commitment to the idea that truth emerges by pitting opposing viewpoints against one another. In Britain, a centuries-old tradition of political cartooning deflates the claims of those in authority, from kings and princes to ministers of the crown and their appointed experts. It was this cultural environment which turned a publicity stunt staged by the agriculture minister, John Gummer, at the height of the 'mad cow' crisis, into a public assessment of his government's credibility. Gummer's attempt to feed his little daughter Cordelia a beef burger before the BBC's television cameras backfired entirely when cartoonists and news programmes seized on his image as the archetype of an overreaching state intent on 'feeding' false reassurances to unsuspecting citizens (for a more detailed account, see Jasanoff 2005).

Moving to the global realm, where the proponents of agricultural biotechnology have positioned both the problem of VAD and the solution of Golden Rice, we are struck by the dearth of institutions and cultural discourses through which a global citizenry can begin to demand accountability. Perhaps the most successful effort of this kind was the coalition that forced Monsanto to retreat from its commitment to developing sterile seed technology, a move that, if successful, would have prevented Third World farmers from retaining and replanting their own seed from year to year. RAFI activists successfully labelled the sterility-inducing device the 'Terminator gene', after the hugely popular science fiction films starring the actor-turned-governor Arnold Schwarzenegger. With a simple act of naming, biotechnology activists brilliantly deployed Hollywood's mass cultural appeal to construct resistance against another perceived vehicle of American power: industrialized agriculture based on the proprietary control of plant genetics. In effect, the Terminator controversy amounted to a very public upstream assessment of a proposed technological development, and at least temporarily brought it to a halt. But just as one swallow does not a summer make, so individual instances of political creativity such as this one cannot take the place of a full-blown constitutional architecture. Given all the difficulties that stand in the way, are there elements of such an architecture that could help to overcome the present institutional deficit in the global governance of biotechnology. If not, where might such elements be most usefully inserted?

Conclusion: a new politics of knowledge

In an important sense, the work has already made much progress. Some four centuries from the beginnings of the scientific revolution, hardly a corner of the world remains completely isolated from the reach of science and technology or impervious to the promise of welfare that goes hand in hand with advancing human knowledge. Science in this sense has helped lay the foundations for a global conversation on the ends and means of progress. The rapid proliferation of global expert networks testifies to the rise of the knowledge society as a cultural formation that transcends nation-states and makes possible the very idea of globally imagined communities. To the extent that we can speak today of 'only one earth', it is science and technology perhaps more than any other form of human activity which have made that singularity a meaningful concept.

The problem for governance, then, is not the spread of techno-scientific cultures in and of themselves, but rather their increasing isolation from other institutions and modalities of deliberation. The danger here is not simply public alienation or apathy in the face of technological change, accompanied by a hollowing out of meaning, intimacy, connection and emotion. Real as these threats may be to the ideal of democratic engagement, more important still is the loss of reflexivity within the scientific enterprise itself, a phenomenon that disables modern science from recognizing, and admitting, how profoundly normative are its visions of progress. Science enters the political playing field seemingly shorn of values and prejudices; automatically coded as a 'public good', it offers no further justification for its existence, nor feels any need to expose its internally generated agendas to wider public inspection. Leapfrogging centuries of history and culture, biotechnology in particular announces its readiness to cure poverty, hunger, disease and death, on scales ranging from Mrs Namurunda's (fictional) weevil-infested fields to a million cases of infant blindness.

I have tried to show that, contrary to this friction-free vision of service to humanity, the capacity of techno-science to deliver salvation depends on highly political acts of framing that may or may not bear much relation to the felt needs of those whom science sets out to help. These framing exercises, moreover, occur in spaces that are often invisible to normal politics, from the research policy division of a multinational corporation such as Monsanto to the boardroom of the Rockefeller Foundation to the editorial pages of *Science* magazine. Attempts to democratize such spaces will pose major conceptual as well as political challenges, for they will require the breaking down of long-held assumptions concerning the neutrality of technical judgements and the confidentiality of business decisions. Yet if science is to fulfil its promise of global problem-solving, then there is no other course than to repoliticize it: not through capture by a narrow range of wealthy special interests, but by opening up science's hidden normative presumptions to authentic and inclusive public debate.

Notes

1 I would like to thank Les Levidow for perceptive and helpful comments on an earlier draft.

2 The patent was licensed to 467 companies during its fifteen-year lifetime. Berg apparently refused to patent any of his work. The George Washington University Law School (n.d.) *Law and Technology at George Washington University Law School*, <http://www.law.gwu.edu/tech/rowland.asp> (visited April 2004).

3 That biotechnology meets imagined needs is evident from such ventures as the production of the 'GFP (green fluorescent protein) Bunny', a rabbit genetically engineered with a phosphorescent jellyfish gene by the Chicago-based artist Eduardo Kac. See <http://www.ekac.org/gfpbunny.html#gfpbunny anchor> (visited April 2004).

4 For a treatment of the role of discourse in underwriting state biotechnology policies in Europe and the United States, see Herbert Gottweis (1998), *Governing Molecules: The Discursive Politics of Genetic Engineering in Europe and the United States*, Cambridge, MA: MIT Press.

5 A misunderstanding of this point runs through the 'science wars' literature taking science studies to task for cognitive and normative relativism. See particularly Mira Nanda (1998), 'The Epistemic Charity of the Social Construc-

tivist Critics and Why the Third World Should Refuse the Offer', in Noretta Koertge (ed.), *A House Built on Sand: Exposing Postmodernist Myths about Science,* New York: Oxford University Press, pp. 286–311.

6 On the dynamics of localization that inevitably accompany globalization, see Sheila Jasanoff and Marybeth Long Martello (eds) (2004), *Earthly Politics: Local and Global in Environmental Governance*, Cambridge, MA: MIT Press.

7 For one example, see National Research Council (1996), *Understanding Risk,* Washington, DC: National Academy Press. See also Sheila Jasanoff (2005), *Designs on Nature: Science and Democracy in Europe and the United States,* Princeton, NJ: Princeton University Press.

14 | Plant biotechnology and the rights of the poor: a technographic approach

PAUL RICHARDS

A right to development?

The vexed issue of plant biotechnology has been debated (in wealthy countries) largely in terms of risk assessment (is it safe?). Development policy experts and multinational companies (displaying varying degrees of self-interest) have attempted to reformulate international debate in terms of needs (Stone 2002). Attention is paid here to plant biotechnology from the perspective of human rights. A right is an entitlement protected by law. The existence of a right implies a duty-holder. Under international law, the state is the main duty-holder, but the international community at times intervenes where rights are not protected by states; for example, where local law and order breaks down. In what ways might human rights impinge upon plant biotechnology? The right to food is enshrined in international declarations. Arguably it has major implications for technology. A right to food could be taken to imply rights of access to relevant genomic information. It might also be invoked to protect the crops of the poor from unintended introgression from genetically modified (GM) crops (the claimed discovery of transgenic constructs in Mexican land races of maize has excited controversy along these lines; Quist and Chapela 2001). Duty-holders may include biotechnology researchers, especially in public sector organizations.

The approach adopted in this chapter is technographic (Richards 2000), as distinct from jurisprudential (see Mohamed-Katerere 2003). Technography is a label proposed by anthropologists and sociologists of technology (Woolgar 1998) to cover the description and analysis of technologies embedded within social situations, and to account for the ways in which this embedding affects agency, collectivity and technological function. Technography, in short, describes technologies from the point of view of how they are actually used, and not from the perspective of how they are supposed to work. The technographic case study in this chapter deals with the zone of post-war recovery in central Sierra Leone, where use of plants is embedded within social and cultural contexts of considerable complexity (Richards 1986). The aim of the technographic analysis is to grasp enough of these contexts to render key technological variables visible and tractable to analysis. Seed issues, it will be demonstrated, are an aspect of an acquired right to self-provisioning. The entitlements upon which this right is based become apparent only via analysis of farming practices. Current biotechnology strategies for rice (the main staple in the region) are assessed in terms of the extent to which they protect or undermine self-provisioning. The chapter does not seek to judge biotechnology. The purpose is to characterize the interests of rights bearers and analyse the responses of duty-holders, thus throwing some light on a debate that must take place between citizens and science if biotechnology is to align itself with human rights.

Technographic case study

The major human rights declarations cover the right to food and other social and economic rights (Klein Goldewijk and de Gaay Fortman 1999; Sengupta 2000). Starvation contradicts the right to life. But a declared right means nothing until it can be acquired. A peculiarity of the situation of the poor in rural African zones of post-war recovery is that the duty-holders – in the absence of a functioning state or viable market institutions – are the poor themselves. The basic entitlement is self-provisioning through subsistence agriculture. Humanitarian agencies may intervene, and thereby become temporary duty-holders, but can rarely supply all groups in the population. Typically, they practise a kind of triage – establishing feeding centres for the most acutely malnourished, providing temporary rations to some (displaced women and children, say) and leaving others to fend for themselves (perhaps the bulk of the population). The concern in this chapter is with this last group. How do they cope? What technological options or legal protections would activate or sustain capacity for self-provisioning?

War in Sierra Leone and its impact on the rural poor Sierra Leone has in recent years taken last place on the United Nations Development Programme (UNDP) human development index. Not only is it the most impoverished country, it is also the most unequal, having surpassed Brazil in that dubious distinction. The huge contrast in life chances between a relatively small number of Sierra Leoneans controlling wealth from the country's alluvial diamonds and the impoverished masses is a root factor in the eleven-year civil war (1991–2002) between the Revolutionary United Front (RUF) and successive government regimes. The conflict came to an end through stalemate and war-weariness. A ceasefire was finally agreed in November 2001, and the disarmament of the factions was completed in January 2002.

The earlier guerrilla campaign (1991–95) mainly disrupted rural communities on the Liberian border. After the 1997 coup, fighting later more or less divided the country along an east–west axis, with rebel forces controlling Freetown, the north and the Kono diamond fields, and government loyalists controlling rural areas in the south and south-east of the country. A roadless tract at the centre of the country under the arc of the Kangari Hills became a no man's land, separating junta forces along the Makeni–Magburaka–Kono axis in the north and the Civil Defence Force (CDF) in the south (from 1997 onwards).

Populations fleeing fighting in 1995–96 – during which time many villages were burnt – began to return in 1997–98, and were more or less fully re-established by 1999–2000, some within rebel areas subject to an international boycott on relief and others in government-controlled areas assisted by international humanitarian agencies. Porter (2003) refers to this boycott on relief as 'one of the most shameful episodes of humanitarian inaction of modern times', but it forced civilian populations to survive through their own initiatives, and now provides an insight into the right to food under conditions of self-provisioning (see below).

Rice genetic resources: a key to pre-war food security A pre-war study, based on field work in 1982–83 and 1987–88, showed that a significant contribution to the food security of indebted and marginalized farmers in Mogbuama, Kamajei chiefdom, came from management of rice genetic diversity (Richards 1986, 1995). Rice is an inbreeder, and produces a wide range of named, stable phenotypes, each with distinct agronomic properties widely recognized by cultivators. A range of varieties is used to exploit different soil and moisture niches along the upland–lowland continuum. Farmers also regularly observe and collect off-types for further adaptive experimentation (Jusu 1999; Richards 1986). Female farmers in the Gambia and male farmers in Sierra Leone are equal in their use of knowledge of rice varieties to exploit a mosaic of soils and moisture facets, but the same kind of interest is not found among male Gambian millet farmers, suggesting that the key factor is the agronomic plasticity of rice, not gender (Nuijten, pers. comm.).

Rice farmers in Mogbuama change varieties at regular intervals, but at any one time each cultivating household retains a portfolio of ten or more distinct types, to benefit from staggered output from three distinct niches (upland, lowland and mid-slope run-off/zone plots). Early rice (ripening in 120 days or less) is important as a pre-harvest hunger-breaker (Richards 1997).

Debt-prone farmers are especially concerned to experiment with early rices (Richards 1986). Some of these early rices belong to the species *Oryza glaberrima* (African rice). Dingkuhn and Asch (1999) ascertained that *O. glaberrima* types from approximately 9 degrees North (the latitude of the West African forest-savannah ecotone) tend not to be photo-periodic. The main swamp and upland rices in West Africa tend to be photo-periodic; that is, flowering depends on day length and not on date of planting or rainfall conditions. Samples planted at different dates all ripen at the same time. This is an advantage on an extensive family farm, planted in stages. But the photo-aperiodic early rices, by contrast, flower a fixed interval after planting. The sooner they are planted the sooner they flower. This gives the farmer the option to develop a moist, low-lying site and plant rice that can be harvested in the hungry season. This food security strategy was first described by European observers in the vicinity of Cape Mount (Liberia) in the seventeenth century (Jones 1983).

Perhaps unexpectedly, informants in Mogbuama recognized that 'strangers' (Mende: *hoteisia*; that is, in-migrants without secure land rights) are among the most committed to experiments in rice variety selection (Richards 1993). The explanation offered is that strangers, being poorer, have more need to overcome food insecurity, and spend more time on the farm making careful varietal observations than citizens, preoccupied with civic and political concerns (political campaigns or court cases). There is some quantitative support for this idea in the agronomic data discussed below.

The impact of wartime humanitarian intervention Mogbuama belongs to the central Sierra Leone war zone, where wartime and post-war humanitarian operations were undertaken by the agency CARE. The area was mainly controlled by the government-loyalist CDF resistance, and some activity was possible during the period of international sanctions (1997–99). The front line with the RUF lay only a few kilometres to the north, however. It was too risky for field agents to travel into interior villages to administer relief directly. Populations were obliged to collect benefits – sometimes by proxy – from secure, vehicle-accessible delivery points. Inputs included seeds and tools, and food to sustain work during the pre-harvest period. Off-road, a number of communities continued to resettle themselves without external assistance, living in intermittent coexistence with the RUF in bush camps (Mende: *sokoikun*, 'corners').

Under the circumstances, CARE was reliant on committees of elders it appointed to oversee relief distribution (village development committees/ VDCs). Supplies intended for the most vulnerable groups were often appropriated by the rural trading elites well represented on the VDCs, and later sold or redistributed to clients and kin, including those living in relatively secure urban conditions. This occasioned much bitterness, and it became clear that arguments over relief supplies exacerbated distinctions between commoners and merchant and chiefly elites, which many people later admitted fed the war. Much village destruction, it was regularly stated, stemmed not from the RUF but from disgruntled elements within local rural populations revenging themselves for past exploitation (Archibald and Richards 2002).

A long history of bitterness over misdirected and misappropriated development assistance unfolded in village meetings. In one case, an entire group of farmers had been denied inputs by the CARE village committee on grounds of their youth. The committee members (all village elders) declared themselves to be the vulnerable target group for whom the supplies were intended. The young people then moved into the bush, creating a 'corner' sufficiently resembling an RUF war camp to strike fear into the rest of the community.

It was clear that a new approach to distribution of food security inputs was needed. CARE opted to start with issues of grievances and rights. Even in remote off-road villages, base-line data show about a third of the population with some awareness of rights issues. A right to food was the single most commonly cited example (64 per cent of all interviewees claiming some knowledge of human rights). Women, youths and children were frequently named as the victims, and chiefs, elders and husbands as the main abusers of rights. Little was ever done about such abuses, people reported, because the main abusers were the local power-holders.

The agency linked this local discussion to input distribution. The deficiencies of the earlier seeds-and-tools scheme were subject to analysis from a rights perspective (in events known as Community Peace and Rights Days) and a new distribution modality devised. Instead of making bulk inputs available to chiefs, elders and family heads via the VDC, every individual willing to farm became entitled to register to receive a small starter pack of quality seed of her or his own choice. A crop scientist/geneticist who had carried out research on farmer seed selection (Dr Malcolm Jusu) was hired as consultant to verify local seed choices, work out a (local) seed procurement strategy, and test the quality of purchases (in earlier distributions up to 90 per cent of groundnut seed distributed to farmers had failed to germinate). Over 95 per cent of farmers now received the seed type of their first choice. Seed lots were distributed at the end of rights awareness workshops, each participant taking home an amount (5 kg) of the selected seed type in a draw-string bag.

A pilot was run in 2001. It was reported that although distribution to individuals seemed at first to threaten even more division, it actually had the opposite effect. Even the youngest family members felt they had a stake in the activity. No individual or family, however marginal in the community, was excluded. Heads of households were obliged to consult with family members in decisions about family farms. This created a framework of cooperation within which people were more able to begin to address some of the more burning issues of exclusion and injustice.

Implemented across parts of three chiefdoms, in communities on either side of the north–south provincial border, the programme was scaled up from 2002–03 (United Nations peacekeeping forces were fully deployed in RUF areas in 2001, disarmament completed and the war declared at an end by January 2002). Even remote villages were covered, with staff now safe to travel on foot and reside in off-road locations. In every village, the entire community above the age of fifteen was enrolled. This inclusive registration provided the sample frame for base-line investigations. Reflecting a full range of social categories in both on-road and off-road locations, the base line provides data to assess post-war food security strategies.

Post-war food security choices The base-line survey contains information on 833 people of fifteen years of age or above randomly selected (sample rate 10 per cent for earlier and 5 per cent for later registrations) from the total registered adult population of thirty-three villages in Kamajei, Bonkolenken and Fakuniya chiefdoms participating in the CARE Rights-based Food Security project (FS/RBA). The sample divides 50:50 between vehicle-accessible and vehicle-inaccessible settlements. In Kamajei, Bonkolenken and part of Fakuniya chiefdom, most villages were displaced in 1995/6, and people returned in 1997/8. In the other part of Fakuniya chiefdom, displacement took place at a later stage in the war (1998–99). Return commenced in 2000 but was not fully complete in some heavily damaged villages at the time of investigation (2002–03).

The basic data sets relevant to understanding local food security options include information on the seed variety choice of the informant, crops grown currently (seasons 2002 or 2003) and prior to displacement (early 1990s), and the soil and land types on which the various types were planted. There is considerable certainty as to the varieties named, since in most cases these were also required for seed distribution, and had to pass the test of client satisfaction. Varieties were collected and identified by Dr Malcolm Jusu, referenced to a base-line collection of 160 rice varieties gathered throughout the country in 1987 by Richards and Jusu, and observed at Rokupr Rice Research Station in 1988 (Jusu 1999; Richards 1997).

Variety choice and niche planting strategies can be compared by gender, civic status (whether migrant or citizen) and age (youth, elder), by pre- and post-war situation, and for people and communities in off- and on-road localities. Information on literacy, languages spoken, off-farm income and access to previous humanitarian programme inputs allows assessment of socio-economic status. Other data include information on participation in village institutions, knowledge of VDCs and awareness of human rights issues.

The results (only briefly summarized here) confirm a number of expected relationships. Women, youth and strangers tend to figure less well in indicators of economic welfare or vulnerability than men, elders and citizens. Off-road villages are generally in a less favourable position than on-road settlements. The most vulnerable group (the group least likely to have off-farm income or access to previous humanitarian inputs) tends to be young women married outside their areas of origin (that is, strangers) living in off-road villages.

Given the importance of rice as the basic subsistence crop in the project area, it is something of a surprise to find that 61 per cent of all seed choices were for groundnuts. By attempting an inclusive distribution of seed rehabilitation inputs based on individual preferences, large numbers of young people and women who depend on groundnuts as a cash crop for their personal needs exercised independent choice. Groundnuts are cultivated on first-year fallow plots after rice cultivation (requiring little extra land preparation) when there is a lull in activities on the household rice farm. The constraint with groundnuts is availability of seed (the seed: harvest ratio is poor, commonly about 1:4).

Groundnut choices reflect a focusing of post-war choices. One variety, *babagida* (named after the Nigerian dictator who first sent peacekeeping troops to Sierra Leone in 1991!), accounted for 85 per cent of all groundnut requests. Before the war, farmers in the sample planted a total of eight types, with the main choice accounting only for about 38 per cent of all seed. After the war, seven types remained in use, with the most favoured variety (*babagida*) now accounting for 54 per cent of all groundnuts planted (prior to CARE distributions). CARE requests represent a further shift towards *babagida*. In other words, the main request to CARE for groundnuts was for a variety the majority already planted.

This focus upon one predominant type, for a crop that mainly supplies a cash income, contrasts with the position for rice, the main food security crop. Farmers in the sample, considered individually, had access to only about two-thirds of the rice varieties per farm they had deployed before the war (2.71 varieties per informant compared to 3.82 per informant before displacement). This spells some loss of niche adaptability when viewed

205

from the perspective of the individual farmer. Farmers requesting rice spread their choices over fifty-three varieties, 73 per cent opting for a rice type they did not currently possess (in other words, they were adding to their portfolio of types). Those choosing rice (*diversifiers*, as distinct from those choosing groundnuts, who can be designated *bulkers*) focused on one favoured type. The data for rice support the hypothesis that successful farming for household food security in central Sierra Leone depends on having the right range or set of varieties, rather than the best single variety (as in the case of market-oriented groundnut farming).

The total number of rice varieties grown after resettlement, though smaller than the number grown before displacement (165 varieties post-war; 231 varieties pre-war), remains large. The use made of the major types remains more or less stable. The top twenty varieties of upland rice, accounting for 71 per cent of rice planted before displacement, represent 71 per cent of all rice planted after return. Seven varieties in the top ten before displacement remain top-ten varieties after return, and the other three were still widely planted. The main difference is that early rices account for only 20 per cent of all post-war plantings, compared to 28 per cent pre-war. Given that early rice is grown as security against hunger, it is hard to reserve seed for replanting. This apart, evidence of a general loss of rice biodiversity due to the war is rather limited. What has been lost is a degree of adaptability through loss of some early rices and through reduction in the total number of varieties accessible to individual farm households.

In a reversal of the usual position, off-road villages (2.79 varieties per farmer) seem to be slightly less badly affected by these changes than on-road villages (2.62 varieties per farmer). And as the cultural stereotype cited above predicts, 'strangers' seemingly have a better position with regard to availability of rice variety choices. The average 'stranger' currently plants 2.78 varieties (2.69 for citizens), and before displacement planted 3.95 varieties (3.81 for citizens). The 'stranger' living off-road has the highest access to rice biodiversity of all (an average of 4.11 varieties per farmer). All other indicators point to the economic marginality and vulnerability of this class of person. Range of rice varieties accessible to strangers emphasizes the importance of a portfolio of rice types as a defence against hunger. From the perspective of the food-insecure, having several rice types is 'smart' – that is, the trend runs counter to other trends in poverty and vulnerability.

Food security in former RUF-controlled areas Some of the smartest seeds in the portfolio are the photo-aperiodic early ripeners belonging to the species *Oryza glaberrima* (African rice). The conventional story is that African rice has no future. It is a 'residual' crop in areas where agricultural modernization is incomplete. But studies of how farmers actually use the material provide a different picture (Jusu 1999; Linares 2002). Discussing the recent spread of *glaberrima* types in north-western Sierra Leone, some of which farmers consider to be 'new' varieties, Jusu (1999) argues that in the absence of *glaberrima* releases from research sources, farmers have improved the plant through their own selection efforts. Likewise, Richards (1986, 1995) documents farmer interest in Mogbuama in screening unfamiliar *glaberrima* types as 'hunger breakers'. Unexciting to breeders, the species is far from 'dead' in the imaginations of the poor.

African rice can be grown on very poor soils, where its vigorous early growth withstands competition from grassy weeds (Jusu 1999). 'Strangers' (including displaced persons) with access only to poorer land tend to favour African rices among their portfolio of choices. In former RUF-controlled areas, where there was little or no international humanitarian activity, the adaptive tactics of 'strangers' became general. African rice now dominates the farming landscape, especially in the Makeni–Magburaka axis, an area commanding the important road to the Kono diamond fields, where the RUF tried, from 1997 to 1998, to establish some basic administrative control (including collective farming).

In September 2003, we asked, in Mayembere, in the former RUF stronghold of Kholifa Rhowalla chiefdom (Magburaka), why African rice was so prominent in a landscape in which Asian rice had been the main crop observed during fieldwork in the 1970s (Johnny et al. 1981). People did not want to farm long distances from the village because of the lack of security, we were told. The uplands close to villages became overused and soil fertility declined. Now only African rice can be grown. Farms are intensively inter-cropped with pigeon pea (a leguminous crop). This improves the soil somewhat and also yields a useful protein-rich foodstuff. The basic local meal has become 'red rice' with a mash of oil palm and pigeon pea. But in any case, an informant added, this type of rice, although it does not yield so much, ripens more quickly. 'We like it because it shortens the hungry season' (Richards, field notes, Mayembere, Tonkolili district, 12 and 13 September 2003).

Summary The technography of self-provisioning in post-war central Sierra Leone points to the significance of two key aspects of food security: range of seed types, and the adaptability of African rice genotypes to low-fertility soils. Proof of the first point is found in evidence (from the CARE data set) that farmers concentrate on a favourable type of groundnut (a cash crop), but opt for diversity of types of rice (the main food security crop). The second point is exemplified by the marked expansion in use of low-yielding but very hardy *O. glaberrima* in RUF-controlled areas cut off from international food aid from 1997.

Implications of technographic analysis: a right to subsist

Douglas and Wildavsky (1982) and Douglas et al. (1998) argue that risk and need always have a social context, and cannot be fully understood without taking that context into account. A key contextual issue concerns the viability of collectivity (how is a coherent and stable group formed and maintained?). Archibald and Richards (2002) develop a similar argument in relation to human rights. They link concern for individual rights in rural communities in post-war Sierra Leone to questions posed by the war itself about the viability of existing (egalitarian and hierarchical) notions of rural social order.

To foreground context in this way is to argue that human rights, properly understood, are more than the enforcement (justiciability) of a declared right in a court of law. Crucially, it involves an attempt to identify the ways in which notions of rights are embedded in local practices – living law, in the phrase of De Gaay Fortman (2001), or rights understood from an inductive perspective, in the language of An-Naim (1998).

The right to food in central Sierra Leone, it is argued, includes as an aspect a right to appropriate seed types (that is, those that best protect the self-provisioning capacities of the poorest and most vulnerable groups). Identifying the right to food as an aspect of living law does not emerge from the analysis of court cases. As people locally point out, there is no redress when rights are abused, because the abusers are powerful within rural society, constituting judge and jury on both village development committees and in customary courts.

The right to food, however, is not acquired in court but in *farming* practice. If external intervention is needed, the duty-bearers are not peace-keeping forces or the officers of the UN special court for war crimes in Sierra Leone, but those who guard and have access to the scientific and technological resources through which self-provisioning can be sustained or improved.

Identifying duty-holders If vulnerable populations derive their right to food through seeds, and if their seeds could be improved by scientific means, who are the duty-holders? The commercial sector is a non-starter. There is little scope for making a profit from seed sales to farmers in war zones. The not-for-profit Danforth research centre (endowed by agri-business) has cooperated on the production of disease-resistant GM sweet potatoes and cassavas for low-resource African farmers, but the future of these varieties is uncertain since there is no agreement on who will pay for the biosafety testing procedures (currently estimated at $5 million per gene, a figure reflecting anti-GM sentiment in rich countries).

Some developing countries have national public sector scientific capacity to link genomics to food security. China has developed rice hybrids and disease-resistant GM rices. But whether these will significantly benefit the most impoverished and inaccessible rural populations may be doubted. Song (1998) found that farmers in isolated regions of south-west China – predominantly women producing maize for domestic consumption or local markets – were more interested in open-pollinated maize types than government hybrids.

War-affected countries, however, generally lack the capacity to benefit from the genomics revolution. In Sierra Leone, war and post-war government funding constraints have rendered the national system more or less dysfunctional. The international agricultural research centres are perhaps the main hope for the application of genetic knowledge to food security in zones of conflict recovery.

Technology strategy In regard to the West African rice-growing region, the main institute is the West African Rice Development Association (WARDA).[1] WARDA has claimed success for a series of rices (*nericas*, 'new rices for Africa'), based on the transfer of genetic features of African rice into Asian rice (Walsh 2001). How should we regard the *nericas*? Is this the kind of seed likely to be embraced by war-displaced rural populations seeking food security?

The idea of selection and breeding for (low-yield but hardy) African rice was proposed by Jordan at the West African Rice Research Station, Rokupr, in 1950, but forgotten as Green Revolution ideas took hold. Revived by Malcolm Jusu (a Rokupr breeder), the idea was elaborated into a research proposal with British aid programme assistance at the outset of the civil war (Jusu 1999; Monde and Richards 1992). It was specifically anticipated that the food security needs of war-displaced farmers would be served by such research, with its stress on conservation, screening and selection of the hardiest genotypes. The proposal was characterized (by EU assessors) as old-fashioned and of 'no scientific interest' (in other words, not GM).

WARDA also planned a programme at about the same time aimed at unlocking the genetic potential of *O. glaberrima* for improvement of Asian rice (Walsh 2001). African rice was ruled out as the target because of the plant's architecture (simple-branched panicles). Inter-specific sterility between African and Asian rice was overcome by using a biotechnology technique (embryo rescue). The resulting *nericas* remain, in effect, Asian rices improved through accessing genes conferring hardiness in African rice.

The WARDA strategy is based on the assumption that farmers will readily abandon a larger number of inferior rices for a smaller number of superior types. This ignores agronomic dimensions of local coping strategies: management of land and labour constraints through the combination and complementarity of different planting materials. The agronomic strategy (Richards 1986) has the advantage that a portfolio of different seeds can be combined and recombined in variable proportions depending on circumstances.

There is no dispute that *nericas* might add to the portfolio of rice variety choices in Sierra Leone. But for this to happen time is needed for farmers to investigate where they best fit. For this reason, the *nericas* cannot be the answer to the immediate needs of resettling farmers. Modern Varieties (MVs) – including a number of International Rice Research Institute (IRRI) short-straw wetland varieties (the classic Green Revolution 'miracle seeds') – were widely distributed by development projects in pre-war Sierra Leone. Most disappeared during the war itself and have not been requested for recovery purposes. The only MVs required on any scale in the CARE base line are long-established varieties (CP4, a tall, late-ripening wetland rice of South-East Asian parentage – the antithesis of the Green Revolution ideotype – introduced in the 1960s, and ROK 3, an upland cultivar selected by a local breeder, G. S. Banya, from material collected in Kailahun and first released in 1972). This suggests that humanitarian agencies are right to be cautious about innovations as part of a recovery strategy.

Technography provides no evidence that food-insecure farmers will cease viewing rice in terms of a *range* of types. From a rights perspective, it can be concluded that for WARDA to fulfil a duty to the food-insecure, it ought to develop a more diversified technology support strategy for West African rice farmers, emphasizing the conservation and effective management of existing 'low potential' types in addition to focusing on input-intensive innovation pathways. A problem is the bias of science towards the excitement of the unknown. Supporting the right to food requires courage to use scientific knowledge to take the path of 'no scientific interest'.

Conclusion

Distinct dimensions of agricultural intensification include intensification of energy inputs and intensification in use of information. Liebig's discoveries in soil chemistry and mechanization combined to provide the basis for modern energy-intensive agriculture. Management of genetic information through scientific breeding and (more recently) developments in functional genomics are important aspects of information intensification. Informatics offers new trade-offs. Energy efficiency can be enhanced through better information on micro-variation in soil fertility, for example, as is the case in modern precision agriculture. The argument from indigenous knowledge studies is that the rural self-provisioning poor have always been precision agriculturalists. A key tool is possession of a range of niche-adapted crop types. Some components of this farmer knowledge may relate, explicitly, to genetic potential (Soleri and Cleveland 2001). Such adaptive knowledge, this chapter suggests, is an important aspect of the acquired right to food exercised by the African self-provisioning poor.

Pro-poor agricultural biotechnology would need to protect and (if possible) enhance such knowledge. Florence Wambugu (a Kenyan proponent of GM) argues that a benefit of new seed technologies for the poor is that the 'technology is in the seed' (quoted in Glover 2003). Under this conception, genetically modified planting materials become the ultimate 'smart' seed. As noted above, 'smart' planting materials have a long history in the West African rice zone. African rice reached the New World – perhaps hidden in the hair of female slaves stripped of all other possessions – to become a back-yard food-security crop in slave households. The ritualized planting of small fields of 'providence rice' by twentieth-century African-American ex-slaves, in places where rice was no longer eaten as a food (Vernon 1993), kept alive the memory of an acquired right embodied in planting materials that not even chattel slavery could extinguish. Disease-free sweet potato or cassava, or *nerica* rices, might or might not serve to enhance this right. But a danger with GM crops is that over-enthusiastic repackaging of genetic information renders the planting material indecipherable to the low-input user faced with highly uncertain conditions (and this heightened uncertainty is now reality for so many African subsistence farmers threatened by war or HIV/AIDS). Stone (2004) argues that a major problem with GM cotton for peasant producers in India is that they do not know how to modify planting strategies for these new seeds in times of drought or rainfall excess. Coherence, predictability and control have been lost. Pyramiding genes into a single, high-performance seed package – the breeding strategy for the *nerica* rices – may risk similar outcomes. Possession of a range of rice varieties allows the *mix* to be varied by the user. Seed as a magic bullet offers no such choice. Either it works or it does not. It is not clear that the new WARDA rices enhance the *versatility* of the poorest of the poor. This might not matter if there were other duty-holders in the field. But war implies the retreat of the market and the collapse of state institutions.

The international agricultural research centres have a unique role in relation to the right to food. This is not to suggest that research on high-yield cultivars substituting for a multiplicity of local types by itself fails to meet human rights standards. The problem would arise only if such activities were pursued to the exclusion of attempts to maintain the range of materials through which the rural poor already exercise their acquired right to food security through self-provisioning.

Note

1 WARDA is itself currently displaced by the war in Côte d'Ivoire from its headquarters in Bouake.

FOUR | **Participation and the politics of engagement**

Commentary

MELISSA LEACH, IAN SCOONES AND
BRIAN WYNNE

Partly in response to the acknowledged problems in the relationships between publics and science, there has been a rush in recent years to increase public participation in issues involving science and technology. Events have been hosted by a variety of organizations employing a variety of techniques – from citizens' juries to consensus conferences, deliberative panels and multi-criteria mapping. Their foci have been different, with some responding to crisis and concerns over risks from technology; some aimed at including citizen input and expertise in particular plans and decisions; and some with a broader mandate to explore wider technology futures and development options.

This section draws together several examples of such initiatives. John Forrester and Steve Cinderby illustrate the use of Geographical Information Systems in the UK and South Africa to incorporate citizen expertise into models – of breast cancer and water quality – and to engage in discussion of the scenarios produced from such combinations of citizen and expert data. Jason Chilvers discusses the use of deliberative and inclusionary processes to engage citizens in debate about waste management options in their local areas and the creation of networks to link such local processes. Audley Genus and Tee Rogers-Hayden show how the Royal Commission on Genetic Modification in New Zealand attempted to offer a space for an open-ended discussion of strategic options, although the limits of this quickly became apparent. Elijah Rusike describes a citizens' jury and scenario workshopping process in Zimbabwe which investigated rural futures, and particularly the role of biotechnologies within them.

Across these cases, a number of questions emerge concerning the terms of public participation, and the models of citizenship these imply. There has been a long history of reflection on these issues in the context of development interventions that have attempted to create spaces for invited participation. First, these reflections have identified invited participation as a social event in which particular types of power dynamics come to prevail, resulting in the exclusion of particular social groups, knowledges or tacit ontologies (e.g. Mosse 1994). Second, such events are often orchestrated, convened in the terms of their host institutions, whether these are local governments, aid agencies or activist NGOs. The effect is often to introduce a certain instrumentalism, whereby citizens are enrolled in a set of institutionally pre-defined agendas where 'science' or 'risk issues' are presented in a particular way. Citizens are cast as those who 'use or choose' among a given array of options, rather than as those who might 'make or shape' agendas derived from their own framing of the issues (Cornwall and Gaventa 2001). Third, a consequence of these dynamics is that participatory processes are vulnerable to framing in terms of the knowledges and life-worlds of the contextually powerful; as Chambers asks, 'Whose reality counts?' (Chambers 1997). Fourth, questions arise about the relationship between invited spaces and wider political processes: whether by their nature invited spaces are isolated and isolating, or whether they are the crucible for broader processes of social and political transformation (Cornwall 2002). This in turn raises broader questions about the institutional and political context within which participation takes place and the ends it is expected to serve: whether it involves manipulation or co-option to support the status quo and divert opposing voices or engenders social transformation will depend on the nature of the state, its relationship with civil society, and the issue in question. Finally, a set of questions arises concerning the relationship between participation and other citizenship rights. It has been argued that the right to participation is a prior right, in that only through participation can people claim other – material, social or political – rights and so become full citizens. It is also argued that the process of participating provides a context for the performance of citizenship, and for social and experiential learning about what it means to be a citizen. The extent to which such action-based learning carries beyond the invited setting into wider political arenas, and engenders broader processes of empowerment and rights-claiming, will, however, depend on the context. As several chapters in this book have noted, there are particular difficulties in 'scaling up' invited participation into global arenas.

As Chapter 2 outlined, different theories of citizenship are linked with particular models of participation. But the converse is also true: that different modes of participation implicitly create different models of citizenship. What has emerged from the long experience with invited participation in development, and which is echoed to some extent in the cases in this section, is that very often the forms of citizenship implied are highly circumscribed.

Much of the debate about public engagement in issues concerning science and technology has been cast in terms of the oppositions between participation and non-participation, scientific expertise and lay knowledge, quantitative and qualitative, and reductionist and holistic. As Andy Stirling argues, however, a more salient distinction is between whether processes are 'open' or 'closed', drawing attention to considerations of power, transparency and accountability in policy justification and appraisal. This applies to any process. Indeed, as he argues, and echoing the development studies critiques above, processes that are labelled 'participatory' may be just as closed as those that are not.

The focus on invited, or orchestrated, participation within both development studies and science studies has perhaps diverted attention from the myriad other ways in which people practise citizenship in relation to issues involving science and technology. These range from pressing perspectives and claims through the law, the media and the Internet to organized activism and protest. These draw on multiple identifications, whether of consumer, green environmentalist, feminist, anti-war, anti-globalization, victim or a host of others. They too may, depending on their form and context, offer opportunities for opening up debate; or in their own particular ways, they may have closing down effects. While these avenues often require organized forms of solidarity and performative citizenship, there may be other more private, hidden or tacit forms of citizenship which find their expression through irony, satire, jokes, hidden transcripts and 'weapons of the weak' (Scott 1985, 1990).

A key question concerns the extent to which these avenues, as complements or alternatives to invited participation, offer a vista of cultural possibilities for new forms of politics and democratic imaginations. One needs to ask whether, and under what conditions, and in what combinations, they offer routes to more vital forms of dissent, to cognitive justice, to genuine negotiation of knowledges, and to political negotiation between ways of life grounded in mutual recognition and respect. This challenge has never been more pressing given that human subjectivities are at the same time being forged through a new politics of the global, and through an increasing pertinence of the politicization of the private self and the body raised by the challenges of new technologies. What is certain is that among this plurality and hybridity, dialogue, reflexivity and a practised form of performative citizenship must take centre stage, recapturing diverse imaginations of the future in the face of pervasive scientizing, globalizing and neo-liberalizing discourses. As Sheila Jasanoff put it:[1] 'I am calling for us to embrace a more complete imagination of the citizen; somebody with a lifecycle, with a history ... someone who knows things and has a capacity to make decisions. If we could elevate that discourse of citizenship then we could revive the political from the decline into which it has fallen in recent years.'

Note

1 In a concluding commentary to the IDS conference 'Science and Citizenship in a Global Context: Challenges from New Technologies' in December 2002.

15 | Opening up or closing down? Analysis, participation and power in the social appraisal of technology

ANDY STIRLING

Participation and analysis in social appraisal

Not without some irony, burgeoning discourses on participation have become a key theme in the globalizing governance of science and technology. As Leach and Scoones discuss (Chapter 2), experience in the North and the South is convergent in several ways. In both settings, the language of 'inclusion', 'engagement' and 'deliberation' is moving into successive political arenas. Beginning in the planning and implementation of specific projects and programmes, a wave of increasing attention to participation is moving through more general frameworks for environmental regulation and the governance of 'technological risk'. New political arenas look set to open up as 'upstream' processes of knowledge production, technological innovation and institutional commitment to technology begin to acquire their own distinctive discourses on participation.

This emergence of new avenues for social agency in the governance of science and technology is presaged in earlier academic trends. Despite the cross-disciplinary differences, understandings of society–technology relationships arising in philosophy, economics, history and social studies paint a common picture (Williams and Edge 1996). Earlier deterministic, linear notions of 'progress' have given way to a picture of contingency (David 1985), social shaping (Bijker 1995), momentum (Hughes 1983), lock-in (Arthur 1989), autonomy (Winner 1977) and 'entrapment' (Walker 2000). The form and direction taken by our science and technology are no longer seen as inevitable and monolithic, awaiting 'discovery' in nature. Instead they are increasingly recognized as being open to shaping by individual creativity, collective ingenuity, cultural priorities, institutional interests, stakeholder negotiation and the exercise of power. The irony is thus intensified. Just at a time when globalization seems to render the governance of science and technology more obscure, remote and inaccessible, so we begin to appreciate the inherent openness to the exercise of human agency and – potentially – to deliberate social choice.

Even if 'deliberate' only from the point of view of incumbent interests, the message is that the directions taken by scientific and technological developments have always effectively been subject to social choice. These choices have, in turn, always been informed by more specific processes (whether explicit or implicit, broad or narrow) of social appraisal. In this sense, then, the advent of new participatory discourses might be seen as an incipient move towards the broadening, diversification and enriching of established practices for the social appraisal of science and technology.

From an evaluative perspective associated with participatory discourses, we are faced with a stark dichotomy. On the one hand (so it goes), there are the established, narrow, rigid, quantitative, opaque, exclusive, expert-based, analytically rigorous procedures, tending to privilege economic considerations and incumbent political and commercial interests (Collingridge 1980; Flyvbjerg 1998; Wynne 1975). Broadly, these may be seen to include approaches such as risk and cost–benefit analysis, technology and lifecycle assessment, as well as Delphi methods and expert advisory committees. On the other hand (so it goes), there are the new, relatively unconstrained, qualitative, sensitive, inclusive, transparent, deliberative, democratically legitimate processes, tending to offer greater emphasis on otherwise marginal issues and interests (such as environmental protection, public health and distributional fairness) (Fischer 1990; Irwin 1995; Sclove 1995). Examples here might be stakeholder forums, consensus conferences, citizens' panels, focus groups and deliberative polls.

There can be no doubting the substance and salience of this dichotomy in many instances. Whether as a cause or as an effect, the emergence of new participatory practices is often associated with increasing acknowledgements of, aspirations towards (and sometimes even achievements in) the greater and more deliberate exercise of a wider agency in the social choice of technology. Many see this as welcome, overdue and insufficient. Yet it is also clear that there exist certain paradoxical, expedient and rhetorical elements in emerging discourses on participation (Irwin 2001b; Levidow 1999; Wakeford 2001). Although the details are complex and diverse, there are some important common questions, which also seem to pervade both Northern and Southern settings. Exactly why are we seeing this increasing interest in participation? Which rationales and motivations are more important for different policy actors? Are there commonalities, synergies or tensions that cross-cut the apparently simple dichotomy? Are there important similarities or differences in the ways in which these styles engage with institutional power? What are the broader social and political implications?

Amid the intensive high-profile activity and discussion, answers to these kinds of question are usually given in terms of the dichotomy itself. Protagonists tend to take up polarized positions, with others constructing intermediate or synthetic positions, which are equally framed according to the analysis/participation dichotomy. There seems curiously little critical attention to the validity and utility of the conceptual dichotomy itself. In particular, there seems to be a neglect of important transcendent and cross-cutting issues, which divide analytic and participatory approaches alike. Some of these may in some circumstances be of greater importance than the dominant distinction between the 'analytic' and 'participatory' categories themselves.

Drawing mainly on experience in the science policy and risk regulation fields in Northern settings, this chapter offers a brief survey of a few key issues. First, it reviews three distinct perspectives on the role of participation in social appraisal and examines the contrasting attitudes to power that are embodied in each. This is then taken as a basis for exploring the extent to which both participatory and analytic approaches raise similar issues of framing and justification. The argument is developed that there exists a crucial general feature in the design and conduct of social appraisal that is equally relevant to participatory and analytic approaches alike, but which remains unduly neglected by each. This concerns whether it is the aim of social appraisal to 'open up' or 'close down' wider policy discourses. The discussion closes by querying the implications of this distinction for globalizing processes of governance in the social choice of technology.

Empowerment, quality and trust

In considering the range of imperatives, rationales and motivations bearing on participation in the social appraisal of science and technology, a useful distinction may be drawn between three types of perspective: normative, instrumental and substantive (Fiorino 1989; Fineberg 1996). From a normative view, participation is just *the right thing to do*. From an instrumental perspective, it is a better way to achieve particular ends. In substantive terms, it leads to *better* ends.

Normative commitments in social appraisal may take a number of forms. Curiously value-laden notions of 'value-free analysis' and emotive appeals to 'sound science' are a common defence of established expert procedures (Byrd and Cothern 2000). In the case of participation, the normative imperatives rest on principles of democratic emancipation, equity, equality and social justice. Invoking authorities such as Rawls (1971) and Habermas (1975), the formal rationale here hinges on a commitment to the empowerment of citizens (especially those with marginal or excluded interests), rather than dominant institutions or elite social groups. At minimum, this rests on the idea that contemporary societies should – as an end in and of itself – be engaging all relevant constituencies in making decisions about scientific and technological choices.

This normative democratic perspective has important specific bearings on the structuring of social appraisal. It is clear, for instance, that from this perspective, the narrow involvement, limited remits, constraining structures, privileged institutional interests and opaque technical procedures associated with expert analysis are all intrinsically problematic in their own right. They conflict with Habermasian principles of 'ideal speech' (1968, 1984), with Rawlsian notions of 'public reason' (1993, 1997) and with a multitude of derived evaluative criteria held ideally to be associated with effective engagement in social appraisal (Clark et al. 2001; Petts 2001; Renn et al. 1995). These deficiencies apply irrespective of the outcomes of appraisal as they actually arise. In short, under this normative democratic view, participation is self-evidently a good thing in its own right, without the need for further justification.

The second type of motivation for greater participation in the social appraisal of science and technology is *instrumental* – as seen from the point of view of incumbent interests. This instrumental utility can take a variety of forms. One is the aim of providing 'social intelligence' concerning the nature of public sensibilities in a particular area of technological activity (Grove-White et al. 1997, 2000). Treated as strategic information, this may help determine the likelihood of adverse responses to particular courses of action. Accordingly, it may aid strategies for the shaping, presentation and implementation of pre-committed policy choices, or it may be useful as guidance on how best to forestall or mitigate negative social reactions.

Beyond enhancing the social credibility of particular choices, another instrumental motivation for participation aims at fostering more general public trust in the institutions and procedures that are responsible for these choices. Reputation management is an important strategic activity for public and commercial bodies alike (HMG 2003). One important element in this often highly competitive arena is a capacity to demonstrate a commitment to or track record in public engagement. Irrespective of any normative or other considerations, this factor alone provides important instrumental incentives for the top-down commissioning of 'participatory' exercises. Themes of credibility and trust have a high profile in the broad academic literature on risk and technology policy (Margolis 1996; Misztal 1996; Seligman 1997). Although more muted in the participation literature itself, these themes are none the less often prominent in the framing of funding bids for public engagement research.

Where corporate interests are highly sensitive to consumer markets, the outcomes of participatory deliberation may have a direct instrumental value in their own right. With careful management of the process, however, sponsoring institutions may sometimes hope to gain instrumental benefits from participatory social appraisal, irrespective of whether the outcomes are actually adopted. Indeed, it is well recognized that the recommendations made in participatory appraisal often remain effectively ignored (Renn et al. 1995). Of course, persistent non-adoption can have a negative impact on trust and credibility. But here there is an interesting opportunity for strategic defence. A crucial difference between instrumental and normative democratic perspectives focuses on the frequent inclusion of a 'policy uptake' criterion in evaluation (Rowe and Frewer 2000). From a normative democratic perspective, non-adoption of recommendations might be interpreted as a failure on the part of the encompassing governance process. A distinguishing feature of an instrumental perspective, on the other hand, is that the delivery of recommendations that are not adopted by incumbent interests is interpreted as a failure on the part of the participatory exercise itself.

The third form of rationale for participatory social appraisal is *substantive*. These types of reason focus on notions such as authenticity, robustness and quality in the choices that actually result from appraisal. Like equity and equality of process, the sensitivity of social appraisal to different epistemological 'ways of knowing', ontological 'ways of being' (Leach and Scoones, Chapter 2) or hermeneutic 'ways of acting' (Wynne 1996) may be seen as normative aspects of empowerment. But the extent to which the resulting technology choices are actually congruent with, and authentically embody, diverse social knowledges, values and meanings is a substantive matter. In this sense, the process of social learning undertaken in appraisal may also be distinguished from more instrumental notions of social intelligence in that it is oriented towards informing the substance of the social choices themselves, rather than their presentation, implementation or associated management strategies. Citizens are engaged as subjects rather than as objects of discourse. The aim lies in the pursuit of more 'socially robust' scientific and technological pathways (Grove White et al. 2000).

In policy circles, expressions of substantive rationales for participation in social appraisal are more positive and decisionistic (Wynne 1997), emphasizing the 'quality' of the resulting decisions (Coenen et al. 1998). Such notions of quality in governance outcomes may remain largely tacit, resting simply on the enhanced breadth and depth of knowledge elicited in participatory approaches. But substantive rationales for participation may also rest on more specific and concrete notions of quality – for instance, involving the degrees of stringency achieved in the protection of human or environmental health. Here, it is reasoned that participation by those groups of workers, consumers or local citizens who stand most at risk may (all else being equal) be expected to condition more rigorously preventive (and, in this sense, 'higher quality') outcomes (O'Brien 2000).

This has particular significance in relation to intractable scientific and technological uncertainties, where wider engagement can be seen as a means to consider broader issues, questions, conditions, causes or possibilities that might otherwise be missed in appraisal (Stirling 1998a; Wynne 1992). Lying at the heart of globalizing discourses on risk, trade and technology, the high-profile issue of 'precaution' is increasingly identified with enhanced citizen and stakeholder participation (Gee et al. 2001). Here, participation offers a means to effect a shift in levels of proof and burdens of persuasion (Fisher and Harding 1999; Raffensberger and Tickner 1999). The rationale for engaging with a wider range of social perspectives arises as one element in the 'broadening out' of appraisal, alongside – and as a means to – a number of other substantive ends. These include considering more indirect (and wider ranges of) effects, extending timescales and geographical scope, examining different sensitivities and scenarios, scrutinizing benefits and justifications (alongside the risks), comparing alternative choices and including strategic issues such as reversibility, flexibility and diversity (Stirling 1999, 2003).

Perhaps the most salient distinction between normative, substantive and instrumental approaches to participation lies in their different relationships with political, economic and institutional power. Normative democratic perspectives tend to hold in common the aim of countering or ameliorating undue exercise of power in social choice (Habermas 1984; Rawls 1971). Instrumental perspectives are aimed uncritically at achieving ends that are conditioned by existing power structures and so – intentionally or not – will tend to support these (Collingridge 1980; Collingridge and Reeve 1986). For its part, a substantive perspective is ostensibly blind to considerations of power, focusing instead on apparently transcendent qualities in the resulting social choices (Coenen et al. 1998). The evaluative implications of these analytic distinctions and diagnoses will vary, depending on the context and the point of view. What all hold in common, however, is that they raise significant and relatively neglected questions about the role of power in social appraisal.

Framing, justification and power

One factor that has contributed to the reduced dominance of established analytic approaches to social appraisal is the progressive erosion of credibility in their status as definitive or value-free (Fineberg 1996; RCEP 1998). This erosion has taken place on several fronts, sometimes assisted by processes of globalization. Worldwide, experience has accumulated innumerable technological risk episodes, in which public concerns were successively ignored, denied, marginalized, 'sedated' (Millstone and van

Zwanenberg 2000) and finally reluctantly acknowledged and confirmed (Gee et al. 2001).

To this may be added the cumulative experience of high-profile expert controversy. As specialisms proliferate and accreditations diversify, so there is ever greater scope for 'boundary work' and other sources of contention (Jasanoff 1990). Yet concealed disagreement is hardly more reassuring. Even where the results of individual appraisal exercises are expressed with fine precision or confident conclusions, comparisons between exercises typically reveal significant divergences (Stirling 1997a). Identified in a wide variety of technology governance arenas, these discrepancies are often large enough to accommodate different performance orderings for the available options, posing important implications for technology choice (Amendola et al. 2002; Stirling and Mayer 1999).

In parallel with these practical, methodological and empirical difficulties, the theoretical foundations in 'rational choice' for analytic approaches to social appraisal are also themselves increasingly demonstrated to be limited and inconsistent. For instance, probability theory underlies the entire activity of risk assessment, yet its applicability is seriously constrained by recognition of intractable states of uncertainty, indeterminacy and ignorance (Funtowicz and Ravetz 1990; Stirling 2003; Wynne 1992). Likewise, the aspirations to definitive 'rational choice' (as embodied in cost–benefit and decision analysis) are increasingly confounded by appreciation of the ambiguities, incommensurabilities and intrinsic impossibilities associated with aggregating divergent social perspectives (Arrow 1963; O'Neill 1993; Stirling 2003). The more extensive and diverse the social and cultural environment, the more pertinent and insoluble these problems become.

The crucial point is that the ostensibly definitive results obtained in expert analysis are now widely acknowledged to be highly sensitive to powerful general 'framing' effects (Goffman 1974; Stirling and Mayer 1999; Wynne 1987). The choice of policy questions, the bounding of institutional remits, the prioritizing of research, the inclusion of disciplines, the accrediting of expertise, the recruitment of committees, the setting of agendas, the structuring of enquiries, the forming of hypotheses, the choice between methodologies, the interpretation of uncertainties, the setting of base lines, the exploring of sensitivities, the definition of metrics, the characterizing of decision options, the prioritizing of criteria, the constituting of 'proof' – all provide ample latitude for contingency or agency. These factors are generally considered external to analysis and so excluded from explicit reflection. Many are essentially subjective in nature and so eminently contestable. Yet they often exert a determining influence on the nature of the results, the full scope of which typically remains concealed or under-acknowledged.

What is sometimes less well recognized is that the design, implementation and interpretation of a typical participatory process also display a similar latitude for contingency and agency (see Scoones and Thompson 2003). Relationships with sponsors, the constitution of oversight, the design of the process, the choice of focus, the partitioning of perspectives, the engagement of stakeholders, the recruitment of participants, the phrasing of questions, the bounding of remits, the characterizing of alternatives, the provision of information, the medium of discourse, the conduct of facilitation, the demeanour of practitioners, the personalities of protagonists, the dynamics of deliberation, the management of dissension, the documentation of findings, the articulation of policy – all provide ample scope for contingent variability, inadvertent bias or the exercise of deliberate conditioning influence. There seems little reason, *a priori*, to distinguish technical analysis and participatory deliberation in terms of their general sensitivity to framing effects.

These issues of framing raise important queries for appraisal from normative, substantive and instrumental perspectives alike. Crucially, they reveal the enormous latitude for the inadvertent tacit effect (or deliberate covert exercise) of power. This challenges normative aspirations (and claims) to 'ideal speech', 'public reason' and 'empowering process', just as much as to 'value-free analysis' and 'sound science'. Indeed, to the extent that the normative aims of participation are assumed of themselves to militate against power, then the challenge might be considered even more pertinent. Likewise, similar questions are raised over the degree to which the outputs of any type of appraisal process – analytic or participatory – may necessarily be expected to display particular substantive qualities (such as equitability or prevention).

In an unusually explicit discussion of the potential role of power in the conditioning of analytic approaches to the social appraisal of technology, David Collingridge (1982, 1983) elaborated on Habermas by highlighting the importance of 'decision justification'. In expanding his account from analytic to participatory approaches to appraisal, and to consider the specific role of framing conditions, this key concept might usefully be elaborated.

Collingridge's undifferentiated notion of justification subsumes two distinct and important instrumental imperatives. These go well beyond the issues of credibility, trust and social intelligence already discussed. First, under what we may term '*weak justification*', incumbent power interests may be quite relaxed about the particularities of a decision. Yet they may none the less experience enormous pressures to allow for effective 'blame management' (Hood 2002; Horlick-Jones 1996). Here, the imperative is to avoid or deflect administrative or political exposure to any blame that may arise in future, if a particular decision were to go awry. To this end, appeals to reified notions of 'legitimacy', 'inclusivity' or 'representativeness' may serve essentially the same function as more traditional invocations of 'sound science', 'authoritative expertise' or 'value-free analysis'. Indeed, to the extent that the credibility of analytic approaches to social appraisal is indeed in decline, there is an increasing incentive to substitute participatory for analytic means to justification (Levidow 1999).

The second form of justification may be distinguished as *'strong justification'*. Here, there is an instrumental imperative not just in relation to decisions in general, but to justify a *particular* decision outcome. Such an outcome may be favoured by incumbent power interests for narrow institutional, parochial cultural or partisan political reasons which it is not expedient openly to declare. Under these circumstances, the deliberate influencing of framing conditions may provide an effective means to secure the desired outcome in appraisal. Such is the manifest latitude for the conditioning of appraisal that there need often be no compromise on, let alone violation of, disciplinary principles, methodological rigour or individual integrity. The point is not that power will always exert this kind of influence, but that this cannot typically be excluded.

Nor do imperatives to strong justification necessarily always need to be explicit and deliberate, even on the part of the incumbent interests themselves. Both analytic and participatory approaches alike subsist in a wider policy context. Incumbent power interests, by definition, enjoy privileged economic, cultural and institutional positions in this wider environment bearing on social appraisal. Such interests are often directly engaged in individual projects through the formal structures of financing, sponsorship, clientship, patronage or stakeholder oversight, as well as in associated general processes of research governance, disciplinary funding, peer review and professional career advancement. Even without postulating direct and deliberate efforts at manipulation or 'capture' (Sabatier 1975; Smith 1999), then, it is typically difficult to rule out the possibility that the design, conduct or interpretation of participatory appraisal will be subject to implicit, but potentially powerful, conditioning pressures. These may often simply operate through the unconscious anticipation of possible actions by powerful interests. This is so even if such actions are never actually perpetrated, communicated or even contemplated. On those occasions where the dynamics of tacit processes in science and technology appraisal are later subject to detailed scrutiny, a host of mechanisms emerge under which the appraisal process effectively 'second-guesses' imperatives for strong justification. This was the case, for instance, with experience in the late 1980s with management of bovine spongiform encephalopathy (BSE) in the UK food chain. The scientific appraisal process repeatedly anticipated the appropriate way to constitute and present emerging scientific questions and findings, so as to minimize the expense, inconvenience, embarrassment and blame falling on government and industry (van Zwanenberg and Millstone 2004).

For reasons that they themselves help explain, these kinds of instrumental imperatives to weak and strong justification are virtually never addressed in the documentation of policy appraisal. As discussed, academic literatures do critically engage with issues of power at more general levels in relation to concepts such as 'expert objectivity' or 'ideal speech'. But specialist academic discourses concerning analytic and participatory approaches do tend to be diffident in fully exploring the more detailed exercise of power through the framing of appraisal. This may lend those rare instances of discussion a certain partisan political or even cynical conspiratorial air. Yet there seems little reason why discussion of the effects of power need be seen as any less appropriate for academic or policy discourse than that of more directly articulated issues such as transparency or rigour. Nor does such discussion carry any necessary political or evaluative connotations. Power may be exerted from different directions to divergent ends. Indeed, under certain instrumental perspectives, motivations towards weak and strong justification are entirely pragmatic and positive aspects of the process of social appraisal and technology choice. The point is not that these are necessarily always normatively negative in their effect, but that they warrant much closer substantive attention.

'Opening up' and 'closing down'

The preceding discussion has explored the role of power in applying pressures for strong and weak justification in social appraisal. It has been shown how this relates to normative, substantive and instrumental understandings of the role and conduct of appraisal. We have seen how, just at a time when globalization apparently makes the governance of science and technology ever more obscure, inaccessible and remote, so we come to appreciate the inherent open-endedness and potential for human agency in the social choice of scientific and technological pathways. It is on this basis that we may now return to the dichotomy with which this chapter began. What conclusions might we draw for the practice or evaluation of participatory and analytic approaches to appraisal, as part of the wider governance of science and technology?

What is curious about approaching the issue in this way is that it quickly becomes clear that – despite their differences – participation and analysis actually hold a lot in common. Both are approaches to social appraisal. Both are subject to normative, substantive and instrumental imperatives. In principle, both are equally sensitive to framing conditions. Yet, as conventionally practised, both have the effect of reducing evaluative diversity. Both are therefore similarly susceptible to processes of justification. Both are applied in institutional environments, which are structured and pervaded by power relationships. Both are vulnerable to 'strategic behaviour'. Yet either approach may be undertaken and presented in such ways as alternatively to conceal and reify, or acknowledge and interrogate, these imperatives, sensitivities and susceptibilities.

One way to think about these cross-cutting alternatives – pervading both sides of the analysis/participation dichotomy – is as a distinction between the use of social appraisal to 'open up' or 'close down' wider policy discourses on science and technology choice.

If social appraisal is about *'closing down'* the process of technology choice, then the aim is instrumentally to assist policy-making by providing a means to weak or strong justification. Whether analytic or participatory, the role of the social appraisal process lies in cutting through the messy, intractable and conflict-prone diversity of interests and perspectives to develop a clear, authoritative, prescriptive recommendation to inform decisions. There is a vulnerablity to 'strategic behaviour' on the part of the practitioners or sponsors in the design and implementation of appraisal. Yet only in this way – so one argument goes – can we achieve the effective management of policy-making, enable an efficient and proportionate allocation of resources and, through mitigating unnecessary conflict, foster a satisfactory level of social and political cohesion. In pursuing this aim, the focus is on defining the right questions, finding the priority issues, identifying the salient knowledges, recruiting the appropriate protagonists, adopting the most effective methods, highlighting the most likely outcomes and so determining the 'best' options.

Whether it takes an analytic or participatory form, the 'output' of this kind of 'closing down' in wider governance processes takes the form of what might be called *'unitary and prescriptive'* policy advice. This involves the highlighting of a single (or very small sub-set) of possible courses of action, which appear to be preferable under the particular framing conditions that happen to have been adopted in appraisal. These conditioning assumptions and sensitivities will typically not be explored in any detail. The outputs will therefore have the instrumental merit of conveying practical implications for policy and clear justification for decision-making.

On the other hand, if social appraisal is aimed at 'opening up' the process of technology choice, then the focus is rather different. Here, the emphasis lies in revealing to wider policy discourses any inherent open-endedness, contingency and capacity for the exercise of social agency. The aim is then to examine the degree to which the results obtained in appraisal are sensitive to different framing conditions and assumptions. Instead of focusing on unitary prescriptive recommendations, appraisal poses alternative questions, focuses on neglected issues, includes marginalized perspectives, triangulates contending knowledges, tests sensitivities to different methods, considers ignored uncertainties, examines different possibilities and highlights new options. Here, the relative lack of structured constraints on modes of expression may present a vulnerability to 'strategic behaviour' on the part of participants. Yet only in this way – so one argument goes – can we ensure the robust informing of governance processes and the achievement of appropriate levels of transparency and accountability in technology choice – unhindered by the smokescreens of justification.

Under an 'opening up' approach – whether analytic or participatory – the 'outputs' to policy-making are delivered as what might be termed *plural and conditional* advice (Stirling 2003). This involves systematically revealing how alternative reasonable courses of action would appear preferable under different detailed 'framing conditions' and showing how these dependencies relate to the real world of divergent contexts, public constituencies, disciplinary perspectives and stakeholder interests. Accordingly, the lack of imperatives for aggregation will relieve pressures to reify notions such as 'objectivity', 'representativeness' or 'legitimacy'. Although the results may be correspondingly ambiguous or equivocal in terms of what constitutes the single 'best' way forward, the openness of the process renders those courses of action that are identified as displaying overall good or poor performance all the more robust as a basis for policy.

'Decisions' or other explicit social commitments will, of course, still need to be made. Here, an 'opening up' approach may illuminate the potential for accommodating more diverse portfolios of social choices (Stirling 1994, 1998b). Attention may be usefully directed at synergies and complementarities between options. Alternatively, the learning thus achieved may offer a fruitful basis for further appraisal oriented more explicitly towards 'closing down'. Either way, it will be much more clear how to apportion responsibility and accountability in decision-making and wider governance processes. In this sense, far from being radical or impractical when compared with established practices for 'closing down', appraisal conducted in 'opening up' mode might be seen as substantively more coherent and normatively more consistent with the prevailing institutions and procedures of representative democracy.

Once the general distinction is established, the specific implications for analytic and participatory approaches seem clear. In an expert analytic approach such as risk assessment, cost–benefit analysis or expert deliberation, many of the same quantitative methods may be employed in 'opening up' as in 'closing down' mode. But instead of aggregating different metrics, methods and perspectives, an analytic orientation towards 'opening up' makes use of techniques such as scenario (Werner 2004) and sensitivity (Saltelli 2001) analysis or multi-criteria mapping (Stirling 1997b; Stirling and Mayer 1999) to reveal the implications of different assumptions and conditions. The reporting of expert deliberation highlights ambiguous findings, contending interpretations and dissenting views (SRP 2003, 2004). Likewise, in participatory appraisal, an 'opening up' approach would employ pluralistic rather than consensual discourse (Bohmann 1996; Dryzek and Niemeyer 2003; Rescher 1993). Deliberation centres on the sustaining and comparing of a diversity of evaluative frameworks, rather than on forging 'common ownership' of a single framework. Appropriately conducted, processes such as scenario workshops (Ogilvie 2002), Q-method (McKeown and Thomas 1988) and deliberative mapping (Davies et al. 2003) all offer practical approaches.

A distinction between 'opening up' and 'closing down' in social appraisal thus pervades both sides of the analysis/participation dichotomy. It is crucially different from notions of 'breadth of process' already discussed in relation to substantive – and especially 'precautionary' – rationales for participation. The breadth or narrowness of an appraisal process concerns the range of *inputs* that are included (such as issues, possibilities, perspectives and options). The 'open' or 'closed' status of an appraisal process, on the other hand, concerns the range of *outputs* that are sustained in parallel and conveyed to wider governance discourses. Of course, there are certain correspondences between the two concepts. All else being equal, an emphasis on 'opening up' may tend to broaden an otherwise 'narrow' appraisal. Likewise, we might expect it to be easier to effect the 'closing down' of appraisal when the process is relatively narrow. This conjunction of 'narrowness' and 'closure', however, may exacerbate tensions with wider policy discourses. When a relatively broad-based process is oriented towards 'opening up' then the challenges will tend to concern the sheer number and complexity of open-ended elements. When a relatively broad appraisal process is subject to 'closing down', then tensions may be expected around the specificity and contestability of the particular axis of closure.

Whatever the result, consideration of these questions of framing, justification and power shows that the distinction between 'opening up' and 'closing down' is of crucial normative, substantive and instrumental importance. In many ways, the distinction may therefore be more salient than conventional contrasts couched in terms such as new versus old, citizens versus specialists, quantitative versus qualitative or analytic versus deliberative. The significance is all the more acute for being subject to such relative neglect in the academic and policy literature. By placing greater emphasis on the acknowledgement, testing, exploration and elaboration of this distinction, we may hope to develop reflective groundings for the pursuit of a more robust, finely nuanced and well-integrated diversity of analytic and participatory approaches.

Globalization, social appraisal and technology choice

The globalizing of the governance of science and technology reviewed in this book presents a compelling imperative for considering the implications of 'opening up' and 'closing down' in social appraisal. As the institutional gradients of power become more acute and extensive, so it becomes more important that due attention be given to processes of justification and closure in technology choice. Highly charged technology-related trade tensions weave between fishery strategies, agricultural practices, genetic modification, intellectually property and the licensing of chemicals. In these and other areas, institutions such as the World Trade Organization, the World Bank and other multilateral forums wrestle with the task of effecting global processes of closure. Favoured procedures include a sophisticated array of analytic as well as deliberative styles of appraisal. Yet – for all the reasons discussed here – there emerge serious challenges in terms of the contingency, contestability and accountability of the outcomes of such appraisal.

In the end, the only way seriously to address these challenges lies in more direct, systematic and explicit attention to institutions and procedures for opening up, as well as closing down, in social appraisal. Only by acknowledging the normative value of pluralism and the substantive value of diversity in appraisal may we hope to achieve more legitimate, robust and truly deliberate technological futures.

16 | Geographic information systems for participation

JOHN FORRESTER AND STEVE CINDERBY

Computer modelling is of growing importance in understanding and find-ing potential solutions to environmental problems ranging from global climate change to local issues of community resource use. Modelling future environments presents a particular problem: namely, how to create socially robust predictions that can also claim to be reliable knowledge about complex futures. One view is that community-inspired solutions are based upon naive etiologies while expert-led solutions are based upon more sophisticated understandings; others view citizen involvement alongside expert assessments as important but differing processes which, if brought together in the right way, can provide a more informed picture. A more open contractual arrangement of this kind between experts and citizens lies at the heart of a methodology called geographic information systems for participa-tion (GIS-P). The early inclusion of knowledge based upon citizen expertise and the 'opening up' of the process (see Chapter 15) can add legitimacy to the reception and uptake of advice based on models and also give rise to better predictions through the widening of assumptions and data inputs upon which the modelling of different scenarios is based.

GIS-P was first used in South Africa to capture and analyse local under-standings of natural resource use (Cinderby 1999). The method was then transferred to the UK where GIS-P was developed in an Economic and Social Research Council (ESRC)-funded study to produce spatial representations of local knowledge about air pollution (Yearley et al. 2003). GIS-P indicates how citizen participation in modelling future environments can contribute to the responsible governance of the environment as well as the creation of a better-informed and involved citizenry.

Previous use of GIS-P in developing countries

Use of geographic information systems (GIS) for environmental re-search has largely been viewed as a critical success by practitioners and their scientific peers. Spatial representation of information undoubtedly enhances precision and communication. Relevant social and cultural in-formation has largely been excluded from environmental investigations, however, and GIS technology has justifiably been perceived as being used to reinforce top-down analyses of development issues. Thus, conventional

GIS has been guilty of not fully addressing and incorporating other bodies of knowledge, questions and experiences, and the social issues relating to these. To address the first of these criticisms, new approaches were developed integrating mental maps showing various interest groups' perceptions of their environment. Mental mapping is a process by which an individual organizes and recalls information about the attributes of their environment. The new dimension is the incorporation of this bottom-up analysis of lay citizens' understandings within the GIS database. Iterative production of citizen maps typically involves members of the local community drawing features of note in a workshop. Features selected for inclusion are dependent on the community group, with any guidance from the outside facilitator being limited to procedural issues. Once the features are produced, their meaning can be interrogated during interviews and the maps subsequently enhanced to represent any greater understanding so generated. The use of spatially referenced base data has allowed these citizen maps to be integrated into a GIS. By overlaying the maps of different interest groups, differing perceptions of the importance of resources and potential areas of conflict can be identified. Combining different perceptions allows for the investigation of the multiple realities of what is thought to be a single issue. Further, resource maps of communities may be redrawn over time to monitor changing resource perception, quality and usage.

It is also possible to incorporate conventional agency-produced information. Comparison may show broad agreement between the official assessments and that of the (often higher-resolution) knowledge of the local communities. In the Namaqualand GIS (Cinderby 1999), information on water quality produced by a hydrological surveyor was combined with information from the local community. Combining different data-sets enhanced the understanding of both the local community and the surveyor. For example, the citizen maps indicated far more water points than had been identified by the outside agency, and to what use the water was being put – information that was largely unknown to the surveyor. Data on water quality were useful to the local communities, as by highlighting where contamination was lowest the use of wells for human consumption could be reassessed and the case for better water supplies could be made more powerfully. Further, as part of the Namaqualand GIS, Landsat satellite imagery was classified to show the levels of green biomass and the types of land cover present. When these data-sets were compared to the community assessments of grazing quality, similar patterns were broadly differentiated. The village assessments, however, contained additional differentiation: areas identified as average grazing land by farmers had physical conditions that should have classified them as good grazing according to the satellite assessment, but additional factors such as wild animal attack or distance from settlement had reduced the attractiveness of the land. This type of qualitative information is usually unavailable in conventional 'expert' spatial data-sets.

The combination of existing environmental information with that obtained from the users of the resource allows greater insight into possibilities and constraints for local development. Combining these multiple viewpoints on to a common map visually increases clarity of communication and allows the potential for local groups to engage on a more level footing with outside agencies.

Current use of GIS-P in the UK

As in South Africa, GIS-P sessions in the UK are conducted by means of citizen groups convened around spatially significant science-based issues that have consequences for participants. The methodology consists of integrating a group discussion to access citizen expertise in environmental issues with a mapping exercise. This allows participants to engage collectively with and criticize different environmental models, drawing on their own local knowledge.

While social issues of democratization and increased trust, and increasing stakeholder involvement in science, are considered laudable themes, they do not necessarily build upon another important potential for increased public involvement in science: namely, enhanced data collection and improved local accuracy – that is, more reliable science. Much work in the fields of environmental policy analysis, health studies and the social studies of science supports the view that people other than official experts have insights into matters of environmental and health impacts (Forrester 1999; Irwin and Wynne 1996; Watterson 1994). Local people have knowledge about mechanisms that are unknown to official experts. This has been further demonstrated in the case of urban air pollution models, where local informants have expertise complementary to that of official modellers (Yearley 2000).

GIS-P has been used successfully in the recognition of problems and in public deliberation of potential solutions, resulting in several notable successes. The air quality management area (AQMA) of one city was chosen using a GIS-P process (Cinderby and Forrester, forthcoming). This AQMA was actually chosen over that identified by the technical modelling process (Yearley et al. 2003). GIS-P has also been used in the analysis of policies resulting from AQMA designation in two other UK cities, and the methodology is being tested further as an engagement and communication methodology in an Engineering and Physical Sciences Research

Council (EPSRC)-funded project looking at better integration of sustainable land use and transport policies in the UK.

GIS-P research is now being extended to women's understanding of environmental risks associated with breast cancer. The iterative process of reframing the women's maps of their lived environments on to a GIS database allows maintenance of the knowledge's integrity while reframing their concerns better to suit the needs of expert and policy communities. This process can embody conflicting principles that are difficult to reconcile. We chose breast cancer as a test issue since, despite recent advances, it still remains the case that women are under-represented in scientific discourse and their voices remain unheard even when the issues are of supreme importance and relevance to their lives. Much of the knowledge that women have of the environmental risk of breast cancer can be located within a traditional scientific paradigm. Yet frequently they have also acquired a 'lay' expert status through the need to know about a disease that has personal relevance (Potts 2001). It can also be argued that citizen engagement in decision-making on this topic makes for stronger science. It promotes greater public understanding of and trust in the exercise of scientific inquiry. Enabling women to participate in the process of mapping breast cancer risk within their local community has allowed an intellectual advance beyond the expert-led view that risk is primarily due to kin-based (genetic) links. Our work is not designed to supplant scientific expert ideas, but to complement them by examining the spatial dimensions of how some women understand and experience the causes of breast cancer. The project also highlights the ways in which established processes of data gathering and knowledge production have been gendered.

GIS-P for global science citizenship

It is contended that 'public contestation almost never leads to demands to dispense with scientific objectivity. Rather the reverse; it intensifies the search for better science' (Nowotny et al. 2001). Evidence from the UK is starting to show citizens from a developed country critiquing the evidence for science-based policy, but often within the self-defined frame of improving the science, not discarding it. In developing countries, where different cultural conditions prevail, on what grounds can locally epistemologically generated understandings face up to Western-backed science? On what terms – mutual exclusion and competition, or complementarity and improvement – do such encounters take place? The techniques described here represent some of the first steps towards an approach offering a new and powerful way of engaging local groups in the planning and decision-making process on a more equal footing with external, technologically endowed agencies and organizations, and their situated bodies of scientific knowledge. GIS-P offers increased communication, and maps can be seen to represent a relatively universal visual language. No previous knowledge about mapping or computers is necessary.

Incorporating participatory approaches within a GIS appears to offer a solution to the criticisms levelled at conventional top-down spatial analysis, including both the undemocratic nature of previous GIS analyses and the representation of single-agency solutions to multiple-reality issues. The use of GIS-P techniques also allows for monitoring of resources and impacts of management decisions on local communities' perceptions through time. A problem, particularly in developing countries, is the relationship between people, resources and policy. The relationship between the natural stock (the environment) and the building blocks of household and wider civil society (physical, financial, human, societal and natural capital) is one that the process of citizen mapping, as used in Namaqualand, can assist in understanding. The form these relationships take in practice at community level is one that may be better understood through the application of GIS-P. Such visualization of linkages would help empower and engage local communities. Further, by linking the expert-understood GIS database to the text of qualitative discussions with local communities, better overall understanding can be achieved. The use of GIS-P in the UK has shown its power as a public-engagement-with-science tool. Citizens do not need to know the science in order to take part in science policy. But when they see expert-data mapped, it is often more easily interpretable, more accountable and more capable of interrogation, and more relevant to their lives.

From the policy-makers' and planners' perspective, the offer is of better understanding of reality, natural and human. Too often policies fail owing to lack of local applicability and exclusion of relevant social realities. For example, how can the use of communal land be planned when the ownership of the land cannot be related to physical infrastructure, such as roads that provide access to markets? Also, how do you determine if people have the assets to enable them to utilize such linkages; for example, through the ownership of, or access to, transport? These are the sorts of data that are mappable on a GIS-P, and the sorts of data traditionally missing from expert analyses because they have seldom been framed in an expert-comprehensible manner. The use of multiple viewpoints on the same issue – including those of local communities and outside agencies – helps not only to address the criticism regarding the democracy of management decisions utilizing GIS but also allows a better insight into the social aspects of management and resource use, greater understanding of environmental stresses (that is, better science citizenship) and more responsible and effective governance.

17 | Democratizing science in the UK: the case of radioactive waste management

JASON CHILVERS

Introduction: professional networks for science and citizenship

Despite powerful justifications, the active involvement of citizens and stakeholders within complex, uncertain environmental decision processes has occurred only very recently in the UK. This chapter draws on a study that has explored aspects of this democratization by following professional actors (participatory practitioners, scientific experts and decision-makers) through networks currently building up around participatory risk appraisal generally and specifically around radioactive waste, and engaging them in critical reflection through in-depth interviews and a workshop process (Chilvers 2004).

Key features of participatory risk appraisal have been described in recent ideal-type conceptualizations of a democratic environmental risk policy process (RCEP 1998; Stern and Fineberg 1996; see also Burns and Uberhorst 1988; Ozawa 1991). These emphasize the legitimate inclusion of citizens, stakeholders and their respective knowledges/rationalities along with the integration of analysis (science) and deliberation (participation) at *all* stages of the decision process, from 'front-end' *framing*, through *assessing*, to *management/action*. By opening up technical policy processes to extended peer review, participatory risk appraisal provides citizens with a legitimate voice in (re)negotiating (social) uncertainties/indeterminacies embedded in science (Wynne 1992), and represents a fundamental re-structuring of the (power) relationship between citizens and specialists (Fischer 2000; Irwin 1995).

In the UK, there is an emergent epistemic community (Haas 1992) of professional actors with recognized competence in participatory risk appraisal practice, comprised of a core group of 'process experts' (participatory practitioners and researchers). These are engaging with decision-making institutions in a range of environmental risk issues in diverse locations. While fragmentation and competition currently limit social learning, actors share broadly consensual beliefs about how science should be democratized which are closely aligned with the ideal-type democratic model outlined above.[1] Their principles implicitly critique many existing participatory approaches for upholding distinctly modernist assumptions, being insufficiently informed by constructivist perspectives on environmental knowledge, and succumbing to what could be termed the 'technocracy of participation'.

In this context, the chapter now offers perspectives on the degree to which science is being democratized by focusing on actors' reflections on past and present practice of citizen engagement in the area of radioactive waste management.

Citizen and stakeholder participation in radioactive waste policy processes

Past practice The current regulatory system for radioactive waste management in the UK involves a separation between government, which sets national policy directions through the Department for Environment, Food and Rural Affairs (Defra), the organizations responsible for the disposal of wastes – UK Nirex Ltd (Nirex) and British Nuclear Fuels Ltd (BNFL) – and regulatory agencies (including the Environment Agency and the Nuclear Industries Inspectorate). This institutional context has its origins in the Royal Commission on Environmental Pollution's 6th Report (RCEP 1976), which recommended that a national radioactive waste disposal facility should be developed and operated by a National Waste Disposal Corporation. Nirex was established in 1982 to assume this role.

After a period of scientific research and site evaluation, Nirex announced its intention to develop a deep underground repository for radioactive waste disposal in 1988, before deciding in the early 1990s to concentrate investigations on the suitability of Sellafield in Cumbria, for which it proposed a Rock Characterization Facility (RCF). This met considerable local and national opposition, and was refused planning permission by Cumbria County Council in 1994. Nirex appealed and a public inquiry ensued. The appeal was eventually dismissed by the Secretary of State in 1997. This represented a significant failure for Nirex, and a massive setback for the UK government in seeking a solution for the long-term management of radioactive waste.

This failure represents a defining moment in the story of radioactive waste decision-making in the UK. Prior to 1997, radioactive waste policy-making was a distinctly technocratic process, dominated by the framings of scientific experts and exclusive dialogue between government, waste management companies, regulators and other professional stakeholders deemed to have sufficient technical competence. Public involvement in decision-making was limited or non-existent (Chilvers et al. 2003; Hunt 2001), and confined to the end of policy processes after definitions, options and assessments had been framed and constrained by decision-making institutions through a strategy of decide-announce-defend (House of Lords

1999; POST 1997). Any engagement was underpinned by a deficit model of public understanding and of citizenship that sought to educate and reassure the public that 'we know best' and 'believe us, we're scientists'. The RCF failure, however, was the crisis that forced institutions to seek help from participatory process experts.

Current practice Since 1997, the radioactive waste participatory risk appraisal epistemic community has evolved rapidly, from tightly defined, highly separated networks around Nirex and BNFL to a more inclusive network around Defra and the UK government's Managing Radioactive Waste Safely (MRWS) process (Defra 2001). This has coincided with the rapid development of citizen and stakeholder engagement practice. In order to gauge the extent of this shift, Table 17.1 presents an analysis of the nature and extent of current participatory practice. It takes seven case examples, nominated as being particularly important or innovative actors, and assesses them against three key aspects of the ideal-type model of participatory risk appraisal outlined in the introduction: who is represented; to what extent are they engaged; and to what degree is science and participation integrated at each stage of the process?

- In terms of *representation*, Table 17.1 differentiates between professional stakeholders, local stakeholders and publics (after Chilvers et al. 2003; Clark et al. 2001), given differences in whom they might represent and differences in their epistemic (knowledge) and ethical (value) claims to participation. The three far-right columns of Table 17.1 provide qualitative scores of the *extent of engagement* and *degree of integration* between analysis and deliberation in the framing, assessing and evaluation stages of each nominated case. The degree of integration is assessed according to three levels:
- *Low or non-interactive integration*: analysis and deliberation remain separate, with no direct exchange or contestation between participants and specialists (for example, written material, remote presentations, face-to-face presentations, expert Delphi processes);
- *Moderate or interactive integration*: direct interaction between analysis and deliberation, and direct exchange between participants and specialists in 'extended peer review' (Funtowicz and Ravetz 1993) (for example, expert panels, various forms of information communication technology);
- *High or active integration*: participants actively contribute 'extended facts' (Funtowicz and Ravetz 1992, 1993) and lay/experiential knowledge to analysis and/or work together with specialists in conducting

239

TABLE 17.1 A comparative analysis of the seven cases of participatory practice discussed by community actors against key aspects of the ideal-type model of participatory risk appraisal.

Case	Representation: who participated and how?	Process description	Framing	Assessing	Evaluation
Spent Fuel Management Options Working Group of the BNFL National Stakeholder Dialogue (Environment Council 2002)	*Professional stakeholders* in workshops and consensus-building processes	High-level engagement in all stages of the process. Active integration in assessing (joint fact-finding; expert representation) and evaluation (deliberative multi-criteria techniques).	**(*) +	** +++	*** +++
Jointly Agreed Sampling & Monitoring working group (JASM) of the BNFL Cricklewood Dialogue (Environment Council 2001)	*Professional stakeholders* in workshops and consensus-building processes	Active integration of analysis and deliberation in assessing stage (joint fact-finding, expert representation) to assess the health risks of radiation leached from spent fuel flasks, as part of nuclear waste transport site mediation process.		** +++	
Monitoring & Retrievability (M&R) Workshops, for Nirex (UKCEED 2000, 2001, 2002)	*Professional stakeholders* in workshops	Previewed (framed) Nirex's work programme on the M&R waste disposal concept. Non-interactive integration (through presentations and written material). Iterative feedbacks between framing and assessing stages between workshops.	** +	+	
Interim Storage of Laid-Up Nuclear Submarines (ISOLUS) Consultation, for the Ministry of Defence (CSEC 2001)	*Public & professional/local stakeholders* in workshops, focus groups and a citizens' panel	Limited to framing stage. Involvement in defining acceptability criteria but limited consideration of alternative options. Apart from expert panel, predominantly non-interactive integration via written material.	**(*) +(+)		

			Analysis (science)	Participant engagement	Integration
National Consensus Conference on Radioactive Waste (UKCEED 1999)	*Public* in a consensus conference	Contributed to framing national policy process on radioactive waste. Involvement in framing issues and questions to address but process design pre-determined. Efforts to achieve integration at non-interactive (written material and presentations) and interactive levels (expert panel).	**(*)	++	(+)
Citizens' Panel on Partitioning & Transmutation (P&T), for Nirex (Hunt and Thompson 2001)	*Public* in a citizens' panel	Framed a review of Nirex's research on P&T. Involvement in defining questions and acceptability criteria but problem/option already defined. Efforts to achieve integration at non-interactive (written material and presentations) and interactive levels (expert panel).	*(*)	++	+
Benchmarking Public Opinion on Radioactive Waste, for Defra (Kelly and Finch 2002)	*Public* in focus groups	Limited to framing stage of national policy process. Sought views on problem definitions and acceptability criteria but removed from decision process. Non-interactive integration between deliberation and analysis (written material).	*(*)	+	

The three far-right columns contain qualitative assessments of the extent of engagement and degree of interaction between analysis (science) and deliberation (participation) in each stage of the decision process, where: * signifies the extent of participant engagement (*** = high; ** = moderate; * = low; = no involvement); and + signifies the degree of integration (+++ = high; ++ = moderate; + = low; = no integration). Bracketed scores indicate where the level is only partially met.

analysis (for example, participatory research, joint fact-finding, expert representation, deliberative multi-criteria techniques).

The analysis in Table 17.1 highlights two key themes. First, and striking, is the significant degree to which publics, as well as stakeholders, are being actively involved in the framing of decision processes – to a moderate or high extent in six of the seven cases. This is involving citizens in processes of extended peer (p)review, often creating spaces that place them in critical interaction with specialists. Participants appear to be playing a key role in defining the issues to be addressed and discussing acceptability criteria, thus expanding the range of perspectives and knowledges that frame policy processes and, in specific instances, influence the shape of scientific assessments. This represents a significant shift towards a more democratic mode of decision-making and is a key indication that science is being democratized.

Second, this democratization is currently being constrained, however, through an almost complete exclusion of citizens from the process of assessing environmental risks and impacts, and the evaluation of different policy options for the management of radioactive waste. The only examples of active participation in assessing and evaluation exclusively involve professional stakeholders, who possess well-developed specialist and procedural knowledges. This is true of the Spent Fuel Management Options Working Group, which actively engaged participants through joint fact-finding and deliberative multi-criteria analysis, and of the JASM working-group process. While these two cases represent an advance in the development of participatory risk appraisal in themselves, the current dependence on scientific constructions at this stage of the policy process is militating against the inclusion of lay/experiential knowledges and cultural forms of rationality.

Conclusions

The evolution of a participation-focused epistemic community in the area of radioactive waste management has coincided with a shift away from the technocratic mode of decision-making that predominated prior to 1997. Although key actors appear to be learning from past failures, however, there is still a long way to go before technical policy processes can be considered fully democratized. Further caution is necessary given that this analysis of current practice has actively focused on innovative-deliberative cases. While significant advances have been made, particularly in relation to front-end framing processes, effective decision-making in issues such as radioactive waste depends on taking seriously the important, and arguably essential, role that citizens can play in 'technical' stages of assessing environmental risks and evaluating management options. This requires the development of analytic-deliberative learning processes that enable citizens' active engagement over longer periods.

Note

1 The focus of these principles includes: the overall shape of the *analytic-deliberative processes*, emphasizing the need for broad participation as early as possible in the process to frame pre-analytic commitments; the need for *science/analysis* to be accessible, relevant and responsive in relation to the deliberative process, and transparent about (social) assumptions and uncertainties; the need for *access to information and specialist expertise* to emphasize diversity and inclusivity, while ensuring deliberative/multi-stream risk communication that is interactive and responsive to participants' needs; and the need for *deliberation* to ensure a highly interactive and critical citizen–expert relationship, and to explore diversity and difference through exposing alternative viewpoints and so 'opening up' the process (cf Chapter 15).

Democratizing science in the UK

18 | Genetic engineering in Aotearoa, New Zealand: a case of opening up or closing down debate?[1]

AUDLEY GENUS AND TEE ROGERS-HAYDEN

Introduction

As in many countries, genetic engineering (GE) has been an issue of controversy in New Zealand. The Royal Commission on Genetic Modification (RCGM) (May 2000 to July 2001) was established as a forum for both public and expert debate, largely in response to demands from environmentalists around the 1999 election (Rogers-Hayden and Hindmarsh 2002). It provides an ideal case study for this part of the book, as the RCGM initially appeared 'open', but on closer inspection can be seen to have been 'closed' owing to significantly unquestioned assumptions shaping the whole process of inquiry, argument and deliberation. It is also of interest for the way in which the debate has gained new momentum since the RCGM, and for what it has to contribute to contemporary thinking about participation in science and technology policy.

The RCGM's apparent openness was largely attributed to its warrant, which required it to investigate possible options and relevant policy changes needed regarding GE. More specifically, its warrant was 'to receive representations upon, inquire into, investigate, and report upon the following matters:

- the strategic options available to enable New Zealand to address, now and in the future, genetic modification, genetically modified organisms, and products;
- any changes considered desirable to the current legislative, regulatory, policy, or institutional arrangements for addressing, in New Zealand, genetic modification, genetically modified organisms, and products'. (RCGM 2001a)

In addition, the template that 'interested persons' (IPs) (those groups presenting cross-examinable evidence) were required to use added to the apparent openness of the participation exercise. The template included a range of aspects of GE beyond physical risks. For example: 'the key strategic issues drawing on ethical, cultural, environmental, social, and economic risks and benefits arising from the use of genetic modification, genetically modified organisms, and products' (RCGM 2001b).

244

The RCGM could be seen as having created a forum to reconcile parties with diverse approaches. Opposing viewpoints were articulated. Proponents of GE expressed their desire for less regulation, suggesting that the risks were acceptable. Meanwhile, environmental groups proposed that the risks were both uncertain and incalculable. Genetic engineering is viewed by these groups as a classic case where the precautionary principle should be implemented, as it fulfils both criteria for precaution: uncertainty and potentially serious irreversible consequences (Rogers-Hayden et al. 2002). The commissioners' response, however, demonstrates the difficulties they experienced in meeting their aim to cater for and render more convergent the diverse cultural and ethical value positions and the views of 'ordinary people', partly because this constitutes a discourse of resistance to and the 'scandalizing' of GE (see Beck 1998 on the making 'real' of ecological risks).

'Expert' and 'citizen' participation

The research summarized here initially focused on the GE controversy, as framed by the RCGM, and based on the submissions made by IPs (see Rogers-Hayden 2003). An issue raised by Beck (1998), however, draws attention to the aspects of citizen involvement. It relates to what Beck (1998: 67) calls 'reflexivity of the hazard potential', in which the 'risky industry' is its own worst enemy, and actually provokes public opposition by its own modes of behaviour, not just by the risks it is generating (see also Wynne 1996). The role of social movements in relation to ecological risks is thus to scandalize the potential dangers of (in this case GE) technology. The commission's report refers to the need to develop a 'shared framework of values', emphasizing the viewpoints of 'as many New Zealanders as possible ... as much as [that] of well-resourced organisations' (RCGM 2001c: 12). Hardly surprisingly, the commission found it difficult to balance the many different viewpoints held by stakeholders and to define an agreed ethical framework within which to accommodate the submissions of various religious, ecological, Maori (indigenous peoples) and Pakeha (European descendants) groups (Rogers-Hayden and Hindmarsh 2002). The extent to which public opinion and representative advice was ignored (9,998, or 92 per cent, of the 10,861 public submissions were against GE) (RCGM 2001c), together with a tradition of non-violent direct action, could explain the nature of public protest following the publication of the RCGM report. For example, such 'scandalizing' took the form of: the destruction of a GE potato trail at Lincoln University Crop and Food Research Institute Laboratory; a pledge by 3,500 'ordinary citizens' to take direct action against GE; the occupation by anti-GE Maori of the offices of the Environmental Risk

Management Authority (ERMA); and a three-week hunger strike by a student in Christchurch. Generally, such actions have been seen as illegitimate by biotechnology firms, research institutes and insurers, which have referred to them as 'eco-terrorism', or 'sabotage', the work of the 'far-left' and 'needless' (*New Zealand Herald*, July 2001 to July 2002).

The case study highlights fundamental conflicts among the various actors with respect to their different concepts of environmental risk, its analysis, the policy-making process and relationships between science, technology and nature. Part of the problem facing the commission lay in how to recognize and reconcile these 'songlines of risk' (Jasanoff 1999), owing partly to the procedures employed to obtain testimony (Rogers-Hayden 2003). Hence, the submission template employed made discussion of interconnected factors associated with adoption of GE difficult, since answers to its questions had to 'stand alone'. This was a process that supported a reductionist approach, where answers to questions could be viewed in isolation from each other. This approach may have been suitable for proponents of GE, but it disadvantaged those, such as the environmental groups, who preferred to present their concerns about GE within a more holistic world-view. Such a perspective emphasizes the interconnectedness of elements of the ecosystem, and of nature with society, and thus contends that arguments about various aspects of GE cannot and should not be artificially separated from each other. From this kind of perspective, it can also be recognized that different citizen positions on an issue such as GM may be rooted in different, perhaps incompatible, ontological commitments, in which case it has also to be acknowledged that conflict needs profound and searching political negotiation, with identities at stake, not only expert authority premised from within one such modernist ontological position (Latour 2000; see also Chapter 1).

Rapprochement also proved difficult because certain groups (for example, proponents of GE supported by scientific experts) saw economic progress and nature as enhanced by GE, while others (environmental groups and lay activists) saw nature to be at risk from the implementation of GE. Moreover, the case study reveals limitations on citizen involvement in building a broader-based understanding of risk connected with different perspectives on governance (see Genus 2000, 2003). These have ranged from reliance on subordination of the citizenry to state and expert authority (the government, scientists, industrialists), through (claimed) equality of people, while subordinating nature (RCGM) to holistic approaches emphasizing the equality of people and nature (environmental campaigners; see Dryzek 1997).

Aftermath and reflection

The RCGM released its recommendations on 30 July 2001. The 1,200-page report suggested that options be kept open (RCGM 2001c). The RCGM found the basic regulatory framework for GE to be appropriate, but suggested the addition of a bioethics council. More specifically it recommended the release of GMOs into the environment under what it termed 'conditional release', where a monitoring and report-back system is integral to the terms of the permitted release. As mentioned above, the issue of GE in New Zealand was not settled by the publication of the RCGM's recommendations.

Since then, the government has worked though the recommendations of the commission, and has met a deadline of October 2003 for lifting the moratorium on GMO field releases. Meanwhile, supporters of GE have continued to encourage the government to loosen the regulation of GMOs, while environmental groups and the public have been involved in protests centring on their demand for New Zealand to become a GE-free nation. A recent development in New Zealand's GE controversy is the announcement that the government will hold a select committee inquiry into the sweetcorn scandal that occurred during the RCGM (Fitzsimons 2002). Further, at the World Summit in Johannesburg (August 2002), the World Bank announced its intention to create an international scientific jury to review the science on issues such as GE, to help governments decide which technologies to use and which to avoid. The 2005 deadline for reporting its findings is seen by environmental campaigners, however, as coming too late in the day to affect choices made in this area, and they have called for governments to effect a moratorium until the World Bank report is published (*New Zealand Herald* 2002).

One may consider the issues raised by the case study in terms of public participation in the risk assessment of technology, Habermas's (1984) notion of communicative rationality, and Beck's (1998: 101) comment regarding the onset of 'discursive modernisation', wherein the doors behind which decisions to invest in risky technology might once have been taken are opened up to politics, and managers can no longer 'rule alone'. Here, the institutionalized actors are frequently more oriented towards success as defined in their own paradigmatic, instrumental strategic terms than they are towards reaching shared understanding, even though they may be willing to *share understandings* in a self-serving way within a seemingly pluralistic process.

Even though the RCGM itself referred to the need to develop shared values, the process by which submissions were collected actually served to fragment the views of those with more holistic positions on the GE/

environmental risk debate. The forum in which views were presented looks on the face of it to be reflexively or discursively modern in terms of possibilities for developing civic science and the deeper social probing of risk (Wynne 2001). On closer inspection, however, the deeper form remains the same as before. The case study exemplifies the working out of a partial, incomplete, modernist rationalization, in which the ontological premises of the powerful institutions are not put in question as part of the social negotiation. Thus, the ambitious expectations invested in the RCGM were thwarted by the recalcitrance of the dominant institutional policy culture which 'closed down' the process. The lay publics here are not the 'cultural dupes' portrayed in the literature on expertise and expert knowledge, a depiction of which Wynne (1996) complains. In addition, this does not look to be a case where any salient and singular 'truth' can be discerned to which rational argument or ideal speech would be deterministically directed. Indeed, analysis of cultural bias and subjectivity (perhaps especially that masquerading as objective scientific claim) should be seen as necessary for understanding the analysis of risk and uncertainty and different protagonists' dealings with each other in scientific and technological debates such as GE. Although it made a rigorous effort to address the uncertainties typically neglected or understated in previous policy assessments, the RCGM nevertheless still reflected the established wider cultural assumption that difference and conflict over new sciences and technologies can be resolved by bringing more powerful epistemic resources to bear, rather than recognizing the need for more demanding, 'opened up' processes of human ontological–cultural self-reflection and negotiation.

Note

1 In part, this chapter draws on Tee Rogers-Hayden's doctoral research. This was supported by a University of Waikato Doctoral Scholarship, a 2001 Federation of New Zealand Graduate Women's Fellowship, a 2002 Claude McCarthy Fellowship, and a 2003 University of Waikato Geography Department Study Award.

19 | Exploring food and farming futures in Zimbabwe: a citizens' jury and scenario workshop experiment

ELIJAH RUSIKE

Much debate about the future of agriculture and what technologies are appropriate is very narrowly framed. Discussions often assume that scientists know what is best and that technology users are simply involved in processes of adaptation and fine tuning. But is this enough? With major changes in the contexts for agricultural livelihoods unfolding across the developing world, setting priorities for agricultural technology development and policy more generally is becoming more challenging. There are a range of new needs associated with changing patterns of labour availability, land pressure, opportunities for off-farm work and health conditions.

Yet technology trajectories are often implicitly imposed. For example, the debate about genetically modified (GM) technologies in the developing world has very often been limited to discussions about the health or environmental risks of one or other GM crop. But the implications of a move towards a more industrialized, commercialized and transnational-dependent agriculture are hidden from view in mainstream regulatory and policy deliberations. GM, however, some argue, entails fundamental changes in the agri-food system, and with this changes in food rights and sovereignty, with major ramifications for people's livelihoods

Given the controversial nature of such new technologies and the far-reaching implications of their adoption, approaches to discussion and deliberation are needed which expand the horizons of debate in terms of scope, content and participants. Such issues, which impinge on the long-term possibilities for livelihoods and ways of living, are not just technical discussions about risk and regulation, but are about the type of future a society wants, with implications for rights and justice, particularly for those who are potentially going to be marginalized by such changes. This requires a coming together of a wide group of stakeholders – scientists, bureaucrats, campaign groups, ordinary consumers and the diversity of producers – to open up debate and suggest options.

Citizens' juries

Citizens' juries have become one of a number of 'deliberative inclusion-ary processes' which have been experimented with over the past decade or so in response to such challenges. Along with scenario workshopping, future search, consensus conferences, constructive technology assessment, participatory policy appraisal and so on, citizens' juries have been proposed as a way of allowing citizens to deliberate on contentious issues

Using a legal-style jury format allows for the panelling of a jury – either as an attempt to provide a representative group of society at large, or as a way of bringing together a marginalized, often unorganized interest group – to discuss a proposal or series of options. The jury is encouraged to cross-examine a series of 'expert witnesses', who present particular positions and evidence. The aim is to come up with a 'verdict', which may or may not be unanimous or consensual; one that represents the 'people's' view (or a particular group's view). The intention is that such a verdict can then feed into wider policy deliberations or campaigning tactics in the broader political arena.

Such an approach was pioneered in the North (see Coote and Lenaghan 1997; Crosby 1996; Wakeford 2002) and has only been recently used in developing-country contexts. Two citizens' juries were held in southern India in 2000 and 2001, and represented important learning opportun-ities for the development of the approach (Pimbert and Wakeford 2002; Wakeford 2000). The 2001 jury, selected largely from smallholder farmers, many of whom were women, and held in Andhra Pradesh, deliberated on a series of pre-prepared scenarios of future agriculture and rural development for the state, including one scenario based on the state government's *2020 Vision* document. The jury rejected this option, putting forward a series of ideals as to what their view for the future might be. This jury process gener-ated much controversy, but also some important reflections on method and approach (IIED 2003; Pimbert and Wakeford 2002). Among these reflections were (from Scoones and Thompson 2003):

- *Issues of representation*: The need to be clear about whom the jury rep-resents, and how it is chosen. Having an explicit bias towards the poor or marginalized is seen as a legitimate standpoint, but this necessarily has to be regarded as a partial view. But even within such groupings, different people will have (inevitably) different views. It is perhaps this diversity of (sometimes dissenting) opinion that needs to be captured and worked with, rather than assuming that 'the poor' or 'smallholders' necessarily speak with one voice.

- *Issues of evidence, legitimacy and authenticity*: With views, 'facts' and 'evidence' so contested, simple arbitration on what is right or wrong is clearly impossible. The process of deliberation itself, whereby alternative framings and understandings are pursued, then becomes key. Diverse views – not just those of mainstream science policy – must be accepted as legitimate and authentic. Through such a process, an 'opening up' (see Stirling, this volume) of debate is encouraged, associated with self-critical reflection on institutional positions and the authority of knowledge.

- *Issues of engagement with the political and policy process*: One critique of many participatory and deliberative processes is that they are often one-off 'events', set up by concerned groups within or outside government, but without any explicit linkage to other political or policy processes. Seeking the links between deliberative, informal spaces and more formal arenas – such as representative politics, bureaucratic processes of policy-making or the legal system – is an important challenge. Alternative modes were suggested, including: the use of one-off, high-profile events to raise awareness and shift the tenor of debate in a policy area (the advocacy ideal); attempts at ongoing deliberation with the aim of influencing those in power through inclusive argumentation (the deliberative ideal); and stimulating local organizations and democratic processes to take up the issues raised from the bottom up (the local democratic ideal).

- *Issues of accountability and transparency*: Designing a process that explicitly seeks to hold government departments, donor agencies and other actors to account, resulting in more responsive policies. The use of 'right-to-information' laws can, for example, be a useful route in ensuring accountability. Yet such consultation mechanisms, such as citizens' juries, can be appropriated and used – like many other participatory processes – to justify actions on the basis that 'the people have been consulted'. The balancing act between being involved and being co-opted is a difficult one to judge.

A citizens' jury in Zimbabwe: exploring farming and food futures

The jury process initiated in Zimbabwe attempted to respond to some of these challenges, while adapting the process to local circumstances – ones that in the period from 2002 proved particularly challenging.

The *Izwi ne Tarisiro* (translated as 'voice and vision' from the original Shona) process was convened by the Intermediate Technology Development Group (southern Africa), a non-governmental organization (NGO) that had been working in Zimbabwe over the past decade or more. The convening partners were: another NGO, the Biotechnology Trust of Zimbabwe (BTZ); a government agency, the Biosafety Board of Zimbabwe, part of the Research Council based in the President's office; and a parastatal organization, the Scientific and Industrial Research and Development Council of Zimbabwe (SIRDC). The aim was to initiate the process with as broad a base as possible, involving both government and non-government actors. An oversight panel was established, which had two members, one a deputy director in the Ministry of Land and Agriculture, the other a former policy head in the same ministry. This provided another link to the government machinery via a ministerial route.

The convening group decided to focus the process on a broad question: 'What do you desire to see happen in the smallholder agriculture sector in Zimbabwe by 2020?' This allowed a broad framing of the debate, and did not constrain the discussions to a particular technological solution (for example, GM or not; irrigation or not, and so on), as had been the case in some past discussions. The process started with a national scoping workshop involving forty-three farmers from sixteen districts, drawn from

---

Box 19.1 Key issues for agriculture and rural livelihoods

- Representation of farmers in national organizations/unions
- Poor coordination of development agencies – government, NGOs, donors, unions
- Lack of participation in policy discussion and debate
- Shortage and prices of farm inputs, including seed, equipment and fertilizers
- Poor infrastructure – roads, telecommunications
- Seed quality and knowledge about new seeds, including GM
- Water for agriculture
- Natural resource management
- HIV/AIDS and its impact on labour
- Access to research knowledge and extension information about new techniques, technologies and markets
- Poor advice from extension agencies, which results in problems
- Piracy of information and resources, such as medicinal plants, seeds
- Lack of access to affordable credit
- Skewed markets and unfair contract farming arrangements
- Lack of agro-processing options for adding value
- Alternative non-farming livelihood options

Source: National scoping workshop (Rusike 2003: 18–20)

---

all provinces in the country. Partner institutions (mostly NGOs) working in different districts of the country identified participants on the basis of a series of criteria. Participants had to be full-time residents in rural areas and farming had to be a significant part of their livelihood; there had to be equal gender representation from each district; and the participant had to have a broad knowledge of rural issues and be sufficiently articulate and confident in discussion in Shona or Ndebele.

The aim was to identify the key issues that affect smallholder farmers, and so to identify key areas where 'expert witnesses' should be called. By allowing a variety of people from across the country to frame the jury process, the aim was to prevent it being dominated by one particular group. It also distanced the convenors from the framing process, allowing them to take on a facilitator role. The key issues identified by the scoping workshop are listed in Box 19.1.

At the close of the national scoping workshop, a jury was chosen by this larger group, with sixteen farmers (ten men and six women) drawn from sixteen districts. These jurors then attended an 'induction workshop',

---

Box 19.2 Expert witnesses at the jury

- HIV/AIDS – University of Zimbabwe, National AIDS Council of Zimbabwe
- Rural livelihoods – ENDA, Zimbabwe (NGO)
- Farming systems – University of Zimbabwe
- Water and agriculture – University of Zimbabwe, Department of Engineering, Agricultural Research and Extension Department (AREX), Ministry of Agriculture
- Training and education – Swedish Cooperative Centre, formerly AREX
- Intellectual property rights – Commutech (NGO)
- Common property and natural resource management – Department of Natural Resources, Ministry of Environment and Tourism; SAFIRE (NGO)
- GM technologies – Biotechnology Trust of Zimbabwe (NGO), Biosafety Board, Research Council
- Farmer institutions – Zimbabwe Farmers' Union, Indigenous Commercial Farmers' Union
- Credit – Swedish Cooperative Centre, formerly ZFU

Source: Rusike (2003: 13)

---

where a lawyer and government officials explained the jury process and the policy-making process to the participants. This allowed the group to build a sense of collective purpose and allowed the demystification of issues of policy, reducing fears and anxieties among participants. Given the sensitivity of some of the issues being discussed, the convenors went to great lengths to allay fears and to involve government officials in the process. The actual jury process occurred over a week, with seventeen specialist witnesses (Box 19.2) making presentations (five government officials, five NGO representatives, five academics and two Farmers' Union officials). Facilitators from the convening organizations used a variety of participatory workshopping techniques to encourage open and free debate.

Concluding comments

The jury forum created a rare opportunity for smallholder farmers not only to interrogate the witnesses, but also to seek understanding on other issues that they had long wished to discuss with officials. By allowing direct interactions with senior officials and other experts, the farmers, in subsequent evaluations, indicated that they felt they understood how things worked perhaps for the first time. The feedback to their local communities was an important part of the wider process.

The process reaffirmed that citizen empowerment and deliberative and inclusive processes can enrich democracy and hold decision-makers accountable for their actions. Jurors used their ability to cross-examine and interrogate the witnesses directly, asking for illustrations and counter-examples to the evidence that they had heard. The questions and concerns raised by the jurors were practically oriented, and although there were diverse opinions expressed, the jury agreed on some basic principles about the local control of food and farming, as well as the importance of indigenous knowledge, practical skills and local institutions. As a member of the oversight panel, with long experience of working in government on policy issues, observed: 'The level of engagement that resulted renders this process a viable method of involving the marginalized at grassroots in consensus building for policy shaping ... Steps should be taken for this process to be mainstreamed as a tool for policymaking by government and other organisations' (quoted in Rusike 2003: 42).

The *Izwi ne Tarisiro* process showed beyond doubt that the citizens' jury, as a tool, is useful in allowing the voice of the poor to contribute to policy issues. The process helped achieve a number of objectives:

- The interaction opportunity created by bringing the policy-makers into contact with ordinary citizens who had been enlightened by interactions with witnesses.

- Direct interaction allowed an exchange that farmers would never have had before.
- Based on the presentations of the specialist witnesses, the farmers have information that they can act on.

List of contributors

Angela Alonso holds a PhD in sociology from the Universidade de São Paulo. She is currently a professor at the Department of Sociology at Universidade de São Paulo and the area coordinator of environmental conflicts at Cebrap (Brazilian Center for Analysis and Planning).   Dr Angela Alonso, CEBRAP, Rua Morgado de Mateus, 615, Vila Mariana, São Paulo, Brazil 04015-902

Jason Chilvers is a lecturer in environment and society at the School of Geography, Earth and Environmental Sciences, University of Birmingham, UK, and was formerly based in the Department of Geography, University College London, where he recently completed his PhD.   Dr Jason Chilvers, University of Birmingham, Edgbaston, Birmingham B15 2TT, UK

Steve Cinderby, Stockholm Environment Institute, University of York, holds an MSc from Cranfield University and has developed participatory GIS techniques for assessing sustainable land management and for enhancing public participation in a range of environmental issues.   Steve Cinderby, Deputy Director, SEI-Y, University of York, York YO10 5DD, UK

Valeriano Costa holds a PhD in sociology from the Universidade de São Paulo. He is currently a professor at the Department of Political Science at Universidade Estadual de Campinas and a researcher in environmental conflicts areas at Cebrap (Brazilian Center for Analysis and Planning).   Dr Valeriano Costa, CEBRAP, Rua Morgado de Mateus, 615 Vila Mariana, São Paulo, Brazil 04015-902

Sarah Cunningham-Burley has conducted research and published extensively in the fields of sociology of health and illness and family sociology for many years. She is currently reader in the Department of Community Health Sciences, and co-director of the Centre for Research on Families and Relationships, University of Edinburgh. She has most recently edited (with Kathryn Backett-Milburn) *Exploring the Body* (Palgrave, 2001) and (with Lynn Jamieson) *Families and the State* (Palgrave, 2003).   Dr Sarah Cunningham-Burley, Centre for Research on Families and Relationships, University of Edinburgh, 23 Buccleuch Place, Edinburgh EH8 9LN, UK

Frank Fischer is professor of political science and member of the Center for Global Change and Governance at Rutgers University. He is the author of *Citizens, Experts, and the Environment: The Politics of Local Knowledge*

(Duke, 2000) and *Reframing Public Policy: Discursive Politics and Deliberative Practices* (Oxford, 2003). Professor Frank Fischer, Department of Political Science, 719 Hill Hall, Rutgers University, Newark, NJ 07102, USA

John Forrester, Stockholm Environment Institute, University of York, holds a PhD from Queen's University, Belfast and researches topics relating to public engagement with the science behind sustainable development and environmental issues. Dr John Forrester, SEI-Y, University of York, York YO10 5DD, UK

Audley Genus is senior lecturer in technology policy and strategy at the University of Newcastle upon Tyne. He has published widely on aspects of public policy and corporate strategy related to decision-making about risky technology. In addition to publications appearing in academic journals, he has written three books, the most recent of which is *Decisions, Technology and Organization*, published by Gower. Dr Audley Genus, University of Newcastle upon Tyne Business School, 2nd Floor, Armstrong Building, University of Newcastle upon Tyne, Newcastle upon Tyne NE1 7RU, UK

Kees Jansen is a lecturer in the Technology and Agrarian Development Group at Wageningen University, The Netherlands. Recent publications include *Political Ecology, Mountain Agriculture, and Knowledge in Honduras* (Amsterdam: Thela, 1998) and 'Crisis Discourses and Technology Regulation in a Weak State: Responses to a Pesticide Disaster in Honduras', *Development and Change* 34(1): 45-66 (2003). He is co-editor of *Agribusiness and Society: Corporate Responses to Environmentalism, Market Opportunities and Public Regulation* (Zed Books, 2004). Dr Kees Jansen, TAO, Wageningen University, Hollandseweg 1, 6706 KN Wageningen, The Netherlands

Sheila Jasanoff is Pforzheimer professor of science and technology studies at the Kennedy School of Government, Harvard University. Her research centres on the role of science and technology in the political structures of modern democratic societies, with a particular focus on the use of science in law and public policy. She has written and lectured widely on problems of environmental regulation, risk management and biotechnology in the United States, Europe, and India. Her books on these topics include *Controlling Chemicals* (1985), *The Fifth Branch* (1990), *Science at the Bar* (1995) and *Designs on Nature* (forthcoming). Sheila Jasanoff, JFK School of Government, Harvard University, 79 JFK Street, Cambridge, MA 02138, USA

James Keeley is a PhD candidate at the Institute of Development Studies, University of Sussex. He is currently based at the College of Humanities and

Rural Development, China Agricultural University, Beijing. He is co-author (with Ian Scoones) of *Understanding Environmental Policy Processes: Cases from Africa* (2003, Earthscan). James Keeley, 13b, Building A, Eastgate International Apartments (Donghuan guoji gongyu), 39 Dongzhong Jie, Dongcheng Qu, Beijing 100027, China

Anne Kerr is a sociologist with a range of research interests in the fields of genetics, ethics and medicine. She has been based in the Department of Sociology at the University of York since 2000, where she teaches in the areas of genetics and society, disability, gender, and science and technology. Among other publications, she is the author of *Genetics and Society: A Sociology of Disease* (Routledge, 2004). Dr Anne Kerr, Department of Sociology, University of York, York YO10 5DD, UK

Melissa Leach is a professorial fellow at the Institute of Development Studies, University of Sussex. Her background is in social anthropology, specializing in environmental and science–society issues. Research interests include social and institutional dimensions of environmental change; gender; knowledge, power and policy processes; health technologies, citizenship and participation, and social and historical perspectives on ecology, agriculture and forestry, particularly in Africa and the Caribbean. Her book publications include (with James Fairhead) *Misreading the African Landscape* (Cambridge, 1996), *Reframing Deforestation* (Routledge, 1998) and *Science, Society and Power* (Cambridge, 2003). Professor Melissa Leach, Institute of Development Studies at the University of Sussex, Brighton BN1 9RE, UK

Jerry Ravetz is the author of *Scientific Knowledge and its Social Problems*. He has also co-authored *Uncertainty and Quality in Science for Policy* with S.O. Funtowicz, and with him has developed the theory of Post-Normal Science. Currently he is a visiting fellow at the James Martin Institute for Science and Civilization, University of Oxford. Jerry Ravetz, 106 Defoe House, Barbican, London EC2Y 8ND, UK

Paul Richards is currently chair of technology and agrarian development, in the Social Sciences Department of Wageningen University, The Netherlands and professor of anthropology at University College London. He is an anthropologist working on issues of technology, poverty and conflict in Africa. He is currently working on ex-combatant reintegration and post-war reconstruction issues in Liberia and Sierra Leone. Professor Paul Richards, Hollandseweg1, 6706 KN Wageningen, The Netherlands

Steven Robins is professor of sociology and anthropology at the University

258

of Stellenbosch. He has worked on issues of rural development, especially in Southern Zimbabwe, Namaqualand and the Kalahari (South Africa), and has written on trauma, place, housing and urban identity in Cape Town. He is currently working on the cultural politics of HIV/AIDS in South Africa.   Dr Steven Robins, Department of Sociology and Social Anthropology, Stellenbosch University, Lettere & Wysbegeerde A Building, Private Bag X1, Matieland 7602, South Africa

Tee Rogers-Hayden is a senior research associate in the Centre for Environmental Risk at the University of East Anglia. Her work focuses on the relationships between new technologies and society. She is particularly interested in genetic modification and nanotechnology, their governance, and deliberation about them. Her doctoral research involved analysing New Zealand's Royal Commission on Genetic Modification as a forum for public debate. She is currently working on the Public Understanding of Risk programme, funded by the Leverhulme Trust, furthering research from the formal evaluation of the UK's *GM Nation?* debate and analysing the development of nanotechnology.   Tee Rogers-Hayden, Centre for Environmental Risk, School of Environmental Sciences, University of East Anglia, Norwich NR4 7TJ, UK

Esther Roquas is a legal sociologist. Her research interests include international regulatory frameworks and processes of transformation in developing-country states; policy-making and science advice; and property and land policy. She is co-ordinator of the Research School for Resource Studies for Development at Wageningen University. Recent publications include *Stacked Law. Land, Property and Conflict in Honduras* (Amsterdam: Rozenberg Publishers, 2002) and 'Devil Pact Narratives in Rural Central America: Class, Gender and Resistance', *Journal of Peasant Studies* 29(3–4): 270–99 (2002) (co-author Kees Jansen).   Esther Roquas, CERES Research School, Wageningen University, Hollandseweg 1, 6706 KN Wageningen, Netherlands

Elijah Rusike works with the Intermediate Technology Development Group – Southern Africa (ITDG-SA). He is based in eastern Zimbabwe, where he is district facilitator of the Nyanga sustainable livelihoods project. He is an agricultural extensionist by training and convened the 'voice and decision for smallholder agriculture' citizens' jury process in Zimbabwe.   Elijah Rusike, District Facilitator, ITDG, Nyanga Sustainable Livelihoods Project, PO Box 215, Nyanga, Zimbabwe

Ian Scoones is a professorial fellow at the Institute of Development Studies, University of Sussex. His background is as a natural resource ecologist interested in exploring the links between ecological dynamics and local resource management with a focus on dryland areas in Africa, particularly Ethiopia and Zimbabwe. Research with an interdisciplinary perspective has involved examining issues of rangeland and pastoral development, soil and water conservation, forestry and woodland management, as well as biodiversity and protected area issues. A social and institutional perspective is at the centre of his work, which explores the linkages between local knowledges and practices and the processes of scientific enquiry, development policy-making and field-level implementation. Professor Ian Scoones, Institute of Development Studies at the University of Sussex, Brighton BN1 9RE, UK

Andy Stirling is a senior lecturer at SPRU, Science and Technology Policy Research at the University of Sussex. His research focuses on issues of risk, uncertainty and accountability in science and technology policy, where he is interested in developing ways to enhance precaution and participation. Dr Andy Stirling, SPRU, Science and Technology Policy Research, Freeman Centre, University of Sussex, Brighton BN1 9QE, UK

Richard Tutton is a sociologist in the Science and Technology Studies Unit (SATSU) in the Department of Sociology at the University of York. His research has focused on the implications of genetic research and technologies for cultural identity and citizenship. He has edited (with Oonagh Corrigan) *Genetic Databases: Socio-ethical Issues in the Collection and Use of DNA* (Routledge, 2004). Dr Richard Tutton, Science and Technology Studies Unit, Department of Sociology, University of York, York YO10 5DD, UK

Murlidhar V. is a founder member of the Occupational Health and Safety Centre (OHSC), Mumbai, established in 1988. He has been a consultant surgeon at the university teaching hospital, Mumbai, since 1990 and is an activist on issues relating to health and safety in the workplace, working with organizations and unions and networking with individuals and community groups. Major area of work include getting compensation for occupationally affected workers of lung and hearing disability, and training of students, doctors and activists in occupational and environmental health. Dr Murlidhar V., Row House 141, Sector 10, Sanpada, Navimumbai 400 705, Maharashtra, India.

Shiv Visvanathan is a senior fellow at the Centre for the Study of Developing Societies (CSDS) in Delhi, India. He is an anthropologist and human rights researcher, whose work has explored the question of alternatives as a dialogue between the West and India. Closely linked to his current work is the attempt to demystify modern science and social knowledge as legitimising categories of organized violence and exploitation. His writings have explored the psychological, cultural and political relations of science; the growing control of society by technology; and linkages between scientific establishment and authoritarian structures of state.   Professor Shiv Visvanathan, Dhirubhai Ambani Institute of Information and Communication Technology, Room No. 1111, Near Indroda Circle, Gandhinagar 382009, Gujarat, India

Brian Wynne is professor of science studies at the ESRC Centre for the Economic and Social Aspects of Genomics, Lancaster University. His work has covered sociology of scientific knowledge in public arenas, such as risk assessment, and public responses to science and technology. His book publications include (with Alan Irwin) *Misunderstanding Science? The Public Reconstruction of Science and Technology* (Cambridge University Press, 1996), and (with Scott Lash and Bron Szerszynski, eds), *Risk Environment and Modernity* (Sage, 1996).   Professor Brian Wynne, CESAGen, Institute for Environment, Philosophy and Public Policy, Furness College, Lancaster University, Lancaster LA1 4YG, UK

Bibliography

ACF (Action contre la Faim) (2002) 'Technical positioning towards GMOs', position paper, Technical Department, Paris: ACF

Adam, B., U. Beck and J. Van Loon (eds) (2000) *The Risk Society and Beyond: Critical Issues for Social Theory*, London: Thousand Oaks and New Delhi: Sage Publications

Adezde, C. (2004) *GMOs Not Answer to Poverty/Hunger in Africa*, <http://twnafrica.org/print.asp?twnID=374> (visited April 2004)

Adger, W. N., M. P. Kelly and N. H. Ninh (eds) (2001) *Living with Environmental Change: Social Resilience, Adaptation and Vulnerability in Vietnam*, London: Routledge

AgBiotechnologyNet (2000) 'Biotechnology crops prevent pesticide deaths in China', October, <www.agbiotechnologynet.com>

Amendola, A., S. Contini and I. Ziomas (2002) 'Uncertainties in chemical risk assessment: results of a European benchmark exercise', *Journal of Hazardous Materials*, 29: 347–63

Anagnost, A. (1997) *Narrative Past-times: Narrative, Representation and Power in Modern China*, Durham, NC: Duke University Press

Anderson, B. (1991) *Imagined Communities. Reflection on the Origin and Spread of Nationalism*, London: Verso

Anderson, W. (2002) 'Introduction: Postcolonial technoscience', *Social Studies of Science*, 32(5–6): 643–58

An-Naim, A. A. (1998) 'Human rights and the challenge of relevance: a case of collective rights', in M. Castermans-Holleman, F. Van Hoof and J. Smith (eds), *The Role of the Nation-State in the 21st Century: Human Rights, International Organizations and Foreign Policy. Essays in Honor of Peter Baehr*, Dordrecht: Kluwer

Anon. (2002) *Castro Hlongwane, Caravans, Cats, Geese, Foot & Mouth and Statistics: HIV/AIDS and the Struggle for the Humanisation of the African*, ANC website, <www.anc.org.za>

Appadurai, A. (1991) 'Global ethnoscapes: notes and queries for a transnational anthropology', in R. G. Fox (ed.), *Recapturing Anthropology: Working in the Present*, Santa Fe: School of American Research University of Washington Press

— (2002a) 'Deep democracy: urban governmentality and the horizon of politics', *Public Culture*, 14(1): 21–47

— (2002b) 'Grassroots globalization and the research imagination', in J. Vincent (ed.), *The Anthropology of Politics: A Reader in Ethnography, Theory and Critique*, Malden, MA: Blackwell

Archibald, S. and P. Richards (2002) 'Converts to human rights? Popular debate about war and justice in rural central Sierra Leone', *Africa*, 72(3): 339–67

Arendt, H. (1963) *Eichmann in Jerusalem*, Harmondsworth: Penguin

Arrow, K. (1963) *Social Choice and Individual Values*, New Haven, CT: Yale University Press

Arthur, W. (1989) 'Competing technologies, increasing returns, and lock-in by historical events', *Economic Journal*, 99: 116–31

Barme, G. (1999) *In the Red: On Contemporary Chinese Culture*, New York: Columbia University Press

Barnes, B., D. Bloor and J. Henry (1996) *Scientific Knowledge: A Sociological Analysis*, London: Athlone Press

Bauman, Z. (1998) *Globalization: The Human Consequences*, Cambridge: Polity Press

Beck, U. (1992) *Risk Society: Towards a New Modernity*, London: Sage

— (1995) *Ecological Politics in an Age of Risk*, Cambridge: Polity Press

— (1998) *World Risk Society,* Cambridge: Polity Press

— (2000) 'Risk society revisited: theory, politics and research programmes', in B. Adam et al. (eds), *The Risk Society and Beyond: Critical Issues for Social Theory*, London: Sage, pp. 211–29

Beck, U., A. Giddens and S. Lash (eds) (1994) *Reflexive Modernisation: Politics, Tradition and Aesthetics*, Cambridge: Polity Press

Bijker, W. (1995) *Of Bicycles, Bakelite and Bulbs: Toward a Theory of Sociotechnical Change*, Cambridge, MA: MIT Press

Blaikie, P. and H. Brookfield (1987) *Land Degradation and Society*, London: Methuen

Blecher, M. and V. Shue (1996) *Tethered Deer: Government and Economy in a Chinese County*, Stanford: Stanford University Press

Bloomfield, D., K. Collins, C. Fry and R. Munton (1998) 'Deliberative and inclusionary processes: their contributions to environmental governance', paper presented at the first ESRC 'DIPs in environmental decision-making' seminar, 17 December

— (2001) 'Deliberation and inclusion: vehicles for increasing trust in UK public governance?', *Environment and Planning C*, 19: 501–13

Bohmann, J. (1996) *Public Deliberation: Pluralism, Complexity and Democracy*, Cambridge, MA: MIT Press

Bohmann, J. and W. Rehg (1997) *Deliberative Democracy: Essays on Reason and Politics*, Cambridge, MA: MIT Press

Breslin, S. (2003) 'Reforming China's embedded socialist compromise: China and the WTO', *Global Change, Peace and Security*, 15(3): 213–29

Brickman, R., S. Jasanoff and I. Ilgen (1985) *Controlling Chemicals: The Politics of Regulation in Europe and the United States*, Ithaca, NY: Cornell University Press

Brock, K., A. Cornwall and J. Gaventa (2001) 'Power, knowledge and political spaces in the framing of poverty policy', *IDS Working Paper* 143, Brighton: IDS

Brockington, D. (2002) *Fortress Conservation: The Preservation of the Mkomazi Game Reserve, Tanzania*, Oxford: James Currey

Brokensha, D., D. Warren and O. Werner (eds) (1980) *Indigenous Knowledge Systems and Development*, Maryland: University Press of America

Brown, P. and E. J. Mikkelsen (1990) *No Safe Place: Toxic Waste, Leukemia and Community Action*, Berkeley, CA: University of California Press

Brunk, C., L. Haworth and B. Lee (eds) (1991) *Value Assumptions in Risk Assessment*, Waterloo, Canada: Wilfrid Laurier University Press

Bryant, R. (1992) 'Political ecology: an emerging research agenda in Third World studies', *Political Geography*, 11: 12–36

Burns, T. and R. Uberhorst (1988) *Creative Democracy: Systemic Conflict Resolution and Policy Making in a World of High Science*, New York: Praeger

Byrd, D. and C. Cothern (2000) *Introduction to Risk Analysis: A Systematic Approach to Science-Based Decision Making*, Rockville: Government Institute

Cabinet Office (2002) 'Risk: improving government's ability to handle risk and uncertainty', London: Strategy Unit.

Callon, M. (1996) 'Four models for the dynamics of science', in S. Jasanoff et al. (eds), *Handbook of Science and Technology*, Newbury Park, CA: Sage

Caplan, P. (ed.) (2000) *Risk Revisited*, London: Pluto

Castells, M. (1996) *The Rise of the Network Society*, Oxford: Blackwell

Certeau, M. de (1991) *Culture in the Plural*, Minneapolis: University of Minnesota Press

Chambers, R. (1993) *Challenging the Professions: Frontiers for Rural Development*, London: IT Publications

— (1997) *Whose Reality Counts? Putting the First Last*, London: IT Publications

Chambers, R., A. Pacey and L. A. Thrupp (1989) *Farmer First: Farmer Innovation and Agricultural Research*, London: IT Publications

Chilvers, J. D. (2004) 'Participatory environmental risk policy-making in an age of uncertainty: UK actor-networks, social learning and effective practice', unpublished PhD thesis, University of London

Chilvers, J. D., J. A. Burgess and J. Murlis (2003) 'Securing public confidence in radioactive waste management: developing a vision for a process of public and stakeholder engagement', in Defra/ESRU, *Managing Radioactive Waste Safely: Participatory Methods Workshop Report – Volume 2: Background Papers*, London: Defra/RAS/03.001/Vol2, pp. 51–97

Cinderby, S. (1999) 'Geographic information systems (GIS) for participation: the future of environmental GIS?', *International Journal of Environment and Pollution*, 11(3): 304–15

Cinderby, S. and J. Forrester (forthcoming) 'Facilitating the local governance of air pollution using GIS for Participation', *Applied Geography*

Clark, J., J. Burgess, A. Stirling and K. Studd (2001) 'Local outreach: the development of criteria for the evaluation of close and responsive relationships at the local level', R&D Technical Report SWCON 204, Bristol: Environment Agency

Clement, T. (2002) Speech on the Myriad gene patent issue by the Honourable Tony Clement, Minister of Health and Long-Term Care, Ontario Government, Canada, 19 September 2001, available online at <www.gov.on. ca>

Cocchiarella, L. (2001) *Guides to the Evaluation of Permanent Impairment*, 5th edn, Chicago, IL: American Medical Association

Coenen, F., D. Huitema and L. O'Toole Jr (eds) (1998) 'Participation and the quality of environmental decision making', *Environment & Policy*, 14, Dordrecht: Kluwer

Cohen, A. P. (1994) *Self-Consciousness*, London: Routledge

Cohn, S. (2000) 'Risk, ambiguity and loss of control: How people with a chronic illness exerience complex biological causal models', in P. Caplan (ed.), *Risk Revisited*, London: Pluto Press, pp. 204–25

Collingridge, D. (1980) *The Social Control of Technology*, Milton Keynes: Open University Press

— (1982) *Critical Decision Making: A New Theory of Social Choice*, London: Pinter

— (1983) *Technology in the Policy Process: Controlling Nuclear Power*, London: Pinter

Collingridge, D. and C. Reeve (1986) *Science Speaks to Power*, New York: St Martin's Press

Collins, H. M. and R. Evans (2002) 'The third wave of science studies: studies of expertise and experience', *Social Studies of Science*, 32(2): 235–96

— (2003) 'King Canute meets the Beach Boys: responses to the Third Wave', *Social Studies of Science*, 33(3): 435–52

Cooke, B. and U. Kothari (eds) (2001) *Participation: The New Tyranny*, London: Zed Books

Conover, P. (1984) 'How people organize their political world', *American Journal of Political Science*, 28: 95–126

Conway, G. (2001) Letter to Doug Parr, Greenpeace, 22 January, <http://www.biotech-info.net/conway_greenpeace.pdf> (visited April 2004)

Conway, G. and G. Toenniessen (2003) 'Science for African food security', *Science*, 299(5,610): 1,187–8

Cooke, B. and U. Kothari (2001) *Participation: The New Tyranny?*, London: Zed Books

Coote, A. and J. Lenaghan (1997) *Citizen's Juries: Theory into Practice*, London: Institute for Public Policy Research

Cornwall, A. (2002) 'Making spaces, changing places: situating participation in development', *IDS Working Paper* 170, Brighton: IDS

Cornwall, A. and J. Gaventa (2001) 'From users and choosers to makers and shapers: repositioning participation in social policy', *IDS Working Paper* 127, Brighton: IDS.

Council for Biotechnology Information (2001) *Golden Rice (A Background)*, <http://www.whybiotech.com/html/pdf/Golden_Rice.pdf> (visited April 2004)

Covello, V. T. (1993) *Risk Assessment Methods*, New York: Plenum Press

Crosby, N. (1996) *Creating An Authentic Voice of the People: Deliberation on Democratic Theory and Practice*, Chicago, IL: Midwest Political Science Association, pp. 157–74

CSEC (2001) *Project ISOLUS Front End Consultation: Final Report*, a report by

CSEC, Lancaster University, to the Ministry of Defence, September. Lancaster: CSEC

Cunningham-Burley, S., A. Kerr and S. Pavis (1999) 'Theorising subjects and subject matter in focus group research', in R. Barbour and J. Kitzinger (eds), *Developing Focus Group Research: Politics, Theory and Practice*, London: Sage

Dalpé, R., L. Bouchard, A.-J. Houle and L. Bédard (2003) 'Watching the race to find the breast cancer genes', *Science, Technology, and Human Values*, 28(2): 187–216

David, P. (1985) 'Clio and the economics of QWERTY', *American Economic Review*, 75: 332–7

Davies, G., J. Burgess, M. Eames, S. Mayer, K. Staley, A. Stirling and S. Williamson (2003) 'Deliberative mapping: appraising options for addressing "the kidney gap"', final report to the Wellcome Trust, June,

Defra (2001) *Managing Radioactive Waste Safely: Proposals for Developing a Policy for Managing Radioactive Waste in the UK*, London: Department for Environment, Food and Rural Affairs

De Gaay Fortman, B. (2001) 'Penibel recht', inaugural address, University of Utrecht, 21 May. Utrecht: Studie en Informatiecentrum Mensenrechten (SIM)

de Sousa Santos, B. (2003) 'The World Social Forum: Towards a counter-hegemonic globalisation', presented at the XXIVth International Congress of The Latin-American Studies Association, Dallas, March 2003 <www.ces.fe.uc.pt/bss/fsm.php>

Dewey, J. (1927) *The Public and Its Problems*, Denver, CO: Swallow

Dienel, P. and O. Renn (1995) 'Planning cells: a gate to "fractal" mediation', in O. Renn, T. Webler and P. Wiedemann (eds), *Fairness and Competence in Citizen Participation*, Boston, MA: Kluwer Academic

Dingkuhn, M. and F. Asch (1999) 'Phenological responses of Oryza sativa, O. glaberrima and inter-specific rice cultivars on a toposequence in West Africa', *Euphytica*, 110: 109–26

Dorrington, R., D. Bourne, D. Bradshaw, R. Laubscher and I. Timaeus (2001) *The Impact of HIV/AIDS on Adult Mortality in South Africa*, Medical Research Council Technical Report, Burden of Disease Research Unit, MRC

Doubleday, R. (forthcoming) 'Institutionalising NGO Dialogue at Unilever: Framing the Public as "Consumer-Citizens"', *Science and Public Policy*

Douglas, M. and A. Wildavsky (1982) *Risk and Culture*, Berkeley, CA: University of California Press

Douglas, M., D. Gasper, S. Ney and M. Thompson (1998) 'Human needs and wants', in S. Rayner and E. Malone (eds), *Human Choice and Climate Change. Vol. 1: The Societal Framework*, Columbus, OH: Battelle Press, pp. 195–264

Dryzek, J. S. (1990) *Discursive Democracy: Politics, Policy and Political Science*, Cambridge: Cambridge University Press

— (1997) *The Politics of the Earth: Environmental Discourses*, Oxford: Oxford University Press

— (2000) *Deliberative Democracy and Beyond: Liberals, Critics and Contestations*, Oxford: Oxford University Press

Dryzek, J. and S. Niemeyer (2003) 'Pluralism and consensus in political deliberation', draft paper for the 2003 annual meeting of the American Political Science Association, August

DTI/Treasury (2004) *A Framework for Science and Innovation 2004–2014*, London: UK Government, Department of Trade and Industry and Treasury

Duckett, J. (1998) *The Entrepreneurial State in China: Real Estate and Commerce Departments in Reform Era Tianjin*, London and New York: Routledge

Dunkerley, D. and P. Glasner (1998) 'Empowering the public? Citizens' juries and the new genetic technologies', *Critical Public Health*, 8: 181–92

Edwards, M. and J. Gaventa (eds) (2001) *Global Citizen Action*, Colorado: Lynne Reiner and London: Earthscan

Elias, N. (1984) *The Court Society*, Lisbon: Handon House

Ellison, N. (1997) 'Towards a new social politics: citizenship and reflexivity in late modernity', *Sociology*, 31(4): 697–717

Endo, Y. and E. Boutrif (2002) 'Plant biotechnology and its international regulation: FAO's initiative', *Livestock Production Science*, 74(3): 217–22

Environment Council (2001) 'Radioactivity monitoring at Brent Yard Railway Sidings, Willesden', a report prepared by Stanger Science and Environment for the Environment Council, October. London: TEC

— (2002) *BNFL National Stakeholder Dialogue: Spent Fuel Management Option Working Group Report*, July. London: TEC

Epstein, S. (1996) *Impure Science: AIDS, Activism and the Politics of Knowledge*, Berkeley, CA: University of California Press

Escobar, A. (1995) *Encountering Development*, Princeton, NJ: Princeton University Press

European Commission (2002) *Science and Society Action Plan*, EC SDME 06/62

European Parliament (2001) 'European Parliament resolution on the patenting of BRCA1 and BRCA2 ("breast cancer") genes', texts adopted by the European Parliament, available online at <www.cptech.org>

Evans, P. (1995) *Embedded Autonomy: States and Industrial Transformation*, Princeton, NJ: Princeton University Press

Evans-Pritchard, E. E. (1937) *Witchcraft, Oracles and Magic among the Azande*, Oxford: Oxford University Press

Fairhead, J. (1992) 'Indigenous technical knowledge and natural resource management in sub-Saharan Africa: a critical overview', paper presented at SSRC project conference on African agriculture, Dakar, Senegal

Fairhead, J. and M. Leach (1996) *Misreading the African Landscape: Society and Ecology in a Forest-Savanna Mosaic*, Cambridge: Cambridge University Press

— (2000) 'Fashioned forest pasts, occluded histories? International environmental analysis in West African locales', *Development and Change*, 31(1): 35–59

— (2002) 'Practising "biodiversity": the articulation of international, national and local science policy in Guinea', *IDS Bulletin*, 33(1): 102–10

— (2003) *Science, Society and Power: Environmental Knowledge and Policy in West Africa and the Caribbean*, Cambridge: Cambridge University Press

FAO (Food and Agriculture Organization of the United Nations) (1990) *International Code of Conduct on the Distribution and Use of Pesticides (Amended to include Prior Informed Consent in Article 9 as adopted by the 25th Session of the FAO Conference in November 1989)*, Rome: FAO

FAO/WHO (Food and Agriculture Organization of the United Nations/World Health Organization) (2002) 'Report of the third session of the Codex ad hoc intergovernmental task force on foods derived from biotechnology', Yokohama, Japan, 4–8 March

Farmer, P. E. (1992) *AIDS and Accusation: Haiti and the Geography of Blame*, Berkeley, CA: University of California Press

Farrington, J. and A. Martin (1988) 'Farmer participation in agricultural research: a review of concepts and practices', Agricultural Administration Occasional Paper 9, London: ODI

Fineberg, H. (1996) *Understanding Risk: Informing Decisions in a Democratic Society*, National Research Council Committee on Risk Characterisation, Washington, DC: National Academy Press

Fiorino, D. (1989) 'Environmental risk and democratic process: a critical review', *Columbia Journal of Environmental Law*, 14: 501–47

Fischer, F. (1990) *Technocracy and the Politics of Expertise*, Newbury Park, CA: Sage

— (1995a) *Evaluating Public Policy*, Belmont, CA: Wadsworth

— (1995b) 'Hazardous waste policy, community movements and the politics of Nimby: participatory risk assessment in the USA and Canada', in F. Fischer and M. Black (eds), *Greening Environmental Policy*, London: Paul Chapman, pp. 165–82

— (2000) *Citizens, Experts and the Environment: The Politics of Local Knowledge*, Durham, NC, and London: Duke University Press

— (2003a) 'Risk assessment and environmental crisis: toward an integration of science and participation', in S. Campbell and S. S. Fainstein (eds), *Readings in Planning Theory*, 2nd edn, Oxford: Blackwell, pp. 418–34

— (2003b) *Reframing Public Policy: Discursive Politics and Deliberative Practices*, Oxford: Oxford University Press

Fisher, E. and R. Harding (eds) (1999) *Perspectives on the Precautionary Principle*, Sydney: Federation Press

Fiske, S. T. and S. E. Taylor (1984) *Social Cognition*, Reading, MA: Addison-Wesley

Fitzsimons, J. (2002) 'Corngate inquiry will clear the air', media release, 17 October

Flyvbjerg, B. (1998) *Rationality and Power: Democracy in Practice*, Chicago: University of Chicago Press

Forrester, J. (1999) 'The logistics of public participation in environmental assessment', *International Journal of Environment and Pollution*, 11(3): 316–30

Foucault, M. (1985) *History of Sexuality*, New York: Vintage

Fresco, L. (2001) 'Genetically modified organisms in food and agriculture: Where are we? Where are we going?', keynote address at the conference on 'Crop and forest biotechnology for the future', Royal Swedish Academy of Agriculture and Forestry, Falkenberg, Sweden, 16–18 September

Frosch, R. A., C. Juma, P. M. Smith, A. G. K. Solomon, M. P. Greene and J. Boright (2002) *Knowledge and Diplomacy: Science Advice in the United Nations System*, Washington, DC: National Academies Press

Fuks, M. (1998) 'Arenas de ação e debate público: conflitos ambientais e emergência do meio ambiente enquanto problema social no Rio de Janeiro', *Dados – Revista de Ciências Sociais*, 41(1), Rio de Janeiro: Instituto Universitário de Pesquisa do Rio de Janeiro

Fuller, S. (2000) *Thomas Kuhn: A Philosophical History of Our Times*, Chicago: University of Chicago Press

Funtowicz, S. O. and J. R. Ravetz (1990) *Uncertainty and Quality in Science for Policy*, Amsterdam: Kluwer

— (1993) 'Science for the post-normal age', *Futures*, 25(7): 739–55

Gaventa, J. and A. Cornwall (2000) 'From users and choosers to makers and shapers: repositioning participation in social policy', *IDS Bulletin*, 31(4): 50–62

Gaventa, J. and A. M. Goetz (2001) 'Bringing citizen voice and client focus into service delivery', *IDS Working Paper* 138, Brighton: IDS

GECP (2001) 'Environmental justice: rights and means to a healthy environment for all', *ESRC Global Environmental Change Programme Special Briefing* 7

Gee, D., P. Harremoes, J. Keys, M. MacGarvin, A. Stirling, S. Vaz and B. Wynne (2001) *Late Lesson from Early Warnings: The Precautionary Principle 1898–2000*, Copenhagen: European Environment Agency

GEF (Global Environment Facility) (2000) 'Initial strategy for assisting countries to prepare for the entry into force of the Cartagena Protocol on Biosafety', Geneva: UNEP/GEF

Genus, A. (2000) *Decisions, Technology and Organization*, Aldershot: Gower

— (2003) 'Building a constructive, reflexive and "reflective" approach to the assessment of technology risks', presented to 'Innovation in Europe' conference, Roskilde, Denmark, 9 May

Giddens, A. (1990) *The Consequences of Modernity*, Cambridge: Polity Press

Gitay, J. (2002) 'Rhetoric, politics, science, medicine: the South African HIV/AIDS controversy', paper presented at the Centre for African Studies, University of Cape Town, 18 September

Glover, D. (2003) 'Biotechnology for Africa?', *Democratising Biotechnology: Genetically Modified Crops in Developing Countries Briefing Series*, Briefing 10, Brighton: IDS

Goffman, E. (1974) *Frame Analysis: An Essay on the Organisation of Experience*, New York: Harper & Row

Gottweis, H. (1998) *Governing Molecules: The Discursive Politics of Genetic Engineering in Europe and the United States*, Cambridge, MA: MIT Press

Grove-White, R., P. Macnaghten and B. Wynne (2000) *Wising Up: The Public and New Technologies*, Centre for the Study of Environmental Change, Lancaster University

Grove-White, R., P. Macnaghten, S. Mayer and B. Wynne (1997) *Uncertain World: Genetically Modified Organisms, Food and Public Attitudes in Britain*, Centre for the Study of Environmental Change, Lancaster University

Grundmann, R. (1996) 'Mending the ozone layer: the role of transnational policy networks', MPIFG Discussion Paper 96/8, Cologne: Max-Planck-Institut für Gesellschaftsforschung

Guerinot, M. L. (2000) 'The Green Revolution strikes gold', *Science*, 287: 241–3

Guivant, J. (1998) 'Conflitos e negociações nas políticas de controle ambiental: o caso da suinocultura em Santa Catarina', *Ambiente & Sociedade*, 1(2): 101–23

Gupta, A. (2002) 'When global is local: negotiating use of biotechnology', in F. Biermann, R. Brohm and K. Dingwerth (eds), *Proceedings of the 2001 Berlin Conference on the Human Dimensions of Global Environmental Change 'Global Environmental Change and the Nation State'*, Potsdam: Potsdam Institute for Climate Impact Research, pp. 238–47

Gupta, A. and J. Ferguson (1992) 'Beyond culture: space, identity and the politics of difference', *Cultural Anthropology*, 7(1): 6–23

Haas, P. M. (1989) 'Do regimes matter? Epistemic communities and Mediterranean pollution control', *International Organization*, 43(3): 377–403

— (1992) 'Introduction: epistemic communities and international policy coordination', *International Organization*, 46(1): 1–36

Haas, P. M. and D. McCabe (2001) 'Amplifiers or dampeners: international institutions and social learning in the management of global environmental risks', in The Social Learning Group (ed.), *Learning to Manage Global Environmental Risks*, vol. 1, Cambridge, MA: MIT Press, pp. 323–48

Habermas, J. (1968) *Toward a Rational Society: Student Protest, Science and Politics*, London: Heinemann

— (1975) *Legitimation Crisis* (trans. T. J. McCarthy), Boston, MA: Beacon Press

— (1984) *The Theory of Communicative Action. Vol. 1: Reason and the Rationalisation of Society* (trans. T. J. McCarthy), London: Heinemann

— (1996) 'Three normative models of democracy', in S. Behnabib (ed.), *Democracy and Difference: Contesting the Boundaries of the Political*, Princeton, NJ: Princeton University Press

Hacking, I. (1995) *Rewriting the Soul: Multiple Personality and the Sciences of Memory*, Princeton, NJ: Princeton University Press

Hadden, S. (1991) 'Public perceptions of hazardous waste', *Risk Analysis*, 11(1): 47–57

Hajer, M. A. (1995) *The Politics of Environmental Discourse*, Oxford: Clarendon

Hannerz, U. (1990) 'Cosmopolitans and locals in world culture', in M. Featherstone (ed.), *Global Culture*, London: Sage

Hannigan, J. A. (1995) *Environmental Sociology: A Social Constructionist Perspective*, London: Routledge

Haraway, D. J. (1991) *Simians, Cyborgs, and Women: The Reinvention of Nature*, London: Free Association Books

Harding, S. (1991) *Whose Science? Whose Knowledge? Thinking from Women's Lives*, Buckingham: Open University Press

— (1998) *Is Science Multicultural? Postcolonialisms, feminisms and Epistemologies*, Bloomington and Indianapolis: Indiana University Press

Hardt, M. and A. Negri (2000) *Empire*, Cambridge, MA: Harvard University Press

Harvey, D. (1989) *The Condition of Postmodernity*, Oxford: Blackwell

Hayden, C. (2003) *When Nature Goes Public: The Making and Unmaking of Bioprospecting in Mexico*, Princeton, NJ: Princeton University Press

He, D.-J., J.-L. Shen, W.-J. Zhou and C. Gao (2001) 'Ying yong dan cixi F2 dai fa jiance mianlingchong dui zhuan Bt jiyin mian kangxing dengli jiyin de pinlu' [Using an F2 genetic method of isofemale lines to detect the frequency of resistance alleles to Bacillus thuringiensis toxin from transgenic Bt cotton in cotton bollworm (Lepidoptera: Noctuidae)], *Cotton Science*, 13(2): 105–8

Held, D. (1987) *Models of Democracy*, Cambridge: Polity Press

— (1995) *Democracy and the Global Order: From the Nation State to Cosmopolitan Governance*, Cambridge: Polity Press

Held, D. and A. McGrew (2002) *Globalization/Anti-Globalization*, Cambridge: Polity Press

Henley, J. (2001) 'Cancer unit fights US gene patent', *Guardian*, 8 September

Hill, S. (1992) *Democratic Values and Technological Choices*, Stanford, CA: Stanford University Press

Hinchcliffe, S., M. B. Kearnes, M. Degen and S. Whatmore (forthcoming) 'Urban wild things: a cosmopolitical experiment', *Environment and Planning D*, 'Society and Space', special issue on boundaries

HMG (Holt, Mulroy and Germann Public Affairs) (2003) *Reputation Management*, Washington, DC, <www.hmgpa.com/reputation.htm>

Hodgson, J. (2002) 'UNEP "buys support for Cartagena", say critics', *Nature Biotechnology*, 20: 205

Holmes, T. and I. Scoones (2000) 'Participatory environmental policy processes: experiences from North and South', *IDS Working Paper* 113, Brighton: IDS

Holstein, J. A. and J. F. Gubrium (1995) *The Active Interview*, Thousand Oaks, CA: Sage

Homewood, K. (ed.) (forthcoming) *Rural Resources and Local Livelihoods in Africa*, Oxford: James Currey

Hood, C. (2002) 'Managing risk and managing blame: a political science approach', in A. Weale (ed.), *Risk, Democratic Citizenship and Public Policy*, Oxford: OUP/British Academy Press

Horlick-Jones, T. (1996) 'The problem of blame', in C. Hood and D. Jones (eds), *Accident and Design: Contemporary Debates in Risk Management*, London: UCL

House of Lords (1999) *Management of Nuclear Waste*, Report of the House of Lords Select Committee on Science and Technology, London: HMSO

Bibliography

— (2000) *Science and Society*, Select Committee on Science and Technology report, session 1999–2000, London, March

Huang, J. and Q. Wang (2003) 'Biotechnology policy and regulation in China', IDS Working Paper, Biotechnology Policy Series, 4

Huang, J., S. Rozelle, C. Pray and Q. Wang (2002a) 'Plant biotechnology in China', *Science*, 295: 674–6

Huang, J., R. Hu and Q. Wang (2002b) 'Economic and farmer health impacts of plant biotechnology development in China', paper presented at the 'Globalisation and the International Governance of Biotechnology' project workshop, Nairobi, November

Huang, J., R. Hu, C. Fan, C. Pray and S. Rozelle (2003) 'Bt cotton benefits, costs and impacts in China', *IDS Working Paper*, Biotechnology Policy Series, 5, Brighton: IDS

Hughes, T. (1983) *Networks of Power: Electrification in Western Society 1880–1930*, Baltimore, MD: Johns Hopkins University Press

Hunt, J. (2001) *Designing Dialogue*, RISCOM II Deliverable 4.5, Lancaster: CSEC

Hunt, J. and B. Thompson (2001) *Partitioning and Transmutation Citizens' Panel*, a report to Nirex by Lancaster University, Harwell: UK Nirex Ltd

IIED (2003) *PLA Notes: Participatory Processes for Policy Change*, London: IIED, February

Illich, I. (1992) *In the Mirror of the Past*, Lectures and Addresses, New York: Marion Boyars

IPPR (Institute for Public Policy Research) (1999) *Models of Public Involvement*, <www/pip.organisation.uk/models.html>

Irwin, A. (1995) *Citizen Science: A Study of People, Expertise and Sustainable Development*, London: Routledge (Environment and Society)

— (2001a) 'Constructing the scientific citizen: science and democracy in the biosciences', *Public Understanding of Science*, 10: 1–18

— (2001b) *Sociology and the Environment*, Cambridge and Malden, MA: Polity Press

Irwin, A. and M. Michael (2003) *Science, Social Theory and Public Knowledge*, Milton Keynes: Open University Press and McGraw-Hill

Irwin, A. and B. Wynne (eds) (1996) *Misunderstanding Science? The Public Reconstruction of Science and Technology*, Cambridge: Cambridge University Press

Irwin, A., H. Rothstein, S. Yearly and E. McCarthy (1997) 'Regulatory science: towards a sociological framework', *Futures*, 29(1): 17–31

Izquierdo, J. (2000) 'Biotechnology can help crop production to feed an increasing world population – positive and negative aspects need to be balanced: a perspective from FAO', in A. D. Arencibia (ed.), *Plant Genetic Engineering: Towards the Third Millennium*, proceedings of the International Symposium on Plant Genetic Engineering, 6–10 December 1999, Havana, Cuba. Shrub Oak: Agritech Publications/Agricell Report

Izquierdo, J. and W. Roca (1998) 'Under-utilized Andean food crops: status and prospects of plant biotechnology for the conservation and sustainable agricultural use of genetic resources', *Acta Horticulturae*, 457: 157–72

Jansen, K. (2000) 'Making policy agendas for safe pesticide use: public and private interests in technology regulation in a developing country', paper presented at the London POSTI conference on 'Policy Agendas for Sustainable Technological Innovation', 1–3 December

Jasanoff, S. (1990) *The Fifth Branch: Science Advisers as Policymakers*, Cambridge, MA: Harvard University Press

— (1999) 'The songlines of risk', *Environmental Values*, 8(2): 135–52

— (2003a) 'Breaking the waves in science studies', *Social Studies of Science*, 33(3): 389–400

— (2003b) 'In a constitutional moment: science and social order at the millennium', in B. Joerges and H. Nowotny (eds), *Social Studies of Science and Technology: Looking Back, Ahead*, Yearbook of the Sociology of the Sciences 23, Dordrecht: Kluwer, pp. 155–80

— (2005) *Designs on Nature: Science and Democracy in Europe and the United States*, Princeton, NJ: Princeton University Press

Jasanoff, S. and M. Long Martello (eds) (2004) *Earthly Politics: Local and Global in Environmental Governance*, Cambridge, MA: MIT Press

Jasanoff, S. and B. Wynne (1998) 'Scientific knowledge and decision-making', in S. Rayner and E. Malone (eds), *Human Choice and Climate Change*, vol. 1, Washington, DC: Battelle Institute Press, pp. 1–112

Johnny, M. M. P., J. A. Karimu and P. Richards (1981) 'Upland and swamp rice farming systems in Sierra Leone: the social context of technical change', *Africa*, 51: 596–620

Jones, A. (1983) *From Slaves to Palm Kernels: A History of the Galinhas Country (West Africa) 1730–1890*, Wiesbaden: Steiner Verlag

Jones, E. and J. Gaventa (2002) 'Concepts of citizenship: a review', *IDS Development Bibliography*, 19

Jusu, M. S. (1999) 'Management of genetic variability in rice (Oryza sativa L. and O. glaberrima Steud.) by breeders and farmers in Sierra Leone', PhD thesis, Wageningen University

Kabeer, N. (1994) *Reversed Realities: Gender Hierarchies in Development Thought*, London: Verso

— (2001) 'Citizenship and the boundaries of the acknowledged community: identity, affiliation and exclusion', *IDS Working Paper* 171, Brighton: IDS

Kang, D. (2002) 'Bad loans to good friends: money politics and the developmental state in Korea', *International Organization*, 56(1): 177–207

Karnik, S. (2001) 'Locating HIV/AIDS and India: Cautionary Notes on the Globalization of Categories', *Science Technology and Human Values*, 26(3): 322–48

Kasperson, R. and P. Stallen (1991) *Communicating Risks to the Public*, Dordrecht: Kluwer

Kay, L. (1993) *The Molecular Vision of Life: Caltech, the Rockefeller Foundation and the Rise of the New Biology*, Oxford: Oxford University Press

Keane, M. (2001) 'Redefining Chinese Citizenship', *Economy and Society*, 30(1): 1–17

Keeley, J. (2003a) 'The biotechnology developmental state? Investigating the

Chinese gene revolution', *IDS Working Paper*, Biotechnology Policy Series, 6, Brighton: IDS

— (2003b) 'Regulating biotechnology in China: the politics of biosafety', *IDS Working Paper*, Biotechnology Policy Series, 7, Brighton: IDS

Keeley, J. and I. Scoones (2003) *Understanding Environmental Policy Processes: Cases from Africa*, London: Earthscan

Kelly, J. and H. Finch (2002) 'Benchmarking public opinion on the management of radioactive waste', Defra Report no. DEFRA/RAS/02.012, London: Defra

Kennedy, D. (2002) 'The Importance of Rice', *Science*, 296: 13

Klein, N. (2000) *No Logo*, London: Flamingo

Klein Goldewijk, B. and B. de Gaay Fortman (1999) *Where Needs Meet Rights: Economic, Social and Cultural Rights in a New Perspective*, Geneva: WCC Publications

Knorr-Cetina, K. (1981) *The Manufacture of Knowledge: An Essay on the Constructivist and Contextual Nature of Science*, Oxford: Pergamon Press

— (1999) *Epistemic Cultures: How the Sciences Make Knowledge*, Cambridge, MA, and London: Harvard University Press

Kriesi, H., R. Koopmans, J. W. Duyvendak and M. Giugni (1995) *New Social Movements in Western Europe: A Comparative Analysis*, London: ULC Press

Krimsky, S. and D. Golding (eds) (1992) *Social Theory and Risk*, New York: Praeger

Kuhn, T. (1970) *The Structure of Scientific Revolutions*, Chicago: University of Chicago Press

Laclau, E. and C. Mouffe (1985) *Hegemony and Socialist Strategy: Towards a Radical Democratic Politics*, London: Verso

Lash, S., B. Szerszynski and B. Wynne (eds) (1996) *Risk, Environment and Modernity*, London: Sage

Latour, B. (1987) *Science in Action: How to Follow Scientists and Engineers through Society*, Milton Keynes: Open University Press

— (1993) *We Have Never Been Modern*, Hemel Hempstead: Harvester

— (1999) *Pandora's Hope,* Cambridge, MA: Harvard University Press

— (2000) 'When things strike back: a possible contribution of "science studies" to the social sciences', *British Journal of Sociology*, 51(1): 107–23

— (2004) *Politics of Nature. How to Bring the Sciences into Democracy*, Cambridge, MA: Harvard University Press

Latour, B. and S. Woolgar (1979) *Laboratory Life: The Social Construction of Scientific Facts*, Beverly Hills, CA: Sage

Leach, M. and J. Fairhead (2002) 'Manners of contestation: citizen science and indigenous knowledge in West Africa and the Caribbean', *International Social Science Journal*, 173: 337–49

Leach, M. and R. Mearns (eds) (1996) *The Lie of the Land: Challenging Received Wisdom on the African Environment*, Oxford: James Currey

Lefebvre, H. (1991) *Critique of Everyday Life*, London: Verso

Leis, R. and E. Viola (1997) 'A agenda 21 diante dos desafios da governabilidade das políticas públicas organizações não governamentais', in U. Cordani, J. Marcovith and E. Salati (eds), *Rio 92: Cinco Anos Depois*, São Paulo: Alphagraphics

Levidow, L. (1999) 'Democratising technology or technologising democracy', *Technology in Society*, 20(2): 211–26

Linares, O. (2002) 'African Rice (Oryza glaberrima): history and future potential', *PNAS*, 99(25): 16,360–5

Long, N. and A. Long (eds) (1992) *Battlefields of Knowledge: The Interlocking of Theory and Practice in Social Research and Development*, London: Routledge

Long, N. and J. van der Ploeg (1989) 'Demythologising planned development: an actor perspective', *Sociologia Ruralis*, XXIX(3/4): 227–34

Lynch, D. (1999) *After the Propaganda State: Media, Politics and "Thought-Work" in Reformed China*, Stanford, CA: Stanford University Press

McAdam, D., S. Tarrow and C. Tilly (2001) *Dynamics of Contention*, Cambridge: Cambridge University Press

McKeown, B. and D. Thomas (1988) *Q Methodology*, Newbury Park, CA: Sage

McNaghten, P., R. Grove-White, M. Jacobs and B. Wynne (1995) *Public Perceptions and Sustainability in Lancashire: Indicators, Institutions, Participation*, Lancaster: CSEC, Lancaster University and Lancashire County Council

Maloney, W., G. Smith and G. Stoker (2000) 'Social capital and urban governance: adding a more contextualized "top-down" perspective', *Political Studies*, 48: 802–20

Mamdani, M. (1972) *The Myth of Population Control: Family, Caste and Class in an Indian Village*, New York: Monthly Review Press

— (1996) *Citizen and Subject: Contemporary Africa and the Legacy of Late Colonialism*, Oxford: James Currey

Mansbridge, J. (1999) 'On the idea that participation makes better citizens', in S. Elkin and K. Soltan (eds), *Citizen Competence and Democratic Institutions*, Philadelphia: Pennsylvania State University Press, pp. 291–328

Marcus, T. (2001) 'Kissing the cobra: sexuality and high risk in a generalised epidemic – a case study', paper presented for the conference 'AIDS in Context', University of Witwatersrand, Johannesburg, March

Margolis, H. (1996) *Dealing with Risk*, Chicago: Chicago University Press

Marris, C., B. Wynne, P. Simmons and S. Weldon (2001) 'Public attitudes to agricultural biotechnologies in Europe (PABE)', EU FAIR project final report, Brussels, <www.pabe.net>

Marshall, T. H. (1950) *Citizenship and Social Class*, Cambridge: Cambridge University Press

May, R. (2001) Government Chief Scientist's address to the Expo meeting, UK Pavilion, Hanover, Germany

Meek, J. (2000a) 'US firm may double cost of UK cancer checks', *Guardian*, 17 January

— (2000b) 'US genetics firm in cancer check deal', *Guardian*, 9 March

Mehta, L. (1998) *Contexts of Scarcity: The Political Ecology of Water in Kutch, India*, DPhil thesis, IDS, University of Sussex, Brighton

Mehta, L. et al. (1999) 'Exploring understandings of institutions and uncertainty: new directions in natural resource management', IDS Discussion Paper 372, Brighton: IDS

Meillassoux, C. (1991) *The Anthropology of Slavery: The Wombs of Iron and Gold* (trans. Alide Dasnois), London: Athlone Press

Merrifield, J. (2002) 'Learning citizenship', IDS Working Paper 158, Brighton: IDS

Mies, M. and V. Shiva (1993) *Ecofeminism*, London: Zed Books

Miller, D. (1988) 'The ethical significance of nationality', *Ethics*, 98: 647–62

Millstone, E. and P. van Zwanenberg (2000) 'Food safety and consumer protection in a globalised economy', *Swiss Political Science Review*, 6(3): 109–18

Misztal, B. (1996) *Trust in Modern Societies*, Cambridge: Polity Press

Mo, J. (2001) 'Protection of plant varieties in China', *Journal of World Intellectual Property*, 4(6): 871–904

Mohamed-Katerere, J. (2003) 'From risks to rights: challenges for biotechnology policy', *Democratising Biotechnology: Genetically Modified Crops in Developing Countries Briefing Series*, Briefing 12, Brighton: IDS

Monde, S. S. and P. Richards (1992) 'Rice biodiversity conservation and plant improvement in Sierra Leone', in A. Putter (ed.), *Safeguarding the Genetic Basis of Africa's Traditional Crops*, Proceedings of the CTA/IBPGR/KARI/UNEP seminar, Nairobi, October. Wageningen: CTA; Rome: IPGRI, pp. 83–100

Monsanto (2000) *'Golden' Crops: Part of a Sustainable Solution to Global Vitamin A Malnutrition*, <http://www.monsanto.com/monsanto/layout/media/00/12-07-00c.asp> (visited April 2004)

— (2001) 'China has tested over 100 biotechnology crops', *Biotechnology Global Update*, 3(12), December

— (2002a) 'China transgenic cotton acreage doubles', *Biotechnology Global Update*, 4(1): 4 January

— (2002b) 'Scientists refute allegations made by Greenpeace study', Biotechnology Global Update 4(6), June.

Moore, D., J. Kosek and A. Pandian (2003) *Race, Nature, and the Politics of Difference*, Durham, NC: Duke University Press

Mosse, D. (1994) 'Authority, gender and knowledge: theoretical reflections on the practice of participatory rural appraisal', *Development and Change*, 25: 497–526

Mouffe, C. (1992) 'Democratic citizenship and the political community', in C. Mouffe (ed.), *Dimensions of Radical Democracy: Pluralism, Citizenship, Community*, London: Verso

— (1995) 'Democratic politics and the question of identity', in J. Rajchman (ed.), *The Identity in Question*, New York: Routledge

Munton, R. (2003) 'Deliberative democracy and environmental decision-making', in F. Berkhout, M. Leach and I. Scoones (eds), *Negotiating Environmental Change: New Perspectives from Social Science*, Cheltenham: Edward Elgar

Murdoch, J. and J. Clark (1994) 'Sustainable knowledge', *Geoforum*, 25: 115–32

Murlidhar, V. (2002) 'Occupational diseases among textile workers of Mumbai', *National Medical Journal of India*, 15(3)

Murlidhar, V. and V. Kanhere (1998) 'Occupational noise-induced hearing loss: the first two cases compensated in India', *National Medical Journal of India*, 11(3): 150

Murlidhar, V., V. J. Murlidhar and V. Kanhere (1995) 'Byssinosis in a Bombay textile mill', *National Medical Journal of India*, 8(5): 204–7

— (1996) *Disability, Impairment and Their Assessment*, New Delhi: Participatory Research in Asia (PRIA), <www.pria.org>

Nanda, M. (1998) 'The Epistemic Charity of the Social Constructivist Critics and Why the Third World Should Refuse the Offer', in N. Koertge (ed.), *A House Built on Sand: Exposing Postmodernist Myths about Science*, New York: Oxford University Press, pp. 286–311

Nandy, A. (1980) *Alternative Sciences*, New Delhi: Allied Publishers

Narayan, D. (2000) *Voices of the Poor: Crying Out for Change*, Washington, DC: World Bank

National Research Council (1996) *Understanding Risk*, Washington, DC: National Academy Press

NEF (1998) *Participation Works!: 21 Techniques of Community Participation for the 21st Century*, London: New Economics Foundation

Nemery, B. (1995) 'Occupational lung diseases', *National Medical Journal of India*, 8(5): 199

New Zealand Herald (2002) 'World Bank to review GE, other technologies', 30 August

— (various dates) <www.nzherald.co.nz>

Nowotny, H., P. Scott and M. Gibbons (2001) *Re-thinking Science: Knowledge and the Public in an Age of Uncertainty*, Cambridge: Polity Press

Nuffield Council on Bioethics (2002) 'The ethics of patenting DNA', London: Nuffield Council on Bioethics

Nugent, S. (2000) 'Good risk, bad risk: reflexive modernisation and Amazonia', in P. Caplan (ed.), *Risk Revisited*, London: Pluto, pp. 226–48

Nyamu, C. (2002) 'Towards an actor-oriented approach to human rights', IDS Working Paper 169, Brighton: IDS

Nyerges, A. E. (1997) 'Introduction – the Ecology of Practice', in A. E. Nyerges (ed.), *Introduction – the Ecology of Practice*, Gordon and Breach Publishers, pp. 1–38

O'Brien, M. (2000) *Making Better Environmental Decisions: An Alternative to Risk Assessment*, Cambridge, MA: MIT Press

Offe, C. (1985) 'New social movements: challenging the boundaries of institutional politics', *Social Research*, 52: 817–68

Ogilvie, J. (2002) *Creating Better Futures: Scenario Planning as a Tool for a Better Tomorrow*, Oxford: Oxford University Press

Oldham, P. (2004) 'Amazonian indigenous peoples and genomics knowledge: Ethical and human rights issues' , mimeo, CESAGen, Lancaster University

O'Neill, J. (1993) *Ecology, Policy and Politics: Human Well-being and the Natural World*, London: Routledge

OST (1999) Minutes of the Advisory Group for the Public Consultation on the Biosciences, UK Government Office for Science and Technology, Department of Trade and Industry, 14 January

Ozawa, C. (1991) *Recasting Science: Consensual Procedures in Public Policy Making*, San Francisco, CA: Westview Press

Paarlberg, R. (2001) *The Politics of Precaution: Genetically Modified Crops in Developing Countries*, Baltimore, MD: Johns Hopkins University Press

Pádua, J. A. (2002) *Um Sopro de Destruição: Pensamento Político e Crítica Ambiental no Brasil Escravista (1786–1888)*, Rio de Janeiro: Ed. Zahar

Parris, K. (1999) 'Entrepreneurs and citizenship in China', *Problems of Post-Communism*, 46(1): 43–61

Parsuraman, S. and P. V. Unnikrishnan (2000) *India Disaster Report: Towards a Policy Initiative*, Delhi: Oxford University Press

Pateman, C. (1970) *Participation and Democratic Theory*, Cambridge: Cambridge University Press

Peet, R. and M. Watts (1996) *Liberation Ecologies: Environment, Development, Social Movements*, London and New York: Routledge

Petts, J. (2001) 'Evaluating the effectiveness of deliberate processes: waste management case studies', *Journal of Environmental Planning and Management*, 44(2): 207–26

Phillips, A. (1993) *Democracy and Difference*, Philadelphia: Pennsylvania State University Press

— (1995) *The Politics of Presence*, Oxford: Oxford University Press

Pickering, A. (1992) 'From science as knowledge to science as practice', in A. Pickering (ed.), *Science as Practice and Culture*, Chicago: University of Chicago Press

— (1995) *The Mangle of Practice: Time, Agency and Science*, Chicago: University of Chicago Press

Pimbert, M. P. and T. Wakeford (2002) *Prajateerpu: A Citizens' Jury/Scenario Workshop on Food and Farming Futures for Andhra Pradesh, India*, London: IIED

PLA Notes (1988 onwards) *Participatory Learning and Action: Notes*, London: IIED

Plough, A. and S. Krimsky (1987) 'The emergence of risk communications studies: social and political context', *Science, Technology, and Human Values*, 12: 4–10

Polanyi, K. (1968) *Primitive, Archaic and Modern Economics: Essays of Karl Polanyi* (ed. George Dalton), Boston, MA: Beacon Press

Polanyi, M. (1962) 'The Republic of Science', *Minerva*, 1: 54–73

Porter, T. (2003) *The Interaction between Political and Humanitarian Action in Sierra Leone, 1995 to 2002*, Geneva: Centre for Humanitarian Dialogue

POST (1997) *Radioactive Waste – Where Next?*, Parliamentary Office of Science and Technology Report, November, London: POST

Potrykis, I. (2000) *Open Letter to Hope Shand and RAFI in Response to Their Press Release on 'Golden Rice' from October 13*, 18 October, <http://www.biotech-info.net/potrykus_responds.html> (visited April 2004)

Potts, L. (2001) 'Lies, damn lies and public protection: corporate responsibility and breast cancer activism', *Journal of International Women's Studies*, 2(3): 1–11

Power, M. (2004) *The Risk Management of Everything*, London: Demos

Quist, D. and I. Chapela (2001) 'Transgenic DNA introgressed into traditional maize landraces in Oaxaca, Mexico', *Nature*, 414: 541–3

Raffensberger, C. and J. Tickner (eds) (1999) *Protecting Public Health and the Environment: Implementing the Precautionary Principle*, Washington, DC: Island Press

Rajan, S. R. (2002) 'Missing expertise, categorical politics, and chronic disasters – the case of Bhopal', in S. Hoffman and A. Oliver-Smith (eds), *Catastrophe and Culture: The Anthropology of Disaster*, New Mexico: School of American Research (SAR), pp. 237–59

Ravetz, J. (1993) 'Science for the post-normal age', *Futures*, 25(7): 735–55

— (1997) 'The science of "What-if?"', *Futures*, 29(6): 533–9

— (1999) 'Post-normal science – an insight now maturing', *Futures*, 31(7): 641–6

— (2003) 'A paradoxical future for safety in the global knowledge economy', *Futures*, 35(8): 811–26

Rawls, J. (1971) *A Theory of Justice*, Cambridge, MA: Belknap Press/Harvard University Press

— (1993) *Political Liberalism*, New York: Columbia University Press

— (1997) 'The idea of public reason revisited', *University of Chicago Law Review*, 64: 765–807

RCEP (1976) *Nuclear power and the environment*, Royal Commission on Environmental Pollution's 6th Report, Cmnd. 6618, London: HMSO

— (1998) *Setting Environmental Standards*, Royal Commission on Environmental Pollution's 21st Report, London: HMSO

RCGM (Royal Commission on Genetic Modification) (2001a) 'Introduction', Warrant, English version, 7 March, <www.gmcommission.govt.nz/intro/warrant_eng.html> — (2001b) 'Submission' ('Interested Persons'), Form 1, <www.gmcommission.govt.nz/inquiry/Form1.doc>

— (2001c) 'Report of the Royal Commission on Genetic Modification', Wellington

Reid, T. (2002) 'The needle and the damage done', *The Times*, 26 November

Renn, O., T. Webler and P. Wiedemann (1995) *Fairness and Competence in Citizen Participation: Evaluating Models for Environmental Discourse*, Dordrecht: Kluwer

Rescher, N. (1993) *Pluralism: Against the Demand for Consensus*, Oxford: Clarendon

Richards, A. (1939) *Land, Labour and Diet: An Economic Study of the Bemba Tribe*, Oxford: Oxford University Press

Richards, P. (1985) *Indigenous Agricultural Revolution*, London: Longman

— (1986) *Coping with Hunger: Hazard and Experiment in a West African Rice Farming System*, London: Allen & Unwin

— (1989) 'Agriculture as a performance', in R. Chambers, A. Pacey and L. A. Thrupp (eds), *Farmer First: Farmer Innovation and Agricultural* Research, London: IT Publications, pp. 39–42

— (1993) 'Natural symbols and natural history: chimpanzees, elephants and experiments in Mende thought', in K. Milton (ed.), *Environmentalism: The View from Anthropology*, ASA Monograph 32, London: Routledge

— (1995) 'The versatility of the poor: indigenous wetland management systems in Sierra Leone', *GeoJournal*, 35(2): 197–203

— (1997) 'Towards an African Green Revolution? An anthropology of rice research in Sierra Leone', in E. Nyerges (ed.), *The Ecology of Practice: Studies of Food Crop Production in sub-Saharan West Africa*, Newark: Gordon & Breach

— (2000) 'Food security, safe food: biotechnology and sustainable development in anthropological perspective', inaugural lecture, Wageningen University

— (2003) 'Controversy over recent West African wars: an agrarian question?', unpublished seminar paper, Institute of Social Studies, The Hague, 6 October

Rimmer, M. (2003) 'Myriad Genetics: patent law and genetic testing', *European Intellectual Property Review*, 25(1): 20–33

Robertson, R. (1992) *Globalization: Social Theory and Global Culture*, London: Sage

Robins, S. (2002) 'Grounding "globalisation from below": global citizens in local spaces', draft mimeo, University of the Western Cape, South Africa

Rocheleau, D., B. Thomas-Slater and E. Wangari (eds) (1996) *Feminist Political Ecology: Global Issues and Local Experiences*, London: Routledge

Rogers-Hayden, T. (2003) 'Deconstructing the Royal Commission on Genetic Modification', unpublished PhD thesis, University of Waikato

Rogers-Hayden, T. and R. Hindmarsh (2002) 'Modernity contextualises New Zealand's Royal Commission on Genetic Modification: a discourse analysis', *Journal of New Zealand Studies*, 1(1): 41–61

Rogers-Hayden, T., R. Hindmarsh and M. Risely (2002) '"Precaution" down under? Marginalising the strong precautionary principle in GE debates in New Zealand and Australia', *Ecopolitics, Thought + Action*, 1(4): 86–97

Romanyshyn, R. D. (1989) *Technology, Symptom and Dream*, New York: Routledge

Rose, N. (2001) 'The politics of life itself', mimeo, London School of Economics

Rosenau, J. (1990) *Turbulence in World Politics*, Brighton: Princeton University Press

Rowe, G. and L. J. Frewer (2000) 'Public participation methods: an evaluative review of the literature', *Science, Technology and Human Values*, 25: 3–29

Royal Society (2004) *Nanoscience and Nanotechnologies: opportunities and uncertainties*, Royal Society report 19/04, London: Royal Society

Rubin, C. T. (1994) *The Green Crusade: Rethinking the Roots of Environmentalism*, New York: Macmillan

Rusike, E. (2003) 'Izwi ne Tarisiro: voice and vision for smallholder agriculture in Zimbabwe by 2020. Report of a citizens' jury', Harare: ITDG

Sabatier, P. (1975) 'Social movements and regulatory agencies: toward a more adequate – and less pessimistic – theory of "clientele capture"', *Policy Sciences*, 6: 301–42

Sabatier, P. A. and H. C. Jenkins-Smith (eds) (1993) *Policy Change and Learning: An Advocacy Coalition Approach*, Boulder, CO: Westview Press

Sachs, W. (ed.) (1992) *The Development Dictionary*, London: Zed Books

Saltelli, A. (2001) *Sensitivity Analysis for Importance Assessment*, EC Joint Research Centre, Ispra, December, <www.ce.ncsu.edu/risk/pdf/saltelli.pdf>

Sandal, M. (1998) *Liberalism and the Limits of Social Justice*, Cambridge: Cambridge University Press

Santos, B. de Sousa (1992) 'A discourse on the sciences', *Review*, 15(1): 9–48

Schlosberg, D. (1999) *Environmental Justice and the New Pluralism: The Challenge of Difference for Environmentalism*, Oxford: Oxford University Press

Schoepf, B. G. (2001) 'International AIDS research in anthropology: taking a critical perspective on the crisis', *Annual Review of Anthropology*, 30: 335–61

Schumacher, E. F. (1973) *Small Is Beautiful: Economics as if People Mattered*, New York: Harper and Row

Sclove, R. (1995) *Democracy and Technology*, New York: Guilford Press

Scoones, I. (ed.) (1995) *Living with Uncertainty: New Directions in Pastoral Development in Africa*, London: IT Publications

Scoones, I. and J. Thompson (eds) (1994) *Beyond Farmer First: Rural People's Knowledge, Agricultural Research and Extension Practice*, London: IT Publications

— (2003) 'Participatory processes for policy change: reflections on the Prajateerpu e-forum', *PLA Notes*, 46: 51–61

Scott, J. (1985) *Weapons of the Weak: Everyday Forms of Peasant Resistance*, New Haven, CT: Yale University Press

— (1990) *Domination and the Arts of Resistance: Hidden Transcripts*, New Haven, CT: Yale University Press

— (1998) *Seeing Like a State*, New Haven, CT: Yale University Press

Scriven, M. (1987) 'Probative logic', in F. H. van Eemeren et al. (eds), *Argumentation: Across the Lines of Discipline*, Dordrecht: Foris Publications, pp. 7–32

Seligman, A. (1997) *The Problem of Trust*, Princeton, NJ: Princeton University Press

Selman, P. (1998) 'Local Agenda 21: Substance or spin?', *Journal of Environmental Planning and Management*, 41(5): 533–53

Selman, P. and J. Parker (1997) 'Citizenship, civicness and social capital in Local Agenda 21', *Local Environment*, 2(2): 171–84

Sen, A. (1982) *Poverty and Famines: An Essay on Entitlement and Deprivation*, Oxford: Oxford University Press

Bibliography

Sengupta, A. (2000) 'Realizing the right to development', *Development and Change*, 31(3): 533–78

Shiva, V. (1989) *The Violence of the Green Revolution*, Dehradun: Vandana Shiva Third World Network with Zed Books

— (2000) *The Golden Rice Hoax: When Politics Replaces Science*, 26 October, <http://members.tripod.com/~ngin/11.htm> (visited December 2002)

Shotter, J. (1993) *The Cultural Politics of Everyday Life*, Buckingham: Open University Press

Singh, K. (2001) 'Participatory research', in M. Edwards and J. Gaventa (eds), *Global Citizen Action*, Boulder, CO: Lynne Reiner

Sirianni, C. and L. Friedland (2000) *Civic Innovation in America: Community Empowerment, Public Policy and the Movement for Civic Renewal*, Berkeley, CA: University of California Press

Skinner, D. (2002) 'Racing the future: science, technology and the politics of difference', paper presented at the EASST conference, York, July

Slovic, P. (1992) 'Rating the risks', *Environment*, 21: 36–9

— (2001) *The Perception of Risk*, London: Earthscan

Smith, A. (1999) 'Policy networks and advocacy coalitions: explaining policy change and stability in UK industrial pollution policy?', *Environment and Planning C – Government and Policy*, 17: 1–20

Smith, A.-M. (1998) *Laclau and Mouffe: The Radical Democratic Imaginary*, London: Routledge

Smith, C. (2000) 'China rushes to adopt genetically modified crops', *New York Times*, 7 October, <www.ag.ohio-state.edu/ipm/trans/10_071.htm>

Sokal, A. (1996) 'Transgressing the boundaries: toward a transformative hermeneutics of quantum gravity', *Social Text*, 46/47: 217–52

Soleri, D. and D. Cleveland (2001) 'Farmers' genetic perceptions regarding their crop populations: an example with maize in the Central Valleys of Oaxaca, Mexico', *Economic Botany*, 55: 106–28

Song, Y. (1998) '"New" seed in "old" China', PhD thesis, Wageningen University

SRP (2003) *First Report,* UK Government Genetic Modification Science Review Panel (SRP), July, <www.gmsciencedebate.org.uk/report/default.htm#first>

— (2004) *Second Report,* UK Government Genetic Modification Science Review Panel (SRP), July, <www.gmsciencedebate.org.uk/report/default.htm#second>

Stengers, I. (1996) *Cosmopolitques, Tome 1: La Guerre des Sciences*, Paris: La Découverte

Stern, P. F. and H. Fineberg (eds) (1996) *Understanding Risk: Informing Decisions in a Democratic Society*, Washington, DC: National Academy Press

Stirling, A. (1994) 'Diversity and ignorance in electricity supply investment: addressing the solution rather than the problem', *Energy Policy*, 22(3): 195–216

— (1997a) 'Limits to the value of external costs', *Energy Policy*, 25(5): 517–40

— (1997b) 'Multicriteria mapping: mitigating the problems of environmental valuation?', in J. Foster (ed.), *Valuing Nature: Economics, Ethics and Environment*, London: Routledge

— (1998a) 'Risk at a turning point?', *Journal of Risk Research*, 1(2): 97–110

— (1998b) 'On the economics and analysis of diversity', SPRU Electronic Working Paper, 28, October, <www.sussex.ac.uk/spru/publications/imprint/sewps/sewp28/sewp28.html>

— (1999) 'On "science" and "precaution" in the management of technological risk', report to the EU Forward Studies Unit, IPTS, Seville, EUR19056 EN, <ftp://ftp.jrc.es/pub/EURdoc/eur19056en.pdf>

— (2003) 'Risk, uncertainty and precaution: some instrumental implications from the social sciences', in F. Berkhout, M. Leach and I. Scoones (eds), *Negotiating Environmental Change, New Perspectives from Social Science*, Cheltenham: Edward Elgar

Stirling, A. and S. Mayer (1999) *Rethinking Risk: A Pilot Multi-Criteria Mapping of a Genetically Modified Crop in Agricultural Systems in the UK*, SPRU, University of Sussex

Stone, G. D. (2002) 'Both sides now: fallacies in the GM wars, implications for developing countries and anthropological perspectives', *Current Anthropology*, 43(4): 611–19

— (2004) 'Biotechnology and the political ecology of information in India', *Human Organization*, 63(2): 127–40

Stott, P. and S. Sullivan (eds) 2000 *Political Ecology: Science, Myth and Power*, London: Arnold

Strathern, M. (1999) *Property, Substance, Effect: Anthropological Essays on Persons and Things*, London: Athlone Press

Syngenta (2000) '"Golden Rice" Collaboration Brings Health Benefits Nearer', <http://www.syngentacropprotection-us.com/media/article.asp?article_id=42> (visited April 2004)

Tarrow, S. (1994) *Power in Movement: Social Movements, Collective Action and Politics*, Cambridge and New York: Cambridge University Press

Taylor, P. W. (1961) *Normative Discourse*, Englewood Cliffs, NJ: Prentice-Hall

Taylor, T. J. (1992) *Mutual Misunderstanding*, London: Routledge

Tilly, C. (1993) 'Contentious repertoires', *Great Britain, 1758–1834. Social Science History*, 17: 2

Toulmin, S. (1958) *The Uses of Argument*, Cambridge: Cambridge University Press

Treichler, P. (1999) *How to Have Theory in an Epidemic: Cultural Chronicles and AIDS*, Durham, NC: Duke University Press

UKCEED (1999) *Citizens' Panel Report on the UK National Consensus Conference on Radioactive Waste Management, 21–24 May 1999*, Peterborough: UKCEED

— (2000) 'Workshop on the monitoring and retrievability of radioactive waste', a report for Nirex prepared by the UK Centre for Economic and Environmental Development, 2 December. Harwell: UK Nirex Ltd

— (2001) 'Workshop on the monitoring and retrievability of radioactive waste', a report for Nirex prepared by the UK Centre for Economic and Environmental Development, February. Harwell: UK Nirex Ltd

— (2002) 'Workshop on the monitoring and retrievability of radioactive waste', a report for Nirex prepared by the UK Centre for Economic and Environmental Development, February. Harwell: UK Nirex Ltd

Van Zwanenberg, P. and E. Millstone (2004) *BSE: Risk, Science and Governance*, Oxford: Oxford University Press

Vernon, A. (1993) *African Americans at Mars Bluff, South Carolina*, Baton Rouge, LA, and London: Louisiana State University Press

Verran, H. (2001) 'Re-imagining land ownership in Australia', *Post Colonial Studies*, 1: 237–54

— (2002) 'A postcolonial moment in science studies: Alternative firing strategies in environmental science and aboriginal land-management practices', *Social Studies of Science*, 32(5–6): 725–59

Viola, E. and H. Leis (1995) 'A evolução das políticas ambientalistas no Brasil, 1971–1991: do bissetorialismo preservacionista para o multissetorialismo orientado para o desenvolvimento sustentável', in D. Hogan and L. Vieira (eds), *Dilemas Socioambientais e Desenvolvimento Sustentável*, Campinas: Ed. Unicamp

Visvanathan, S. (1984) *Organising for Science: The Making of an Individual Research Laboratory*, New Delhi: Oxford University Press

— (2002) 'Transfer of technology', *International Encyclopedia of Social and Behavioral Sciences*, Amsterdam: Elsevier

Wade, R. (1990) *Governing the Market: Economic Theory and the Role of the State in East Asian Industrialisation*, Princeton, NJ: Princeton University Press

Wadman, M. (2001) 'Europe's patent rebellion', *Fortune*, 1 October

Wakeford, T. (2000) *Indian Farmers Judge GM Crops*, London: ActionAid

— (2001) 'A comparison of deliberative processes', *PLA Notes*, 40, London: IIED

— (2002) 'Citizens juries: a radical alternative for social research', *Social Research Update*, 37

Walker, W. (2000) 'Entrapment in large technical systems: institutional commitment and power relations', *Research Policy*, 29(7/8): 833–46

Walsh, J. R. (2001) *Wide Crossing: The West Africa Rice Development Association in Transition, 1985–2000*, Aldershot: Ashgate (SOAS Studies in Development Geography)

Wapner, P. (1996) *Environmental Activism and World Civic Politics*, Albany, NY: State University of New York Press

Warren, D., L. Slikkerveer and D. Brokensha (eds) (1995) *The Cultural Dimension of Development: Indigenous Knowledge Systems,*, London: IT Publications

Wasserman, H. (2003) 'New media in a new democracy: an exploration of the potential of the Internet for civil society groups in South Africa', in K. Sarikakis and D. Thusssu (eds), *Ideologies of the Internet*, Cresskill, NJ: Hampton Press

Watterson, A. (1994) 'Whither lay epidemiology in the UK public health and practice? Some reflections on occupational and environmental health opportunities', *Journal of Public Health Medicine*, 16(3): 270–4

Werner, R. (2004) *Designing Strategy: Scenario Analysis and the Art of Making Business Strategy*, Connecticut: Praeger

Whatmore, S. (2002) *Hybrid Geographies: Natures, Cultures, Spaces*, London: Sage

Whestphal, P. S. (2002) 'Your money or your life', *New Scientist*, 175(2,351): 29–33

White, G. (1988) *Developmental States in East Asia*, Basingstoke: Macmillan

Whiteside, M. (2002) *Divided Natures*, Cambridge, MA: MIT Press

Wilde, R. D. (2000) *De Voorspellers: Een Kritiek op de Toekomstindustrie*, Amsterdam: De Balie

Wilkinson, S. (1998) 'Focus group methodology: a review', *International Journal of Social Research Methodology*, 1(3): 181–203

Williams, B. (1973) *The Problem of the Self*, London: Cambridge University Press

Williams, C., P. Alderson and B. Farsides (2002) '"Drawing the line" in prenatal screening and testing: health practitioners' discussions', *Health, Risk and Society*, 4(1): 61–75

Williams, R. and D. Edge (1996) 'The social shaping of technology', *Research Policy*, 25: 865–99

Wilsdon, J. and R. Willis (2004) *See-Through Science: Why Public Engagement Needs to Move Upstream*, London: Demos

Winner, L. (1977) *Autonomous Technology: Technics Out of Control as a Theme in Political Thought*, Cambridge: MIT Press

Woolgar, S. (1998) 'A new theory of innovation?', *Prometheus*, 16(4): 441–53

World Bank (1993) *East Asian Miracle: Economic Growth and Public Policy*, Washington, DC: World Bank

Wynne, B. (1975) 'The rhetoric of consensus politics: a critical review of technology assessment', *Research Policy*, 4: 108–58

— (1987) 'Risk perception, decision analysis and the public acceptance problem', in B. Wynne (ed.), *Risk Management and Hazardous Waste: Implementation and the Dialectics of Credibility*, Berlin: Springer

— (1989) 'Frameworks of rationality in risk assessment', in J. Brown (ed.) *Environmental Threats*, London: Frances Pinter, pp. 45–78

— (1991) 'Knowledges in context', *Science, Technology and Human Values*, 19: 1–17

— (1992) 'Misunderstood misunderstanding: social identities and public uptake of science', *Public Understanding of Science*, 1: 281–304

— (1996) 'May the sheep safely graze? A reflexive view of the expert–lay knowledge divide', in S. Lash, B. Szerszynski and B. Wynne (eds), *Risk, Environment and Modernity: Towards a New Ecology*, London: Sage (Theory, Culture and Society), pp. 44–83

— (1997) 'Methodology and institutions: value as seen from the risk field', in J. Foster (ed.), *Valuing Nature: Economics, Ethics and Environment*, London: Routledge

— (2001) 'Creating public alienation: expert cultures of risk and ethics on GMOs', *Science as Culture*, 10: 445–81

— (2002) 'Risk and environment as legitimatory discourses of technology: reflexivity inside out', *Current Sociology*, 50(3): 459–77

— (2003) 'Seasick on the Third Wave? Subverting the hegemony of propositionalism', *Social Studies of Science*, 33(3): 401–18

Xue, D. Y. (2002) 'A summary of research on the environmental impacts of Bt cotton in China', report published by Greenpeace and the Nanjing Institute of Environmental Sciences, Hong Kong: Greenpeace

— (2003) 'Zhuanjiyin mianhua huanjing shifang dui shengwu duoyangxing de yingxiang diaocha, shiyan he duice' xiangmu yanshou zongjie. Guojia huanbao zongju yanjiu xiangmu. Guowai shengwu anquan xinxi' [Biodiversity impacts of environmental release of GM cotton: research, trials and countermeasures], summary of project findings, State Environmental Protection Authority Central Office project, *International Biosafety*, 8: 26–31

Yearley, S. (1994) 'Social movements and environmental change', in M. Redclift and T. Benton (eds), *Social Theory and the Global Environment*, London: Routledge

— (2000) 'Making systematic sense of public discontents with expert knowledge: two analytical approaches and a case study', *Public Understanding of Science*, 9(2): 105–22

Yearley, S., S. Cinderby, J. Forrester, P. Bailey and P. Rosen (2003) 'Participatory modelling and the local governance of the politics of UK air pollution: a three-city case study', *Environmental Values*, 12(2): 247–62

Young, I. M. (1989) 'Polity and group difference: a critique of the ideal of universal citizenship', *Ethics*, 99: 250–74

— (1990) *Justice and the Politics of Difference*, Princeton, NJ: Princeton University Press

Index

Index

293

Rock Characterisation Facility (RCF), 238–9
Rockefeller Foundation, 184–5, 186, 190, 192, 194
Rodoanel project (Brazil), 167, 169, 173–5, 177, 181
Roosevelt, Franklin D., 'Four Freedoms', 52
Rosenau, J., 32
Rosgen company, 103
Royal Commission on Environmental Pollution (UK), 238
Royal Commission on Genetic Modification (New Zealand), 215, 244–8
Royal Society, 1985 Report, 22

Sachs, W., 7
safety, 43–53; as constitutional issue, 41; globalization of, 52; supplanted by risk, 44
safety science: as new focus for politics, 52–3; corruption of, 53; methodology of, 45–6; trajectory of, 46–8
Saha, Meghnad, 87
Santos, Boaventura, 85
São Paulo, 180; environmental issues in, 167–82
scenario workshops, 230, 249–55
Schwarzenegger, Arnold, 196
science: accountability of, 190; alternative, 93; as culture of modern policy, 72; as means of production, 43; as practice and performance, 19; as public good, 197; class-bound nature of, 52; commercial culture of, 69; corruptions of, 48–50; critique of, 20, 85 (as human rights problem, 89; in India, 87–91); democratic legitimacy of, 9; democratization of, 5, 6, 21, 88, 115, 197, 234 (in UK, 237–43); dissident, 97; key to profitability, 186; mistrust of, 5, 22; of occupational diseases, 130; politicization of, 41, 43, 50–2; politics of, 90; publicly framed in terms of risk, 81
science advice, third category of, 143–5
science and citizenship, 3–14; in global context, 15–38

science and technology studies, 4–5, 6, 15–38; third wave of, 18
science and technology, governance of, 218
science shops, 22
science studies, third wave of, 80
Science, 155, 186, 191–2, 197
scientific advisory committees, 144
Scientific and Industrial Research and Development Council (Zimbabwe), 252
scientific citizens, 36
scientific knowledge: as policy culture, 77–80; assumed universality of, 76
scientificic rationality, Western, 18
scientific temper, 88
scoping workshops, 252–3
Scott, J., 192
Scriven, M., 61
seed: blackmarket, 163; control of industry, 159; controversy about, 184–8; distribution to farmers, 203–4; price of, 161; smart, 211; sterile technology, 196
seed security, 100
self-provisioning: as right, 200, 201
Sellafield, waste disposal in, 238
Sen, Amartya, 193
SEPA organization, 163
Shand, Hope, 192
Shiva, Vandana, 85, 90, 184–6, 186–7, 194
sickle cell anaemia, 92
Sierra Leone: impoverishment of, 200; post-war recovery in, 199–200
Sirianni, C., 31
small is beautiful, 23
social appraisal, framing of, 223–7
social intelligence, 221
social process theory of cognition, 56
socially embedded citizen, 23
Society for Participatory Research in India (PRIA), 130, 134, 136, 138, 139, 140; campaign on disability assessment, 137
Sociology of Scientific Knowledge (SSK), 4, 5, 8, 12, 67
Sokal, A., 83
solidarity, 14; creation of, 30
Song, Y., 209
South, epistemology of, 12
sound science, 220, 225, 226